LYDIA LUNCH: THE WAR IS NEVER OVER
A COMPANION TO THE FILM BY BETH B
NICK SOULSBY

A Jawbone book
First edition 2020
Published in the UK and the USA by
Jawbone Press
Office G1
141–157 Acre Lane
London SW2 5UA
England
www.jawbonepress.com

ISBN 978-1-911036-45-6

Title page photograph by Christina Birrer.
Jacket design by Paul Palmer-Edwards,
www.paulpalmer-edwards.com.

Printed by Everbest Printing Investment Ltd.

1 2 3 4 5 24 23 22 21 20

CONTENTS

INTRODUCTION

When every last vestige of life has been wrung from a historical moment, someone wealthy will pay to whack a monument on top. It's a symbolic gesture indicating that a personage, place, or idea is nothing more than dead concrete, so safely anodyne that the comfortably well heeled can memorialise it as a pointer to long-departed youthful passion. The same process occurs in music and our wider culture. Martin Luther King—a figure hated by millions who went on to contest the role of capitalism in racial submission—has been whitewashed into a secular saint acceptable even to Donald Trump; Kurt Cobain's gun fetishism and conservative libertarianism is muted to make him a liberal icon; Bob Marley has been so emasculated he stands for little more than sunshine and marijuana.

Watching Beth B's film *Lydia Lunch: The War Is Never Over*, what awed me was seeing someone so keenly aware that the core function of our creative industries is to enact that process of sanitisation; to render an artist—by middle age—fêted but ineffective, applauded yet void. Lydia Lunch has, more or less politely, declined that pressure for some four decades. A devotion to nomadism, physical and intellectual, seems to have made her immune to the drag factors that tell humans to buy a couch, sit down, shut up, and repeat themselves ad infinitum.

Instead, what Lydia has created is a wildly diverse wealth of emotional, intellectual, and artistic expression. The daunting sprawl of her work stems from a very deliberate desire to seize every opportunity to create and to share. Therefore, anyone approaching Lydia can choose whether the path lies through her half a dozen major books, or the dozen further works she has written; whether it is found in the couple of hundred music releases she has issued; if the live experience of Lydia's near continuous touring is what ignites the spark; or if it's the dozen or more films she's been in; the extensive photographic work she has exhibited; the theatrical productions, workshops, spoken-word performances, and even séances.

SELF-ALCHEMY

The performance of, and testimony to, pain is ever increasingly ingrained across modern music. The bookshelves heave with biographical studies of undesirable life circumstances. Our TV schedules are loaded with presentations of hurt. The internet is awash with both symptoms and confessions of psychic injury and impairment. Bipolarity is a fundamental requirement of modern musical lyricism, with the most commercially dominant music washing back and forth between triumphalism and despondency. While Lydia was an innovator and a forerunner of the public performance of trauma, her fundamental purpose differs significantly from much of the acting out engaged in across the modern domain of faux-celebrity and (un)reality viewing.

Growing up in Rochester, New York, at a time of significant upheaval in American life, Lydia endured years of abuse at the hands of her father while her mother worked nights as a nurse. In speaking about it as a core component of her early spoken-word performances, specifically in the piece 'Daddy Dearest', Lydia did not wear it as a badge of honour symbolising her rise, nor did she apply it as a wax polish making her successes shine brighter. In some cases, trauma is used as a reinforcement of privilege excusing one's behaviour and refusing responsibility for what one does. Lydia's presentation, by contrast, was stark, factual; it placed responsibility where it was deserved and never asked for pity or exception.

The traumas we experience as children become the grooves and indentations into which our ongoing development is poured. Life and further experience in some cases will modify the topography of our personalities, soften the deviations in the terrain, but the initial marks are always there. In other cases, there's no amount of life that will cement over the cracks, and the marks scored in us will always bisect our souls. But that does not mean it is all we are; each individual is a world entire, in which that pain is just one feature. The whole of a person cannot be summed up by reference to only one flaw, no matter how catastrophic. In the case of Lydia, she is not some mere automaton reproducing a childhood trauma. The suggestion would seem insulting, a casual denigration of a significant body of work. What's important is what an individual does after a moment of trauma.

Trauma—in Lydia's projection, and made very clear in Beth B's film— is a cut made on a soul, an imposition. It is not something rubbed out to leave a perfect clean spirit, nor something defeated by therapy, willpower, or medication and left in the past. Trauma as a foundational stone of a personality is built into personality, unavoidably a component of who someone is. The question is the extent to which it can be mitigated, used, responded to, or controlled—but it cannot be erased. Lydia's strength and aggressive resistance is a positive reaction she has forged, a movement away from disturbance, and a declaration of control over and responsibility for oneself. By refusing to let the harm done to her dominate her, she freed herself from fear or inhibition and was able to decide who she intended to be.

Beth B, in creating the film *Lydia Lunch: The War Is Never Over*, has not just documented Lydia's ongoing struggle, she has also made another mark in her own reckoning with past events. The exercise of male power within her own family, and her mother's subsequent breakdown and reinvention as an artist, left enduring marks on Beth. Encountering Lydia in late-70s New York City was a revelation to her, with Lydia appearing to personify a new model for womanhood—one that could exercise will, possess and satisfy desire, live without apology. Exploring control, power, sensuality, and violence through her films culminated in recent years first in *Call Her Applebroog*, a 2016 documentary portrayal of her mother, the artist Ida Applebroog. *Lydia Lunch: The War Is Never Over* is a logical counterpart to, and next step after, that film.

1977–84

Heading to New York City as a teenager runaway, Lydia was motivated to start a band after seeing no-wave outfit Mars enact their tightly rehearsed and practiced maelstrom of sound. Lydia initiated a spell of time in which her energies were devoted to a succession of bands of her own. Teenage Jesus & The Jerks are relatively long lasting—a full two-and-a-half years. The band coexists for a year of that with a side-project, Beirut Slump—an apparent opportunity to spend time with friends, the creative's alternative to slouching in front of a TV. From there, the wheel revolves ever faster. *Queen Of Siam* is a one-off studio project; 8 Eyed Spy get started around the same time, then cease abruptly barely a year later. Devil Dogs have a bare four-month lifespan, then 13.13 make it through two line-ups in six months before Lydia terminates the effort. The Agony Is The Ecstasy are whittled down from a four-piece, to a three-piece, to closure inside not much more than eight weeks; In Limbo last no longer.

It is fair to take Lydia at her word—that she's a conceptualist—so what we're seeing is the traditional focus on 'the band', or on a particular career path, here plays a vastly reduced role compared to the importance of the specific idea Lydia is seeking to express. Most bands merely exist, then seek the ideas to occupy the unit, with an ongoing cost resulting in terms of the money needed to keep a band afloat, the energy needed to negotiate competing artistic views and personal desires in order to coexist. Lydia reverses this equation at a very early stage. 'The band' is not the critical element; the players are steered to the degree necessary to realise the result, but are given freedom to act within those overall boundaries. The players can change so long as the sound or message is delivered, the desired tour executed, the recording made.

The bands in question are, to this day, brutal propositions. Teenage Jesus & The Jerks still sound alien, stripped down to a minimalism not reached even by the hardcore of Minor Threat and the like. Beirut Slump are a maximalist proposition but seesaw in a queasy, unsettling slalom ride that defies easy listening. Lydia pivots in the opposite direction with *Queen Of Siam*, splitting down the middle between the big-band side of the album and the nursery rhyme side. 8 Eyed Spy too are relatively catchy, rockist, despite possessing a scrappy and fun edge aided by exquisite selection of cover songs. Devil Dogs play blues music with a violence that would make The Stooges proud, while likely making them wince. The Agony Is The Ecstasy, from the one live release visible, make a hellish racket, while

In Limbo lurch back toward the pace of George Romero's zombies, like the nursery rhyme vibe of the *Queen Of Siam* album crawling under wire entanglements.

The other strand of Lydia's activity that dominates this early spell is her willingness to act as muse within the film works of others. Across these few years, Lydia brings her confidence to the camera, giving herself to the filmmaker's vision while retaining her own power of interpretation. By the time Lydia returned permanently to New York City in 1984, she had appeared in eleven films, portraying either herself or a range of characters inhabiting the tropes of torturer or private eye, as seen in Beth B and Scott B's films *Black Box* and *Vortex*. What's most noticeable about Lydia's film work is the slim line between playing a character and simply being Lydia Lunch. Her rising confidence is also visible, but so much is there at the start, in Vivienne Dick's *Guerillere Talks*, where she launches her statements at the camera with a word-perfect virtuosity matched by her casually cinematic physical motion.

1984–90

The earlier period of Lydia's career, though commencing as a New York story, is interrupted by a lengthy spell living in the UK, a brief diversion to Germany following The Birthday Party to Berlin, then a footloose bounce back and forth between London and the USA. In 1984, Lydia moved back permanently to New York City, but by now was performing so many gigs, so many shows, that it's fair to say she lived mainly on the road.

The nature of her work changed too, with spoken word becoming the core mode of her creative expression, possessing a directness and an ability to detail and elucidate a topic that song form would never match. Lydia achieved the underestimated feat of appearing to speak off the cuff, in the moment, while making each word, pause, emphasis, and diversion deliberate in delivery and intention. The uncompromising nature of the subject matter required this deftness of touch, no matter the degree of fury being expressed, in order to lead audiences into terrain where they might be uncomfortable, and to persuade them to endure, digest, and witness. Spoken word also came with the added advantage of requiring a minimum of equipment, props, or participants, removing expense as a barrier to genuine independence from label funding and obligation.

Lydia's musical work became much more focused on the studio, with Jim Thirlwell (aka Clint Ruin, Foetus, J.G. Thirlwell, etc.) her primary collaborator across a run of releases. She would increasingly guest with other artists, or release/re-release her recordings and those of others she admired on her own Widowspeak imprint. This approach tightened her control over the strategic aspects of a project, and the financial, while freeing Lydia of the entanglements required to keep a band unified, motivated, fed, clothed, and housed. The Harry Crews project of autumn 1988 exemplifies the new approach: a one-off setup, on this occasion with no plans for studio recording (though a live album was released as a document) and a set number of dates on a particular continent in a relatively tight timeframe. It was also one of the increasingly rare times, after the conclusion of her early bands, that Lydia picked up a guitar rather than concentrating on vocals. Her belief became that if she was to play guitar, it had to be because the project specifically required her unique style in order to complete the sound.

Lydia's film work also underwent a significant evolution at this time, as she moved from only acting in other people's films to writing and orchestrating them too. Her collaborations with Richard Kern on four films between 1984 and 1988 is the most obvious example, but one can also point to the full-scale theatrical productions she staged with Emilio Cubeiro, 1988's *South Of Your Border* and 1990's *Smell Of Guilt*. The most obvious unifying factor between her film, theatre, spoken word, and writing is the exploration of sexuality and control, pushing out to extremes that would genuinely shock audiences. This was an era where pornography was not as readily available as it is now, where TV and video were intensely sanitised, which meant the creation of a film like *Fingered* was truly transgressive.

1991–2000

Bookended by Lydia's departure from New York City, the 90s saw her living in New Orleans, San Francisco, Pittsburgh, and finally Los Angeles. This time period began with the formation of her first and only true band of the decade: Shotgun Wedding. The band came about after a reconnection with Rowland S. Howard and very much followed the model set by Harry Crews (and, before that, by the In Limbo and The Agony Is The Ecstasy bands.) Recording an album in May, the band toured Europe in November and December, then disbanded. Lydia's approach was to document a project to whatever extent it required, then to move on. The decade saw numerous spoken-word tours, with music releases and tours a relatively minimal part of the mix.

It's hard to recall the thrill among musicians when electronics reached a state of maturity that would allow an entire album to be made without other instruments being required. A major evolution in Lydia's art came with her embrace of the potential of technology. Having already experienced the studio-based conjuring of Thirlwell, Lydia was ahead of many of her peers in the underground. Collaborations with Shock Headed Peters and that band's David Knight and Karl Blake would be succeeded by the full album, *Matrikamantra*, created by Joe Budenholzer. This allowed Lydia to tour with taped backing woven into a range of temporary live line-ups, with saxophonist Terry Edwards regularly at the centre.

Lydia had also begun, with 1982's *Adulterers Anonymous* (written in collaboration with Exene Cervenka), to release more of her writing into the world. By the time of 1992's *Incriminating Evidence*, her dexterity with words meant her writing style was tightly aligned to her spoken-word performances. Every word on the page looks like it could be performed out loud to an audience; there's no flab, no wording that might look poetic on a page but feel clumsy in the mouth. Lydia sees herself primarily as a writer, with the medium of expression changing to meet the demands of the words. Reading her various collections of essays, articles, and spoken-word routines, there's a very strong authorial voice and a tenacious grip on the key point expressed, the minimum of digression or talking around rather than directly to an issue.

What also began to take place was an underlying generational shift, with new musicians coming through who had been fans of Lydia's work and now sought to involve her in their own creativity. Increasingly, a new, geographically and nationally disparate community would form, with Lydia as the common thread linking a range of collaborations and guest appearances. Her status also changed, with a lot of coverage dwelling on her as an icon whose meaning went far beyond music. She would be recognised as a voice for female empowerment, for emancipation of victims of abuse against their aggressors, as a political voice equally at home decrying war as she was recounting memories of sexual hedonism and pleasure rebellion in *Paradoxia* (1997).

2000–20

Across this young century, Lydia's work has sprawled ever outward, taking existing threads in fresh directions. A core development has been the recombination of Lydia's spoken word, her interest in film and photography, and her experience of theatre to create multimedia performances in which her words are matched to music (live or recorded) or overlaid with imagery (from collaborators such as video artist Elise Passavant), as Lydia's skill as a narrator is given full-rein in what is, essentially, a one-woman theatre piece. Her spoken word has continued under such glorious names as *Blood Is Just Memory Without Language: Songs Of Sex, Sorrow, And Rage*, *The Real Pornography*, or *Horribly True Confessions*, among others.

While working extensively as a guest artist or being sampled by other musicians, Lydia continued to form short-lived bands for one-off tours. The most surprising development of the past decade, however, was the resurrection of 'the band' as a core part of Lydia's creative expression. An extended period working with The Anubian Lights in the early 2000s, followed by a brief diversion with a line-up called The Willing Victim and repeated periods of touring with Terry Edwards, James Johnston, and Ian White, culminated in the formation of Big Sexy Noise and a ten-year run of regular touring. Furthermore, Lydia formed Retrovirus in 2012—with a current line-up of Weasel Walter, Tim Dahl, and Bob Bert—as a vehicle for the mutilation and fresh performance of her extensive back catalogue.

Lydia's written work has expanded significantly with a handful of new volumes in the last ten years. She has staged workshops and communal events with friends and associates like Zoe Hansen and Jasmine Hirst, and was even invited to perform her album *My Lover The Killer* at the Deutsche Oper Berlin, in a curious merging with the opera *Carmen*. Her musical works have encompassed everything from blues works with Cypress Hill, to improvisation with Weasel Walter or Medusa's Bed, to the full-on rock of Big Sexy Noise, even initiating performances of the music of Suicide with Marc Hurtado.

When I interviewed the band Melvins a few years back, Buzz Osborne made the point that, in his opinion, most musicians are lazy; that he didn't think producing an album every couple years, working a stage for a couple hours every second night, was a particularly hefty workload. Lydia's constant explosion of activity, her apparent ability to live on planes and in tour buses, certainly illustrates what a creative personality with an enviable work ethic can achieve.

BETH B'S WAR IS NEVER OVER

Beth's film is not another rock-music biopic or standard-issue documentary. The music flies out of the speakers, mostly as accompaniment to the welter of ideas visible in Lydia's life, her persona, the themes she chooses to foreground in her work. The talking heads don't recount 'good time tales'; again and again they impact the audience with memories that make one laugh in sheer surprise, that reinforce the core themes of trauma, sexuality, sensuality, gender, and the differing expectations placed upon a woman. The salacious rock-star biography in which male icons do as they will with an identikit cast of strippers, hookers, and models is accepted and winked at. A discomfort lingers when hearing of Lydia's far less exploitative appetites; her desire for pleasure, satisfaction, for what she wants from whom she wants it. That is not Lydia's problem or Beth's problem. It's our problem. We've been trained to look away from female sexuality in action unless it's performed with one eye on the demands of a male audience. Beth doesn't shy away from it; she celebrates it, delights in a life lived untidily and without glib resolutions.

What I also see in the film is Lydia's enduring self-reliance, as well as her a forging of 'a family of choice'. The latter concept is what lies beyond blood and obligation. It's the people we invest energy in keeping contact with, spending time on, and giving energy to, whether that's in the form of an open ear or a well-timed hug. Lydia is indeed the fearsome survivor of legend, but I've been struck by the vast affection in which she is held, the numerous individuals who credit her as a mentor and as a friend. The making of community, the belief that other people are worth it, is a heavily underrated act of will. Witnessing my father, grandfather, and godfather die in rapid succession, all within fourteen months, I learned that many moments in life are so deep that all we can give is our time and presence to those enduring. Lydia is a giver. Her deep well of energy is hauled up and shared with those around her. That kindness is hugely underrated in this world.

BRINGING WORD TO THE PAGE

My own journey with this book began with an invitation. Having interviewed Lydia in 2015 and 2017, and having interviewed Beth during the latter year, I was surprised and delighted to receive an email from them asking if I would be open to writing a companion to Beth's film. What has made me persist—writing weekends, working long into the night, interviewing individuals around the demands of a full-time job—has been my admiration for the accomplishments of Lydia and Beth. I don't believe the cliché of the suffering artist—most trauma creates nothing beyond broken lives—but I'm impressed by the rare individuals who can take something negative and transmute it into something of beauty that makes others feel less alone in their pain. I feel that's what Lydia and Beth have done in their respective works.

Across the course of the past year, I had the pleasure to listen to, read, and enjoy the remembrances of eighty individuals. It's hard to describe, in a world dedicated to 'broadcasting', the positive energy stoked by hearing people speak of their work, their passions, their experience of the world. My thanks go to each individual in the contributors section for giving me enough of their spirit to make me want to stay up for the umpteenth night to share their voices with an audience. I hope I have done justice to their words. At this point I also need to acknowledge Beth B's kindness in granting permission for the extensive series of interviews she personally conducted for her film to be used in this book: thank you Beth!

I would also like to draw the reader's attention to the extraordinary website FromTheArchives.org. Hans W has singlehandedly grafted long and hard to create the only comprehensive listing of the key dating associated with Lydia's work of which I am aware. Without this site I believe the overall outline and structure of Lydia's career (and that of several other artists he has focused on) would be unrecoverable. My thanks go to Hans for his supportiveness throughout.

As ever, my thanks go to Elizabeth, for her eternal good grace and kindness in a world that often encourages the worst of people. Likewise to LiveNirvana.com, for showing me what motivated fandom can achieve when individuals focus on sharing knowledge rather than accumulating power. Of course, my thanks go to Tom Seabrook and Jawbone Press, for their eternal patience, skill on multiple fronts, and deep supportiveness. Also, thank you to the ever-awesome Isabel Atherton, for always making time to share her wisdom and help me pursue my curious literary path.

My final thank-you goes, obviously, to Beth and to Lydia. I've always wanted the books I create to be a passion, not just another careerist obligation or an imposition forced upon me. It would have been easy for Beth and Lydia to simply treat me as a pair of hands executing their bidding. Instead, at all times, they graciously gave me the opportunity to make a work that would complement the film, while standing on its own two feet. It was beautiful to discover two people who have achieved so much across so many years, and who had the confidence to make room for someone else to make something to accompany their respective passions. Thank you Beth, and thank you Lydia.

NICK SOULSBY, DECEMBER 2019

BABY DOLL

LYDIA LUNCH I'm thirteen years old and it's a blizzard and I'm standing in front of the Monroe Movie Theatre—an X-rated movie theatre a little bit from downtown—and I'm waiting for the bus. I'm in a rabbit-fur jacket, short skirt, platform boots. It's a whiteout and the bus isn't coming, and a car circles around and asks me if I want a ride. I'm like, 'No, I'm waiting for the bus.' He circles around again. 'I said I'm waiting for the bus.' He circles around the third time and says, 'The bus isn't coming. Where are you going?' I said, 'Straight up the road a mile.' He's like, 'Get in.' I do.

He looks like Robert Blake with a cheese-grater complexion. His car is littered with fast-food wrappers and junk, and the first thing he says to me is, 'It's not about sex.' I said, 'It better not be.' 'What are you doing?' I said, 'I'm trying to get out of here.' I meant not only from the bus stop—I'm trying to get out of Rochester. He goes, 'I guess you need money for that.' I'm like, 'Yes, I do.' And he puts, I don't know whether it was a twenty or a fifty—because even twenty dollars in '73 was a lot of money—on the dashboard. I'm going just one mile up a straight road and twilight is falling and it's white and blue and we're driving, and he says, 'Tell me a story about your sisters.' I start making stuff up. And we're driving, and two, three blocks from my house is this park, and we drive to the top and again the snow is falling and it's azure blue and it's beautiful. And I'm talking, and he takes a dead cigarette out of the ashtray.

He just says, 'Open your mouth.' I do. And he puts it in my mouth. I have no fear at all. And then he says, 'Now get out of the car,' and I do. He opens the trunk and pulls out a shotgun, 'Lick the car tires,' and he holds the shotgun to my head, and I lick the car tires. Really, at that point, I was so dead in so many parts that I had no fear, so I smiled. And I licked the tires. And then I don't know whether he came or not, but he said, 'Oh my god, that was so beautiful ... you know it's not about sex?' And that's when I knew, no, it wasn't about sex, it was about power. And, in that moment, I had the power. And he lifted me gently and he put me in the car, and he goes, 'Can I have your phone number?' I gave it to him, and he drove me home, of course, at the corner. He called me a few days later, but I'm like, *I won, and I will always win, and I'm afraid I can't see you, my friend.* He wanted to take me up to Watkins Glen State Park to shoot photos—I knew I would never come back from that. After that, I thought it was important to tell stories, because they're not always about sex, even when I talk about sex, but they are always about power and the imbalance. If I had been frightened, I would have been shot.

*

JASMINE HIRST The 80s, everyone was utterly silent about the way women were treated, about the everyday violence, about what we had to put up with. We didn't even talk about it privately because it was just so normal. At this point in my life, I believe I've met only one woman who experienced not one form of sexual abuse, harassment, or exploitation in her life—it's a given that if you're female you've had some sort of experience. The culture in Australia is a rape culture.

BETH B I'm interested in anything where there's power and control—out of control! It has fascinated me from childhood because I was battling this from a young age. I came out of a household, and a time, where women were seen and not heard. They were the sex kitten, the housewife—they were not employable in the way they are today. My father came over from Vienna escaping the Nazis, and he was oppressive and dominating and scary, he frightened me. He would hit, yell, berate, and I was a very fiery young girl who would stand with my hands on my hips and say, 'No!' Our home was a typical 50s household—male-dominated, with the women scurrying around servicing the father's every whim. My mom did that until she had a nervous breakdown, was hospitalised, was suicidal, when I was thirteen years old. So many women of that time had breakdowns, committed suicide; so many women I know from that time had mothers who had breakdowns or became completely depressed. Do the shopping, have dinner ready, take care of the kids. I grew up not having an example of a woman who had a voice. She had to figure out her own identity, and, in some ways, the foundation of much of my work comes from that dynamic that I grew up with. I understood at a young age that I would not allow that in my life. I've been in battle mode since I was young, figuring out how to survive in that power structure. You take that rebellion with you everywhere you go, into every future relationship that may not pose a threat, but you're wired for threat, and you're wired to react—which often doesn't serve you well in life. Where Lydia and I have taken similar paths is in the self-therapeutic nature of our work.

CATHI UNSWORTH Where I grew up, in Norfolk, in England, child abuse was rife. The nurses used an expression, 'NFN'—'Normal For Norfolk'—which meant inbreeding. A lot of people I went to school with suffered hideously and were passed around their own families at very young ages. I wrote about it in one of my books, *Weirdo*, but made it happen to older children because I didn't think people could stomach that it was happening to junior-school-age kids I knew. There's something about the British national character that's like a battered wife with too many children, her husband down the pub drinking away the money while she tries to hold it all together—that's how I thought of the society I grew up in. People pretended it wasn't happening, but it was really obvious where I grew up. The culture of the 70s was misogynistic and quite violent about both women and children—neither had many rights.

VIVIENNE DICK In Ireland, at that time, you were very much a second-class citizen as a woman. Once I got into filmmaking, I saw film as a mode of expression that was really controlled mostly by men. There were very few women making films, and this continued all the way until years later, teaching film in Galway. The students, both male and female, favoured male protagonists when writing scripts. I was shocked by this. It was like there was a block on a story being told from a woman's perspective, or a woman telling her story. It wasn't just in film, it was across all the arts. My boyfriend at the time—who was French—introduced me to a lot of contemporary art, and we went to a lot of interesting galleries in France, Germany, and the UK. Most of the work I saw was by men—and it's not that I don't like work by men, I like a lot of work by men—but as a woman you feel, *Why is that?*

CARLA BOZULICH I prefer to see the things that happened to me as a child and as a young woman—which were very severe things—as my responsibility. Not that I did them all to myself, but I want to own the possibility of healing. If I'm feeling pain or feeling 'done to' by a memory, I can't control my own healing, and fuck that! I don't want to live the rest of my life powerless like that. I really can't speak for Lydia, I don't know why she does what she does, but I don't feel she is exorcising her demons. Her work has changed drastically, so you can't say one thing about Lydia and have it cover the span of her career. When I listen to Teenage Jesus & The Jerks, I hear a playfulness and a petulance and how fun it must have been to fuck with people that hard. Fun! I think her work is way more powerful now, but I still don't think she's exorcising demons except maybe *your* demons, you know?

BETH B When people speak of mental illness, of trauma, there's this horrifying idea—perhaps sold to them by big pharma—that you take this, or you do this, and you'll be cured! There is no cure. Trauma resides in the body—it's always there, looking for a way to come out again. If you arrest it with medication then it will just come out at another time, another place. There's the notion that you go through rehab and you're cured, but the reality is in the phrase 'in recovery', it's always a work in progress.

LYDIA LUNCH The sentence I came up with that made the most sense to me is that, sometimes, when you need the smallest, most tender action or attention, and you don't get it, you will look for the biggest monster in the room. Now, what the fuck? Really, what you need is the tenderness you were denied as a child, but as a defence mechanism, if you're not going to get it, you look for something monstrous to compensate in a reverse and negative way. Trauma is greedy, so it's like, *OK, if you can't calm me down, I'm going to fuck you up.*

We're all victims of the family in one way or another. It's an imperfect system. Coming out of our generation, the 50s, parents of that generation didn't have the knowledge or the tools for nutrition, and they didn't talk about the abuse they had suffered. Usually abuse is transgenerational. Once I realised that my father's behaviour, and my mother's ... not denial but blindness to it, that it didn't start with them, I had a better understanding of how the world works in general. Once you've been damaged it's really hard, no matter how many years of psychological investigation, of public psychotherapy, of emotional release, there is always some form of trauma that lives in the body and that will manifest in one way or another. Even if, intellectually and psychologically, you've understood that the repercussions of this are worldwide, from the beginning of time, there's still always some mark or scar because trauma is a greedy emotion. If you've been traumatised, even if you've been steady, you're steady for five years, and then—trauma. This happens with people that have alcohol or drug abuse problems, they might be sober for quite a long time, but then that greedy, needy, trauma is like, *Hey, what about me? What about me?* That's something I've been working on and fighting my whole life.

KATHLEEN FOX As a late teen and as someone in my early twenties who did not speak about any of the sexual violence that had occurred in my life to that point, just the very fact that Lydia was out there was a comfort to me until I was able to be comfortable enough with my own self to be who I was as a person and control that anger and never be afraid of anyone again and not ever have to be a victim again.

BETH B Lydia became a model for a lot of women, then and now, to move out of the fear and into the expansive possibilities of having a voice and doing it unapologetically. As a young woman I was always apologising for myself, apologising for any small little thing that was wrong or out of the realm of what was supposed to be. In a way, I do have to say it gave me a lot of permission, to know that we could translate that fear into rage.

There needs to be more support for women's stories. You see all the shit put out in films, and there are so many stories about men—why can't we hear women? There should be a space for the voice of aging women, too, because that's an even worse situation. Our culture just does not want to hear from women over a certain age. The taboo of menopause, being grey, becoming invisible—I really had to choose to be grey-haired because it's a political choice. Women cannot go grey, cannot wrinkle, cannot have age spots, they cannot have a dry vagina, because none of it is sexy, and we have no use in our culture for women who are not sexy. It's so sad. I'm of that age where I understand I am a powerful female, but I am invisible to the wider world—that's the next battle in my life because I am the silver fox and I still have a vagina between my legs! It's the last taboo!

KEMBRA PFAHLER Lydia was bareness and rawness around sex and presentation and her being herself. It's 'To thine own self be true.' She has such a fearlessness about her, and her sexuality is just about being fearless. Courageousness isn't a big part of everyone's life, and most of us live in fear completely. I personally was so afraid of my own sexuality—I was so self-hating when I was developing as a young lady. I hated being female. I hated having to be recognised as a part of the female population. I remember being asked in college, 'What is your opinion, representing fifty percent of the world, as a woman?' And he was looking at me and asking me how I felt, and I remember saying, 'Are you talking to me?' Because I had no idea what he meant.

BETH B In my film *Lydia Lunch: The War Is Never Over*, sometimes it's shocking, realising that it was the early 80s and Lydia was having to battle to be heard, to talk about the abuse and the power from her father, to God, to the patriarchy—that structure was so huge, we couldn't open our mouths to question it. She was doing it before Oprah—nobody was speaking about it, it was forbidden. Some of my work has been about women and hysteria. Sometimes we have to become a little hysterical, because when you're not being heard it just sits like a knot tied within you, and it can come out in these very disturbed ways. With Lydia, it came out in the beautiful form of poetry. With me, it came out in my films where the female protagonists were trying to grapple with what was expected of them—the things we have learnt are normal, that make us comfortable even if it's a horror story—and the desire, the need to break away from that which otherwise destroys and oppresses us.

CHAPTER ONE

FREUD IN FLOP

IN THE AFTERMATH OF NEAR BANKRUPTCY, NEW YORK CITY ENACTS DRASTIC CUTS TO SERVICES AND WELFARE. LOW RENTS ONLY ENHANCE ITS ALLURE TO ARTISTIC WAIFS AND CREATIVE STRAYS ...

LYDIA LUNCH My father was a bible salesman; he was not Catholic. I went to Catholic school; that did not make me a Catholic. By nine, God was out—maybe it was the priest's fingers up under my dress as he smelt of whisky and cigars? Or maybe it was those four-hundred-page bibles my father sold, reading those while I suffered stomach aches from trauma he bestowed upon me? My mother, in silence, and deafness, and stupidity, didn't see what was going on—as mothers usually don't.

I was very lucky to grow up in Rochester, New York, because of a few reasons. First, I experienced the race riots of '64 and '67 right outside my front door. At that time there were like eighteen cities in America having race riots. I didn't remember the riots of '64 because I was five, but I remember the riots of '67—1967 was pretty defining. There were a lot of protests, there were women being elected into Congress, Janis Joplin throwing down at the Monterey Pop Festival.

I remember there was a horror movie playing, and then the riots broke out and my father's car was set on fire and he sent me up to my attic bedroom, and I don't know whether or not 'Light My Fire' was on but that was also a year of a lot of musical protest. It impacted me greatly. You know there was a helicopter that crashed a few blocks from my house? Five thousand people were arrested, and I was talking to my cousins about what they remember, because they lived in the suburbs, I lived in the epicentre. And they said, 'What about '64?' And I had to go back and look at photos from 1964 of the Catholic school I went to around the corner, with police blockading it. It reminded me that from the age of probably five—my first riot—to the age of eight, I was living in a war zone, and protest somehow was given to me: the sense of protest.

CARLO MCCORMICK We had a protest movement in America—the anti-war movement, the civil rights movement—and we had a lineage of that. Lydia comes out of the race riot moment, something way more out of control, way less progressive. Really, it was, *Burn the ship down!* instead of, *Sit down for a better world!* We consume culture in a very passive way, and Lydia would hate the idea that people would come to be entertained by her. If she was going to put herself out there, she wanted everyone in the room to have equal stakes in the game. Most people play a polite game of cards; Lydia would throw all the money in the pot: *Show me what you got.* She liked this discomfort that gets people out of their normal ways of receiving and processing information.

LYDIA LUNCH It was at the age of six that really I had a moment of consciousness that this was not right. I don't mean only the riots, I mean my life— something was wrong here. The trauma zone of a family with a father who was basically, at that time, outside of all society, a petty criminal, and pretty insane.

Also, what was interesting, or what I learned after many years, about my father is that he stopped drinking very early. But he was an outlaw, and you had to respect that. I mean, he was a door-to-door salesman, always a different job, always gambling, banned from a fifty-mile radius of his home town … and, from a very early age, my father would sneak into my room and do things nobody should do to their child, while my mother was working as a night nurse. Of course, when you're that young, you have no idea what's going on, because you have a sense of wrong but you also have a sensation of pleasure—how do you divide that? What does it do to you when you're stuck in this limbo?

BETH B It's also that concept that a parent figure is the person you're supposed to trust, right? I mean, at that age, you don't have the information to know, *Is it right, is it wrong?*

VIVIENNE DICK In my film *Beauty Becomes The Beast* (1979), Lydia plays the part of a young girl, and there is a reference to child abuse. We never actually spoke about it, but later Lydia publicly acknowledged she had been abused as a child, and I think she was surprised that this had come out in the film.

LYDIA LUNCH What started happening then, at ten, eleven, was there were a lot of rock concerts. By the age of twelve I befriended a college radio DJ and started getting free tickets to rock concerts. Out of guilt or whatever, my father would drive me to these concerts. I'm twelve and I would go see Roxy Music, Slade, KISS, and I befriended the promoter, I get backstage, and I tell my father to pick me up at two o'clock in the morning—as 'the favourite one', I was allowed to do anything I wanted. You have to balance what is being stolen and what has been given to me. And when you realise that it's not really a personal thing, it's a genetic traditional historical insanity, it's easier to deal with it in some ways. And then, of course, you get the consciousness to just say, 'Leave me the fuck alone, motherfucker!' And, of course, I had a boyfriend, who was a weightlifter, by the age of twelve, and that kind of ended that.

Another important thing about growing up in Rochester was a place called the House Of Guitars, which was started by three brothers, and they started by stealing guitars. Late 60s, early 70s, they would do commercials, and I got to be on one of these commercials. It's also where I was first discovered, in a sense. At the age of thirteen, I was already pretty goth— I'm wearing big rosary beads, black, all in black, black slicked-back hair, hanging out at the House Of Guitars, and a photographer walks in and says, 'I want to shoot your picture.' Me and my girlfriend lived across the street, and they shot our pictures and put them up in the University Of Rochester Institute Of Technology, and it caused a scandal: *Get these satanic girls off the wall!* I'm like, *Yes ... my first taste of negative attention, fantastic.* The same girl, Lori, my good friend from across the street—at thirteen, it was her dad that drove us to the Greyhound station so we could ride away to New York.

*

BETH B I was living in San Diego, California—the pit of hell and ultra-conservatism. I was in school at University Of California Irvine and really needed to get out of California. I was accepted into the School Of Visual Arts—I knew New York was the place I had to go. I felt so uncomfortable in my skin in California without knowing why or what that even meant, then, as soon as I got to New York, I felt, *OK, I'm home! This is what I've been looking for my whole life.* To go from the lethargic leaden sunshine to the dark, dank, urine-infused streets, this really appealed to me—a gravitational pull. That's where I found like-minded people who were interested in exploding all the myths surrounding this concept of the *happy family.* I realised so much of what had been injected into my brain through environment and culture was all a lie. What was extraordinary about that time in New York was that there were all these outsiders gravitating to the city, the collective unconsciousness, an energy that meant people knew that was the place to go to find others who were disenfranchised.

LIZ SWOPE Bobby [Swope] and I went to Eckerd College in St Petersburg, Florida. Gordon Stevenson was a close friend who also attended Eckerd along with Mark Cunningham, Lucy Hamilton, and Arto Lindsay.* I am eighteen months older than Bobby and had dropped out of college but lived in St Petersburg. As graduation was approaching, and we were interested in art and music, New York City seemed the next logical step. It just seemed there were a lot of like-minded people who just happened to be there at the time. Manhattan is really a small place, and our paths eventually crossed.

LUCY HAMILTON The music scene was extremely compelling. And that

---

* Members of no wave–associated bands Beirut Slump, Teenage Jesus & The Jerks, Mars, Don King, and DNA.

inspiration permeated all the visual and performing arts downtown. As an artist who wanted to make a difference, and because I felt like an alien already, I was twenty-one, and I wasn't striving toward being a conventional career girl—it was natural to become part of it. Mark and Arto were roommates, and they graduated and decided they wanted to go to New York; I left college and decided that's where I wanted to go; then other people had their own paths to New York City. It's always been an alluring city.

CARLO MCCORMICK It was a place of abandonment, and in that void that was left it became a really fecund place. It still had the vestiges of being one of the entry points to this melting point, so you had this rich multicultural tapestry, then you had a generation of people who did not fit in with this smug, complacent, post-hippie, bloated America. All these different groups that couldn't fit into small-town America, they were all coming with a fair amount of baggage, and they all had some lightbulb epiphany moment: *I'm not alone.* In that, community was formed, the commonality of otherness, it just became really ripe for collaboration.

JIM THIRLWELL Avenues B, C, and D were the war zone. There were entire blocks that were demolished, buildings that had been burnt out—it was like a cancerous mouth that had its molars ripped out. I loved that quality. Everything on the street was just like a bomb had hit it.

KEMBRA PFAHLER The Lower East Side really was, essentially, a war zone, and it was a playground that was wide open to finding what I call 'available'. Some people were making the best use of what was available. There was so much detritus on the streets because all the buildings were either burnt down or exploded. There were drug places every other building; one building after the next was empty; taxicabs wouldn't take you to the Lower East Side; people weren't sitting in restaurants outside on the sidewalk. There was a lot of stoop-sitting, people walking around the streets at all hours, 24/7, night and day. And to use that old slogan, 'real recognises real', I gravitated toward the people whose work I loved.

BETH B New York City was a playground for us in its state of decay and abandonment—there was a freedom, a search for identity. What it left for people like myself was a space to dispel the past and recast our identities. Everything that had seemed impossible in my life suddenly became possible because there was nothing to lose.

JAMES NARES The downtown below Fourteenth Street was a free-for-all. There were endless abandoned buildings you could just go in—there were no doors. I made a film where I strung a pendulum up in the street; I just took the street and made this thing that would have killed you if you'd walked into it. I remember Eric Mitchell making films that he approached like Andy Warhol paintings.* He did this one, *Car Crash*, where we found an old abandoned car on the Lower East Side—a common sight, a car jacked up on cinderblocks and the wheels taken so it'd just be sitting there with no wheels. We clambered in, threw ketchup and chocolate syrup all over each other—I was in the front seat with my head through the window, Eric opened the hood and put his head in the hood. Michael McClard filmed it with a sun-gun—a very bright light attached to the camera, like cop lights flashing—and he circled the tableau filming.† There was a whole bunch of homeless people who saw it and were going, 'Oh my god, this is awful!' It was absurd, but they thought it was real.

LYDIA LUNCH People came to New York from St Petersburg, from Ohio, from various places, and they came to a city that was basically the asshole of America at that point. It was bankrupted. I called it Beirut On The Hudson. It was purposefully bombed out by the real estates, the banks, the police department, the fire department being shut down so that they could get

---

* Mitchell was a significant figure in the no-wave film scene, creating works including *Kidnapped* (1978), *Red Italy* (1979), and *Underground USA* (1980). He was part of the Collaborative Projects (Colab) artists group and went on to acting and multimedia art.
† McClard was a fellow filmmaker who worked on *Kidnapped* and *Red Italy* alongside Mitchell, and acted in John Lurie's *Men In Orbit* (1979) and James Nares's *No Japs At My Funeral* (1980). He directed Lydia, James Chance, and Teenage Jesus & The Jerks in the short film *Alien Portrait* (1979).

rid of all those rent controlled apartments that housed minorities, weirdos, artists, musicians. Crime was rampant. The police department had been closed down, and then we had the blackout of '77, which is unlike anything else we've ever seen. It was a heat wave that caused a blackout that went on for days, and the looting was unbelievable.

VIVIENNE DICK New York looked like Berlin at the end of the Second World War. A lot of the buildings were burnt out by the landlords because they couldn't pay the tax, so they'd set fire to the buildings then collect the insurance. Then the buildings were knocked down, so there was rubble everywhere, then people built community gardens in some of the sites. Quite a few people I know got their foothold in New York in these buildings with no electricity or running water, then they'd help refurbish the buildings alongside organisations that were helping to house people, and they got the buildings up and running, then bought them off the state for next to no money—but they had to put money into the building, they had to invest.

THURSTON MOORE New York City was devoid of any economic support from the US government. The street life, everybody was on the same level of poverty, in a sense. You knew who the rich people were: they were either the lucky ones who actually kind of made the grade in whatever they were doing, which was a very rare occurrence—it was only fascinating because it was so unusual.

LUCY HAMILTON Downtown was abandoned; it was filled with drug dens and totally affordable. Of course, the Wall Street contingent—also full of drugs—was in lower Manhattan, but it was evacuated by six o'clock. There was no oversight. The neoliberal Reaganomics movement came in and said you have to get rid of all of this—let the corporations 'help you out'—and eliminated most social programming. This was a huge turnaround because NYC previously had many social services, offering a free college education and free hospitals. The trajectory led to immense real-estate development, making the city unaffordable.

CARLO MCCORMICK It was an old port town, which always allows a tremendous amount of darker energies—port towns are just weird that way. It had this huge 'white flight'—something like six million first-and-second-generation immigrants, largely white, left. The city lost its economic base.

KRISTIAN HOFFMAN The second floor above CBGB's was a kind of flophouse for drunkards and homeless people. The people who hover temporarily resided there, and they hated the racket of CBGB's and the ever-increasing lines, and the noise of rock wannabes hanging around. So, what would they do? Why, of course: light their mattresses aflame and throw them out of the second-storey window at us! Oh, how we laughed.

JIM THIRLWELL I didn't find it particularly dangerous. There was a real sense of community, the arts and music community played out there, a lot of creativity and it was easy to start a gallery or a performance space. A lot of that DIY, a strong underground happening.

RICHARD KERN I came to New York in 1978, '79—something like that. The first day I arrived in New York, I had this whole image, being from the South. I had a pocketknife in my pocket, and I had my hand clenched on it, and I was so afraid. I had to go to East Eighty-Second to meet someone, so I walked from Port Authority to East Eighty-Second clenching that knife, just thinking if anyone talked to me, they were gonna try to kill me.

BETH B That was the feeling in New York at that time. I had a knife put to my throat. I was walking home at two in the morning, after waitressing, and then, of course, I got a guy with a knife that took my money. But it was sort of like the Wild West, wasn't it?

ROB KENNEDY The Lower East Side was Ground Zero for the impact of New York City going bankrupt. People took over buildings and lived as squatters. There was a lot of violence and prostitution; dope—by which I mean heroin and coke—was cheap and plentiful. Shooting galleries were a thing, before AIDS, and if you OD'd they would just toss you out of the window. In the winter, people huddled around burning trashcans to stay warm. Visually, economically, morally it was hell.

RICHARD KERN SoHo was just like a big scary wasteland—at night, especially. It was all dark, and there's plenty of parking … my street, for example, East Thirteenth Street in the East Village, I had a car, and I could pull up anytime day or night and there's a parking spot. There's a lot of parking spots because the only other cars were all getting stripped. The first apartment I got over there, I went in the daytime. There's a big line of people waiting to rent the apartment. I was the only one that had cash, so I got the apartment. And I came back at night, and there was like a million drug dealers there.

KID CONGO POWERS Living on the Lower East Side, it was quite dangerous to be out and about—there were a lot of muggings, you took your life in your hands, the danger of death and murder … how exciting! It depends what kind of young person you were, I guess. Lydia has always said that the people who were making art and music at that time, if they hadn't been doing that, a lot of them would probably have been out murdering, so it's probably best they were making music. It really was a pressure cooker, and the idea was to be as extreme as possible. Everyone was doing some kind of transgressive artistic ritual, and there was an audience there to respond to it. I was attracted to how direct everyone was in New York. I longed for that as a teenager—people said it was harsh, but I thought it was just direct. There was a dark humour to the city, and to the people in it, which appealed to me.

*

LYDIA LUNCH It was in '73 or '74 when I first ran away, at thirteen, to New York. I was here for just a week or two. I knew I had to go back and get money because I didn't want to end up doing what I knew I'd be forced to do at that age …

   When I was on St Mark's Place, I see somebody in an Iggy Pop T-shirt and it's Stiv Bators, but he wasn't Stiv Bators yet, and he was living in

Cleveland.* I started talking to him because I was very forthright like that, and if I saw anybody who looked cool, I talked to them. We became pen pals and then, a few years later, we just seemed to end up in New York at the same time again.

I started hanging out with Dead Boys because, of course, they were a great rock'n'roll band. And then they wrote a song called 'I Need Lunch'! This was before I had a band—I was already notorious. I was a teenage runaway in New York, and we were all extremely poor. Some of my first friends were living in a fur vault building in Hell's Kitchen. I was underage but I had a fake ID, so I decided I would get a job for a couple of weeks in a bar, so I could steal food. I would literally go in there for two weeks, steal the food, run out, and run over to my friends in the band Mink DeVille. One day, I was walking down the sidewalk in front of CBGB's, to bring this pilfered booty, and Willy DeVille just said, 'Lydia Lunch! Lydia Lunch!' I don't know how it stuck, but I didn't choose it.†

THURSTON MOORE You talk to the guys that worked at Bleecker Bob's record store that had this band called Jack Ruby. Jack Ruby was a really important band in '75, '76, for people like Lydia and James Chance—they were sort of a precursor of the aesthetic of no-wave music.

ROBIN HALL Jack Ruby started in '73, with Chris Gray and me and a guy called Randy Cohen. Even though the New York Dolls had been everybody's inspiration to some extent, there had been different strains of stuff, and I still don't think many people were doing what we were doing—there was just Suicide and Jack Ruby. A lot of the attitudes of no wave, we had—we were kind of 'proto no wave'—but one of the reasons we didn't keep going was,

---

* The founder of the key CBGB's punk band Dead Boys, Bators died on June 4, 1990, at age forty, after being hit by a car in Paris. The song 'I Need Lunch' (co-written by Bators with guitarist Jimmy Zero) would appear on the album *Young Loud And Snotty* (Sire, 1977), then on various later retrospectives in live and/or demo versions.

† Willy DeVille returned to the Lower East Side in 1974 and founded Mink DeVille. They became the CBGB's house band 1975–77 and were fellow travellers alongside the key NYC punk bands of the era.

we felt we were working in a vacuum. Over the next three or four years, the people who were looking for that kind of thing found each other.

THURSTON MOORE The Jack Ruby guys worked at Bleecker Bob's, which was the locust for buying new records at that time, and they always tell the story of Lydia, at sixteen years old, banging on the gates: 'Let me in! I wanna look at the records!' She was always right there. She wasn't trying to do anything except to be where the visionaries were, because she knew she was that as well.

ROBIN HALL My earliest memory of her is when she showed up at Jack Ruby rehearsals—I don't think she had started a band yet. She was really good at mythologizing herself right from the beginning. She said she was sixteen, that she was a stripper—nobody knew what to believe and what not to believe. She was brilliant at that! I was definitely intimidated by her. I couldn't figure out how a sixteen-year old could be that intimidating! Lydia was almost fully formed, in some ways, from the time she arrived in New York. I recall this incredibly charismatic young woman who owned any room she was in.

*

PAUL ZONE I knew Lydia as just another girl who was on the scene. It was such a small circle—there weren't that many in the crowd except for other friends, people we knew. It was what I call 'the grey period'—the dark time transitioning from the end of the glam era into what became punk. Everyone was only just starting their bands, or wanted to start bands. There was so much going on, but it all happened so quick. By the late 70s, most of the big punk bands had their record deals and were out on the road, they weren't around anymore, so that opened up the door for no wave and for these new bands. It's why the late 70s blossomed to a lot of different things that took over from the New York punk scene.

THURSTON MOORE Lydia comes up with no wave: 'We don't play new wave, we play no wave.' She says that. The no-wave scene is called the no-wave scene, as opposed to being a part of the punk-rock scene, which is kind of misleading because it's all concurrent. Teenage Jesus & The Jerks and The Contortions are happening by the end of '76, so it's not post-punk, it's not something happening after punk, it *is* punk … but it's no wave.

ROBIN HALL The years 1978–80, I feel it's one of the most amazing three years in music—it was incredibly exciting. That whole scene revolved around Tier 3, Hurrah, and Mudd Club; 8 Eyed Spy, The Raybeats, Bush Tetras, but also bands like The Individuals, The Bongos, The Feelies—all the Hoboken bands. Everyone was hanging out, but it was a very mixed bag.

LYDIA LUNCH When I got off the Greyhound bus in '76, I went to this club I had read about in, like, *Rock Scene*, or *Circus*, or *Creem* magazine, called Mothers. And I walked in and there was Wayne County, who, for some reason, I had written a letter to, and he had written me back in upstate. I'm like, *I'm home.** There was a horrible band playing but I've got nothing, I've got one small suitcase and two hundred bucks—though that was a lot of money in those days—so I picked up the lead singer, said, 'I'm an orphan,' and he said, 'OK. You can come and stay with us in Chelsea,' thinking he had scored big. They had a big loft in Chelsea. I did him once, and then Kitty Bruce—Lenny Bruce's daughter—was moving out of a loft there. I just skedaddled right up to her loft, and a few nights later I went to Max's Kansas City, and Suicide were playing, and I just knew I was home. I mean, I'd never heard of Suicide. There were ten people there, and I just introduced myself, because that's what I would do. Then they became my friends, and Martin Rev would give me vitamins—I was younger than his son. What I can't remember about that period is how all of us never got carded, always got in for free. How did we do that? I guess because they wanted the 'bait'. I have never paid to get into a club in my life.

THURSTON MOORE Seeing those bands—The Contortions and Mars and DNA—

---

* Wayne County (now Jayne) was an early pioneer of punk with the band Wayne County & The Backstreet Boys, another staple of the scene around Max's Kansas City and CBGB's.

at the time, it's hard to explain how shocking it was, because rock'n'roll was all about Robert Plant swinging his microphone and his hairy chest. To see Arto Lindsay with math glasses on, playing just completely anti 'the electric twelve-string guitar' and just freely—to me, I thought it was not just the future, it was so now I didn't even think about the future or the past. It was just, like, in the moment. It was just so *now*.

WEASEL WALTER No wave was deconstruction of rock'n'roll music—it took the parameters and pushed them into surreal and nihilistic extremes. It wasn't even a cohesive movement but it was fashioned into one by the press, and by history. It was a bunch of people deconstructing rock music at the same time, and it came out of a tradition of avant-garde art, free jazz, Fluxus, John Cage, and a lot of twentieth-century artists who pushed music past what people expected new music to be. There's always some staid form that needs to be mocked and destroyed and turned on its side, and there's a beauty in that.

KEMBRA PFAHLER What no wave was, for me, was essentially a contrarian gesture against classic rock. If classic rock was *verse, chorus, verse, chorus, guitar solo, verse, chorus*, no wave was against the idea that this kind of rock'n'roll should be popular and listenable. It was in direct contrast to that, and it was an innovation about minimalism, pain, unlistenability, unpopularity, fast-speed futurism, and kind of rethinking what music was entirely at the time. We had all of these sort of no wave, new wave, punk, rock'n'roll paradigms. We needed to have everything wiped. If it was a chalkboard, it needed to be erased.

JIM SCLAVUNOS Suicide used to allow Teenage Jesus & The Jerks to support them sometimes. They were one of the very few bands that would allow us to support them, because most CBGB's and Max's bands regarded us as room-clearers, which is not really what you look for in the support act.

LYDIA LUNCH Suicide inspired me greatly because of the drama, because of how untraditional it was, because of how frightening they were—though not to me. They were perfect! Then I saw Mars, and Mars ... that told me, *All right, I need to have a band.* Here were four insane people onstage, playing music as if they were all in different bands. Well, as a contrarian, I decided I had to have a band that was so precise and so tight yet with that mania in there too.

WEASEL WALTER A band like Mars, they got progressively more savage and mutated as time went on. They started out as this one-two-chord Velvet Underground tribute band, and, by the end of their career, had evolved into a bunch of wild animals, slobbering and detuning their guitars. Lydia's take was more of a control-freak take—she started with the words, a lot of rage, and these very short, cruel bits of poetry, and she wanted the impact of the music to match the impact of the words.*

LUCY HAMILTON This stuff may sound incredibly chaotic but it was actually thoroughly rehearsed. Mars rehearsed constantly. There was improv but it was based on a structure. And we didn't use any effects—it was all straight, two guitars, a bass, and drums. I had learned piano as a kid—you always give the girl a piano, so she doesn't leave the house. I hated the lessons, and my parents gave up after a couple of years. The piano is great, though, as far as it lays it all out—you can see the scales and the chords. When I started to play guitar, I was able to transpose this. Sumner [Crane] was a trained musician and a great blues guitarist and singer. Mark [Cunningham] began playing trumpet in kindergarten; his uncle was a jazz drummer who got him started. Then Nancy [Arlen] was a painter and had no experience in percussion—I met her at a dance class by Simone Forti.

*

LYDIA LUNCH I was flitting from place to place. Making ten dollars a day on the street, begging for money, claiming I was working for the Cancer Foundation or whatever. All you'd need was ten dollars a day at that point.

---

* Active from 1975 to 1978, Mars were the first of the core bands most associated with no wave and the *No New York* compilation, and a truly unique musical proposition.

And some of the guys who were later in The Contortions and The Raybeats were living down in Tribeca when it wasn't Tribeca yet, when it was in no man's land. They had a loft, and there was an abandoned building beside them, and it had a landlord's number on it. I went and talked to the landlord—I'm seventeen—and convinced him that until he sold the building he might as well let me move in. There was no electricity or running water. I ran the electricity from the people next door, from Jody Harris and Donny Christensen, and took baths at their house.

BETH B I paid $162 for a thousand square foot loft, then met some people who helped me renovate it. I was waitressing at a great restaurant where I met Arturo Vega, who, at the time, was managing the Ramones—and he was the cook! That was emblematic of how people met—everyone was working these jobs, just trying to get by making money however they could. It created an entirely different sense of community because people were out on the streets, so you'd just run into people and they'd say they're off to some party, you'd get there and Jack Smith would be performing, or they'd be going to Max's Kansas City and The Cramps would be playing.*

RICHARD EDSON If you wanted to spend your days doing the work you wanted to do—for me, a lot of it was rehearsing and practising, photography and writing—you gave up your comfort and you gave up some of your safety to live as cheap as possible. Three of us were living in an apartment and we were paying $270 a month, so I just needed to find $90 and enough for food. Sure, we put up with a lot of shit. First night I moved in, I was robbed—my bass and amp were gone by the time I got back. Another time, I caught somebody in the apartment and had a fight—I even knew who he was, and he'd just got out of jail.

VIVIENNE DICK I didn't have any money, and there was cheap rent, which

---

* Smith was one of the first exponents of the camp and trash aesthetics via his films and played a key role in the underground arts movement of the 60s. He died of AIDS in 1989, aged fifty-six. Drag culture owes much to his inspiration.

allowed people to make other work. You had a little job like a waitress, but with that money you could live, and you had all this time. Life wasn't expensive, but you still had to have some kind of job—but you worked as little as possible, so you had free time to do other things.

KID CONGO POWERS Everyone I knew had three or four different jobs. If you weren't a stripper, a prostitute, some kind of sex worker, then you belonged to catering agencies, or you were a bartender. You worked wherever you could work.

BETH B I was working at a house of prostitution, in two different locations in New York City, as a phone receptionist and essentially the madam of the house. The men would come in, I would introduce them to the women, get them condoms, take their money, tell them when time was up, and I'd do the telephones—I'd talk to the men and try to get them to come in. I did an art installation about that at Artists Space very early on, about 1977, where I recorded myself and these men on the phone. I had all these different seductive female personalities I created to try to get them to walk in the door. I was shocked because I never even knew there was such a thing. I was coming from sunny San Diego, where I'd never even heard of drugs and prostitutes—I really was so naïve. This job was a hardcore education for me.

A lot of the men were coming in to be dominated, and, again, at first I was like, *A dominatrix? What's that?* I remember this one boy—and he really was a boy, beautiful, maybe nineteen, twenty—and he went up to the session, then he comes down nude, completely naked, on his hands and knees, on a leash, being led by the dominatrix and into the bathroom, where he proceeded to lick out the toilet. I just kept thinking, *My god, what happened to this poor child?*

It really hit me: what is this abuse that had occurred? What was this iniquity of power in people's lives that brings them to a point where they need to be completely dominated or completely submissive, and they will pay for it? It wasn't just young blonde boys—I was seeing lawyers, I was seeing businessmen, Hasidic Jews. I was seeing everyone from all across the board. I worked there for a couple of years, and it really made me look at the world in a different way. It was like an epiphany for me—it was very cathartic. I'm still making films that are about that.

LIZ SWOPE Lydia was much younger than most of us, and she definitely had a great look, with her black hair and this aggressive street-tough thing. We certainly weren't punk, we wore more thrift clothes—so she made an impression! Hearing different stories she would tell, you had to be impressed—she seemed like a survivor. She'd clearly had challenges, and, at that age, decided to forge ahead, come and live in the city. She had a casual look, tight leggings, she always seemed to have spiked heels on, then she'd wear sweatshirts with the neck cut out or the sleeve cut off, over a bodysuit.

BETH B Lydia, just in her presentation, was so sexually provocative, with her miniskirt up here, and the spiked heels. And in some ways, I know for me, she really represented this anti-feminist. Feminists had become almost like women mirroring men in order to be accepted. She just broke all that loose: *We own our sexuality, we own our sex; I can do whatever I want with it and project whatever I want.* She taught me that there was nothing shameful in that. We didn't have to be bad girls to do that. We can just embrace ourselves as women.

LYDIA LUNCH The most outrageous thing as a sixteen, seventeen-year-old in New York was the number of guys that were dragged into the bathroom at CBGB's. And how many times I got kicked out by Hilly Kristal's wife, Karen, screaming at me, 'Get out of here!'* I'm like, 'I'll get out soon enough, leave me alone, I'm working!' I was dead set on having as much fun as possible. To me, fun and pleasure was always the ultimate rebellion against whatever injustice, whatever trauma, whatever annoyances. I always rebelled with pleasure. I was a hedonist from the age of twelve. I was very sexually aggressive. I became sexually promiscuous in order to

---

* Hilly Kristal was the proprietor of CBGB's.

wash the taste of my father off my hands. And I was pretty successful—I was a successful predator. I liked a lot of anonymous sex. I would pick up guys, tell them a fake name, go to their house, their apartment, rip 'em off, disappear when they were in the bathroom, and laugh all the way home.

It was a way for me to express different sides of my personality because I had many different characters I needed to express, and the best way to do that was through anonymous sex. I don't think it was acts of violence. It was actually demanding my pleasure from whoever I felt like having it from—and rarely, if ever, was I denied. So this was not a cycle of abuse—this was a cycle of pleasure. Who was getting abused? The men I was ripping off, I guess. But, really, I'm a hot sixteen, seventeen-year-old, so who's losing on this equation? I'm getting my rocks off—where's the loss? Couple of dollars here and there—they had jobs, I didn't, and I had one night to make the money and they had 364 days to make up what I stole, no biggie.

KEMBRA PFAHLER When you're talking about female predatory behaviours, I've never heard of Lydia doing anything with people who were not consenting adults. There are so many boring female traditions: don't call the person first, don't ask them to marry, don't have this or that kind of sex in the first hour that you meet the person—there are so many different rules! I don't believe that women should ever compare themselves, or their behaviours, sexually. I tell women in my life that anything they want is in front of them, they just need to take it, whether or not that's perceived as predatory, just take what you want. All I've seen Lydia do is just take what she wants, and maybe that's perceived to be a masculine behaviour.

CARLO MCCORMICK Lydia's probably got a bigger set of balls than I do. There are all sorts of ways in which a woman is *supposed* to attract a man and maybe entrap them—the Doris Day model of sexual politics. Lydia was kind of predatory in a way, like the kind of really gnarly guy who goes out and tries to get a girl drunk so he can bang her, this really callous thinking. Lydia adopted that way of sexual conquest. It's a weird thing of maintaining control in a really chaotic situation—that's sort of been the dynamic in her life.

RUDI PROTRUDI I moved to New York in '77, and I was involved in CBGB's and Max's and Hurrah, Ritz, Peppermint Lounge. I had seen Lydia outside the Mudd Club—they had a guy at the door selecting who was cool enough to come in. She was stood outside the door, making a very loud announcement that she would fuck any guy that was in the line if he was under eighteen—it made quite an impression!

JIM SCLAVUNOS There was a different attitude toward sexuality in the 70s, following on from the 'free love' movement: there was a much more social component to promiscuous sex. It was seen as just one of the many ways in which you could interact with people. It wasn't just that we were all very horny and young, it was also that there was a social model at that point that we were all kind of playing into. Multiple partners was much more of a norm in the pre-AIDS era, across all the sexes, hetero, homosexual, bisexual, and anything in between. And the club scene of the time reflected that. As much as the punks had a sexual identity, they were part of that whole sexual culture of the time as well. There were some aspects of punk at the time that were quite asexual, but Lydia was a groupie, and, when she first came on the scene, she kind of made her reputation as a groupie. And it's fair to say that she enjoyed having sex— and having sex with a lot of different people.

CHAPTER TWO

TEENAGE JESUS

FOLLOWING A JANUARY 1977 MARS GIG, LYDIA FORMS TEENAGE JESUS & THE JERKS. WHILE CYCLING THROUGH MEMBERS, THE BAND ENACT A STARK VISUAL AND MUSICAL AESTHETIC.

JAMES NARES Cynicism was definitely the attitude that ruled. Lydia, onstage, was the high expression of that. Lydia would insult the audience—James Chance would beat up the audience. Songs and shows were short. If the audience said they liked it then they seemed unhappy with that. But there was a higher purpose! It felt reasonable to be cynical and out for yourself and negative about things and expressing feelings about other people that were kind of truthful but not nice. New York was dangerous and we loved it, because it kept people we didn't want there away, so it was great that people were scared.

BETH B The late 70s were all about alienation and negativity: *Fuck you! I'll harm you if you come any closer!* But none of us knew what we were doing. We were like deer in headlights, feeling we had to smash into those headlights and not even knowing why. That's what was necessary. When I was in my twenties I didn't have a clue why I behaved the way I did, why I was attracted to what I was attracted to, but my art was a way of working that through, unconsciously.

RON ATHEY I've been looking a lot at the 60s, and the 60s as they manifested in a mainstream way in the 70s, because the people who ruined punk were the Orange County, Inland Empire scene of assholes. I rejected all that. That was the era of generation gaps, like, all the peace and love bullshit didn't work. Fuck you! There's nothing left. It was the beginning of that nihilism, and you can be a depressive nihilist or you can be an assertive nihilist. And it's interesting to look at a lot of those responses that led into the early 80s.

LYDIA LUNCH Part of what appears to be so nihilistic about that period is, we were products of our generation, meaning the Vietnam War, Kent State, the Summer Of Love being butt-fucked by the Summer Of Hate, Manson, Nixon, Watergate … we felt the 60s failed us! Our parents failed us! The country failed us! We came together as a rallying force to document, as exorcism, the dilemmas we were living at the time.

THURSTON MOORE The attraction of the late 70s in New York was, it was a time where you found energy in things that were nihilistic because the peace-and-love chants became burnt out through bad drugs and immaturity, and the exploitation of ideologies that were actually based on these beautiful concepts of Buddhism or whatever—it becomes a bit exploited, and it turns into bad seed, you know?

DON BAJEMA Lydia is fundamentally about love, she just isn't about bullshit. Most people can't differentiate between the two on all kinds of levels, self-serving levels, acquisition, fairy tales and romances. Lydia has a clear understanding of what love is and an innate aversion to bullshit. My background is trailer parks, I didn't have one single family unit, I was adopted out of a home for unwed mothers, I went through a lot of families, all my uncles were veterans of combat in World War II and were very troubled. I grew up with only a brief breath between childhood and being an adult. My father was overseas a lot and my mother was very sick psychologically. But I had a break when Vietnam came because it generated an amount of political rage in me, a sense of right and wrong, and that gave Lydia and me common ground against things that didn't support life and love as it's supposed to be. Lydia might shock you with things she says about abuses— she's always been someone who is happy to say she'd be just as happy if they dropped the bomb to get it over with—but there's something else inside, demanding that she create something out of all of that, which is what she's done for all this time and will do until her last breath.

*

KID CONGO POWERS I had befriended Kristian Hoffman, who had been in Los Angeles, recording with Bradly Field.* Bradly said, 'You should come to New York and stay at my place,' and they were living with Lydia. He probably thought I'd never come, but I just got on a Greyhound bus one day and showed up—I guess I sent a letter. I met Lydia, but she was off doing her thing, she was busy—I just slept there, and I had things to do too. But after a while all the other people I was staying with fell away, and I was still staying there, so, finally, Lydia talked to me. I was a very sullen teen, my head looking to the ground, shy. I remember her saying, 'You're as crabby as I am—I like you!'

LYDIA LUNCH Somebody gave me a broken guitar or a broken bass—I don't know who—but I was already living with James Chance, who took me in, and I just started writing the music for what became Teenage Jesus & The Jerks. How I devised the songs, it was all a basic temper tantrum. I wanted to make some of the angriest yet most precise, bitter, traumatising music—a scream from the bowels. I met Bradly Field when he was setting a homeless person on fire outside of a pharmacy, and I stamped the person out. I'd heard about Bradly because he'd come from Cleveland, as a lot of people at that time did—like Miriam Linna, who was in The Cramps. Actually, at this point, The Cramps had asked me to be their drummer because I had red hair, and I'm like, *I'm starting my own band* ... so they got Miriam Linna because she had red hair.

MIRIAM LINNA Twelfth Street and First Avenue, I was subletting from an old friend from Ohio, then Lydia and Bradly moved in briefly. There was no

---

* Hoffman founded the band Mumps and went onto be one of Lydia's key collaborators in the 80s. He was Field's partner, and they lived together in the apartment where Beirut Slump would later rehearse.

rent—we were squatting. We got kicked out when the guy whose apartment it was came back unannounced and found us in the kitchen, making a mess. Lydia was pouring ketchup on sanitary napkins and throwing them at the ceiling. I was not interested in no wave at all but was friendly with many people in those groups. And Lydia was responsible for ending my time in The Cramps, when me and Phast Phreddie Patterson walked in on Lydia and Lux Interior *in action*—quite a shock! I got the blame for bringing my sleazy roommate round.

PAUL ZONE Bradly Field told me, 'Oh, me and Lydia have a band now with James—did you know? We're called Teenage Jesus & The Jerks.' I said what a great name it was, and he told me that Lydia was Teenage Jesus—but of course.* They were the only band at the time who sounded anything like that—who had that minimalist sound, that way of putting things together. James didn't last long in the band, but it didn't make any difference to how the band sounded, and he went on to his own wonderful career.

LYDIA LUNCH James Chance was in the original incarnation of Teenage Jesus, but I found out very quickly he was hot and Teenage Jesus was very cold. He wanted to mingle with the audience, and I inspired him to start his own band, which I'm very happy I did, because then he formed The Contortions.

KRISTIAN HOFFMAN Lydia said, with a generosity she was not often credited with at the time, 'You are too talented for this band. We don't really have room to accommodate everything you're capable of! You should have your own band.'

LYDIA LUNCH Bradly did not want to play drums. I had to force him and teach him how to bang out a drum—one drum. It's what I insisted upon, and he could barely play one, but we didn't need more—we needed one drum and one cymbal, because it was basically about the guitar, the rhythm, and the

---

* Field remained the drummer for Teenage Jesus & The Jerks until the European tour of June 1979, when Johnny O'Kane took over percussion.

lyrics or the song titles. And the bass players! I had a few—they came and went. The first one I had was rather musical. He was from Japan, and his name was Reck. He was too musical, actually, for Teenage Jesus. And then we had Gordon Stevenson, and then eventually Jim Sclavunos, who was the most appropriate. I remember walking to the stage the first time and, of course, having never been onstage before, feeling a bit nervous, and that's when I decided that it's not my job to panic. It's my job to *cause* panic.

JAMES NARES Gordon Stevenson on bass, Bradly Field with one drumstick and one drum, and Lydia—it was great. Lydia was something to behold. She was very sexy, roundish, wearing these tight leather dresses and very openly sexual in her behaviour. She had that lovely laugh! She was yelling at the world and you wanted to support her—you couldn't help but love her for what she was doing. It seemed wholly justified, her anger.

PAT IRWIN I had never seen or heard anything like Teenage Jesus. It was an assault, a combination of pure emotion and energy—it killed me, it just tore me apart. The songs were so short they would end before they started—I loved every second of it. None of this fake Chuck Berry stuff—and I loved Chuck Berry by the way—but none of this note-bending rock'n'roll stuff. It was a completely unique vocabulary. The Contortions were more of a musical unit. They were more like a real 'band' than Teenage Jesus—as unique as they were, The Contortions were more traditional-sounding. Teenage Jesus were deconstructing rock'n'roll. It was magnificent.

KEMBRA PFAHLER Listening to Teenage Jesus affected me viscerally. It gave me stomach aches. My brain needed to sort of rewire itself to comprehend what I was actually experiencing. That was a good thing, and difficult. It was definitely one of the most un-entertaining yet entertaining experiences that I've had.

EXENE CERVENKA If you had a record player then you probably had old records. You had to go to New York to find out what was going on—that's where I found out about Lydia. I didn't know her name, she wasn't famous or anything … or maybe she was famous in New York at the time, she was eighteen or so, she was really young. It was a small world back then, a very tight little group—a few other people were involved—then there were those other bands who circulated around that really powerful group of people. It was amazing what was coming out of that nexus in New York. My sister's husband, Gordon Stevenson, joined Teenage Jesus, and my sister Mirielle managed them for a minute, then Lydia married a good friend of mine, Johnny O'Kane from Florida. Then my sister stopped managing them, and Johnny and Lydia broke up, and my sister started going out with Johnny— we'd known him since he was fourteen when we were growing up—then my sister died, in '80.

LYDIA LUNCH Why was Teenage Jesus frightening? That baby-face? That seventeen-year-old in a slip and high heels playing guitar? I scared a lot of people, and especially the older male musicians. The ones I didn't scare were like Robert Quine, who played guitar with Richard Hell. But Richard Hell, David Byrne—they would run from me. They didn't know what to make of it. I mean, not everybody would run, some would run toward me, but …

*

JIM SCLAVUNOS In school, I met a whole bunch of like-minded individuals—a lot of them from Minneapolis—Chris Nelson, Philip Dray, and Seth Goldstein. They were all attending New York University, alongside me, in the film department. We were all quite interested in what was going on in the clubs, and we wanted to have some way of actually getting into the clubs, so we thought, *Why don't we start a fanzine? Then we can just blag our way into the clubs.* So, we had this magazine called *No Magazine*. The subtitle of it was 'Instant Artifact Of The New Order'—a little bit of on-trend flirting with fascism there, but all in keeping with the punk spirit of the times, no ideology involved.

One day, Chris was telling me about this Lydia Lunch character: 'Oh, she's really mean. The band was really great, we want to interview her, but she was really mean, and we think you should interview her.' Maybe they thought I was a big sucker. Maybe they thought I could handle a mean lady. Anyway, I met her at CBGB's. She was very terse but not altogether impolite. And I said, 'Lydia, I'd love to see your band and interview you.' And she said, 'This is where we're playing, you can talk to me at such and such time.' This was post-Reck, so the line-up at the time was Lydia, Gordon, and Bradly. We arranged an interview and it appeared in *No Magazine* no. 3, albeit in a rather artistic way, because it was kind of chopped up and spread out through the whole magazine. We were a funny magazine, and we tried to make every issue quite different. That particular issue had Mao Tse Tung on the cover, and it was printed in red ink, and it was all very kind of collage-y.

KID CONGO POWERS I listened in on Teenage Jesus rehearsing: they were these very militaristic, very timed events. It was a real process: *This is what we're doing, this is how we're going to do it.* The music was gorgeous but also quite psychotic, coming from some other planet but still coherent—it invited you to learn a different language. The songs were so minimal, shorter than anyone's, but anyone could understand the expression. How could such basic music be so difficult? There was a desire not to be hated, but to not pander to anyone.

JIM SCLAVUNOS One of the prerequisites of being allowed to join Teenage Jesus was that I had to be deflowered by Lydia—she wasn't going to have any virgins in the band. Secondly, she clearly wanted to know what she was getting involved with, and there's no better way to get to know somebody than to have sex with them. Lydia had taken an interest in me, and, one time, when The Gynecologists had performed, she cornered me in the men's room and made her intentions pretty clear: she wanted to fuck. Unbeknownst to her, though, I was a virgin. I confessed to her that I was feeling a little bit unprepared to satisfy her request, or demand—her command. This only peaked her interest even more. She saw this as a mission to be accomplished, and she set up an appointment for deflowering me. I was meant to come to this appointment fully prepared to perform the act in question, but also she requested some additional supplies: a couple of cans of Reddi-wip, Coca-Cola, and some chewing gum. My mind was racing: *What kind of kinky stuff is this going to be? What has she got in mind? What could possibly ensue in this romantic rendezvous, the momentous occasion of my deflowering?*

I arrived at her residence on Delancey Street, which was painted entirely black inside. She lived on the upper floor, and she had a little cubbyhole loft there—her little nest that had been built into this loft apartment. I presented her with the supplies, and she immediately squirted some Reddi-wip into her mouth and drank some Coca-Cola—it was just her dinner! No kinkiness whatsoever—that was just what she subsisted on. She had peculiar dietary habits around that period. She lured me up into her boudoir, and she was very gentle and understanding with the act of seduction, and she successfully accomplished the deflowering without any trauma. I thought I was in very capable hands, and so did my girlfriend at the time who, because she didn't want to have to deal with that, said, 'Yeah, go to Lydia—let her do it. I don't want the responsibility.'

There might have also been a second act, the performance of a blowjob, in which, once consummated, she informed me that my cum tasted like clouds, which was very poetic. After all that, she asked me to hand her a book for the post-coital relaxation period. As I was sitting there, kind of decelerating from this exciting passage in my life, she started telling me about her avid interest in neurosurgery—how she had an amateur's interest in it and how she would be really interested in finding people that would be willing to be operated on. I took a quick glance around—I didn't see any scalpels. I figured she was just testing the waters, but it was enough to make me feel like, after I had composed myself, it might be time to leave.

LYDIA LUNCH It's just what I was. I still had my sense of humour! I was still very funny! I was still having a very good time, but I was not making music to involve art. This was tantrum alienation. This was me exercising my hatred and anger. This was an indictment against authority. This was *The Bad Seed*—one of my favourite films as a child, and it was the song I started playing when I got a piano.* It would drive my mother insane. I felt Teenage Jesus needed to express part of who I was, and that was this black haired, traumatising, sadistic, baby-face killer. I scared people.

---

* *The Bad Seed* (1956) is a psychological horror film, based on a 1954 novel, about a murderous eight-year-old girl.

JIM SCLAVUNOS Lydia and I agreed early on that the music was most effective when it sounded like a good hate-fuck—that's was the sort of spirit of it. Just really hard, and sort of an ugly sexy. At least that's what we thought—I don't know if anyone else found it very sexy. Her guitar sound was quite unique, a key part of the Teenage Jesus sound, and the thing that created the continuum through the various line-ups. She wasn't much for tuning—I used to tune her up once a month but, frankly, it sounded a lot better when it was out of tune. It's just that when the strings got too slack she had trouble creating her signature sound. For Bradly, one drum and one cymbal was more than enough for him, and he set about playing them like a windup monkey—but a very intuitive windup monkey. And me, well, I didn't know how to play bass. I had a vague understanding of the scales and the notes, and I could usually roughly detect the tonal centre of what Lydia was either singing at me or squalling away on the guitar. I took what I had heard on Reck and Gordon's recordings with the band and did my own version, with a much more aggressive approach. I tried to treat the bass like a blunt instrument, an instrument of attack, much like Lydia's guitar. I played with a very thick pick, I played it very hard and very aggressively, and I usually went through the PA. I didn't have an amp.

Of the nine or ten people that would attend our shows, two of them were very regular attendees: the Seidman Sisters. They were two very young ladies that were stationed on either side of the stage with baseball bats, and their function was, if anyone tried to take a photo, they were meant to threaten them with their baseball bats. Not that, I suppose, we really minded having our photos taken, but it was a bit of posturing that felt appropriate.

LYDIA LUNCH The shortest Teenage Jesus set was seven minutes. The longest was thirteen. You did not need more. 'Less Is More' was one of the songs. The first song I ever wrote—I don't think I ever performed it—was called 'Popularity Is So Boring'.

CHRISTINA BIRRER I'd seen Teenage Jesus & The Jerks in Chinatown, out in LA. It was very raw, very performance-based—out to shock, in some ways—and that's what I was attracted to, that ambience. I'd lived in New York City from 1976 to 1978, and I saw lots of performance pieces, whether it was Laurie Anderson, Patti Smith, Robert Mapplethorpe's photography, Kathy Acker's writing—and I thought Lydia had that same thing, but in a very primal way. She was using the punk thrash, but all her projects were very text-based. She's always been working textually with things, as opposed to staying within, in the 'song' way of looking at the world.

*

THURSTON MOORE when I first heard of Lydia, I was living on Thirteenth Street, between A and B, and she lived nearby. And I started seeing the name of her band in print. I thought Teenage Jesus & The Jerks was the most audacious and *wrong* kind of name there could be. And then I read an interview that she had done pretty early on, in *SoHo Weekly News*, where she was really badmouthing Patti Smith as a barefoot, smelly hippie. I thought that was completely crossing the line, because what we were doing at that time, with groups like Patti Smith, or Blondie, and Talking Heads, was really sort of creating an identity away from anything that came before. It was all new, it was new wave, it was punk rock—and this was not. This was something else. It was almost like it was too soon, you know?

I was really curious about her, and then they put this first single out, and there was a review of it in *Hit Parader* magazine, who used little icons for their reviews. So, it would be, like, a guy cheering if the record was great, but if the record was just completely terrible, it would just be a dirty boot kicking. That seven-inch got reviewed, the writer's name was Ed Naha, and it was a very pronounced boot-kicking: *This sounds like cats howling before they're killed.* He was just like, *This is the worst sounding thing I've ever heard on record.* I was with J.D. King of The Coachmen, and we just said, 'Wow, we gotta hear this. I mean, this sounds incredible, that's the best review I've ever read of anything!' We ran over to Free Being Records on Second Avenue. We both bought the single. I thought the record was more hardcore than any punk record I've ever heard, and I was hearing them all.

JIM SCLAVUNOS There was a lot of cross-fertilisation among the no-wave bands, like Mars—Sumner Crane in particular. He was dating Lydia on and off all through that period of time, and I'm sure there was an interplay, some kind of dialogue, however fraught with psychodrama that might have been. They had a very kind of complex relationship, both being very complex personalities and unique personalities, to say the least.

KRISTIAN HOFFMAN Lydia and I hit it off for some reason, likely because she was friends with most of the crazies I was closely involved with: James Chance, Bradly Field, Gordon Stevenson, Diego Cortez, various members of Mars. Her relationship with Sumner Crane was interesting! She was playing Herman's Hermits on the turntable, of all things—she said at the time they were her favourite band—and Sumner was on some sort of government providence for the mentally unstable at the time. There was a lot of slamming doors and screaming. I think Lydia liked it that way!

JIM SCLAVUNOS It's hard to summarise Sumner. He was a very odd man with some brilliant ideas and made some amazing work in his time, not least of which was his work as a member of the band Mars. But we all knew each other, and some of us knew each other intimately. So you had The Contortions, DNA, Mars, us—the classic *No New York* configuration.

RICHARD EDSON There was a huge amount of diversity in New York at the time, different scenes, and there was a difference between the SoHo component and the East Village component. One was more from the street—Jean-Michel Basquiat, Madonna, Liquid Liquid, Richard Hell, Richard Kern—totally out of the East Village; I identified much more with them than I did with Rhys Chatham and Glenn Branca. A lot of the SoHo kids came from money—they were being supported, so they had nicer lofts, better clothes, better equipment.

THURSTON MOORE There was a bit of a civil war between bands that were coming out of the East Village and bands coming out of SoHo. I remember Glenn Branca telling me that at the Artists Space gig for Teenage Jesus, Lydia was wearing a leather vest and coming up and just smashing into him, bumping into him, and looking at him going, like, *Excuse me!* And knowing that it was this guy in this band, so that was her way of introducing herself.

JIM SCLAVUNOS *No New York* came about after a show at Artists Space.* Eno was present and he saw the bands, he wanted to record all of them, but he wound up recording just four. What connected us—Mars, DNA, Teenage Jesus, The Contortions—was Mark, Gordon, Arto, and me going to the same college; then we met Lydia, Bradly, and James early on. We shared rehearsal spaces, amplifiers, and instruments, and we performed together. The four bands were very different, of course. We also knew all those SoHo bands, like Theoretical Girls and UT and the Y-Pants, Rhys Chatham when he went solo, and The Gynecologists. I was tarred with the SoHo brush for a while by dint of being in The Gynecologists. I wasn't at the meeting, but I believe Lydia and James somewhat conspired to keep those bands off *No New York*, assuring Brian Eno that their coterie was far more important than any of these SoHo bands. I don't know if that's true, but that's what I gathered, by rumour. For my part, I liked a lot of those bands, but I could kind of see the point of how the four bands that ended up on *No New York* really embodied a certain kind of mentality and a particular approach that was less about art and more about action and emotion and attitude.

BOB BERT After I got out of high school, I went to the School Of Visual Arts and learned how to become a silkscreen printer. I became a fine art silkscreen printer, and eventually I ended up working for Warhol and printing his artwork. By 1978, I've moved to New York, I had an apartment for $115 a month. I was at work one day, and this girl that I worked with showed up with that *No New York* record. I just looked at it and I said, 'Hey, this is the new thing, you know?' I saw the front cover of the record and was floored by it. I saw the back cover, which floored me even more. I was immediately in a trance.

MARC HURTADO *No New York* was different because it used real instruments— but for destroying rock'n'roll. It was new, pure, and beautiful—more like

---

* The show in question took place on May 6, 1978, as part of a festival of local bands. Brian Eno was in town producing a Talking Heads album and, impressed by various performances he witnessed, proposed the idea of a compilation documenting some part of the scene. The album was recorded rapidly and came out the same year.

surrealism or Dada than rock'n'roll. Everything on that compilation was incredible. Lydia was a great writer, and the noise of the guitar was like the scream of a baby, of an infant—it spoke to my heart because my own personal life was complicated, it hadn't been easy. Discovering something like that, at sixteen, I didn't know she was young like me, but it felt like a message direct *to* me. That first impact was incredible.

JIM THIRLWELL I left Australia in 1978 to move to London, but even then I was aware of Lydia, having heard about Teenage Jesus, the no-wave scene, and of *No New York*. When you look at the back cover, the pictures of the people and their names, it looks like mug shots from an insane asylum. That was very compelling.

*

THURSTON MOORE Supposedly they played a gig supporting Wire on some bill at some punk club in London. What Lydia's connection was, I don't know, but they got to customs in London with their guitars, and the customs official said, 'Why are you coming here?' 'We're just visiting.' 'Why are you carrying these guitars?' And Lydia, to her genius, said, 'Well where we live in New York, it's so dangerous that we don't feel comfortable leaving our musical instruments in our apartments, so we're carrying them with us.' And he let them in.*

CHRISTOPH DREHER SO36 was emerging as the most important concert venue in Berlin. It was run by Martin Kippenberger, the painter. Written on the Berlin Wall in huge letters was that Teenage Jesus & The Jerks were playing at SO36.† This relation to New York and no wave started quite early on. When

---

* Teenage Jesus & The Jerks briefly visited London in December 1977 and performed at the Roxy, the Vortex, and one unknown venue with Wayne County & The Electric Chairs and Generation X, among others.

† Teenage Jesus & The Jerks embarked on a European tour in June 1979, with their final performance taking place on June 30, 1979, after which they broke up. Lydia was hospitalised with a serious medical issue and performed the final three shows from a wheelchair.

I went to America in 1980 with a film I made at film academy, I was in San Francisco and I met DNA, who were playing on three consecutive days to a relatively small audience, for twenty minutes, and I was totally impressed—the most exciting thing I'd seen in years. From San Francisco, I arranged a tour ending in New York. There I got in touch with DNA and met a whole load of people, including, I believe, Lydia.

JIM SCLAVUNOS The type of aggression that Teenage Jesus & The Jerks were staging was a very particular type of violence. We were one of the most minimalist of bands at that time. We were minimal in terms of our setup, and we were very static. It was supposed to be intense and confrontational, but without actually engaging the audience directly, if we could avoid it. There were occasionally moments of outreach, such as when Lydia threw a glass of water at some fellow in the front row.*

LYDIA LUNCH I was very ill and touring with Teenage Jesus. I literally had to go from a wheelchair to the stage. Somebody was taking my photo, I asked them two or three times to stop. They didn't. I picked up a glass and threw it, and it smashed against the camera, which was held to their face. Now, this is justifiable. I don't just get into a rage and start breaking things. I just don't get into a rage and start hitting people. A lot of us have a natural sense of violence, as human animals conceived in a violent act, born and baptised in blood, our first cries slapped out of us—the first act of creation being the Big Bang. I think there is violence I've tried to deal with in my own life, understanding my need to watch other people be violent, or inspiring them to violence. It's exercising my own violence without having to get my hands dirty.

JIM SCLAVUNOS And I remember, at the gig in Berlin on that same tour, I remember kicking some poor fellow in the face. But, generally, we didn't participate in any kind of repartee with the audience. We just glared at them. It was supposed to be cold and brutal and static and intense. And these shows were not very long. They were, like, ten to thirteen minutes, tops.

---

* The glass hit the promoter, and the gig was promptly cancelled.

A funny thing, on the live binaural recording that Charles Ball did of us at CBGB's, at the end of the one of the songs, there's this pattering of applause and somebody shouting, 'Less! Less!'

LYDIA LUNCH I had a lot of natural violence, although I've never done anything out of just anger—I've never thrown a plate, hard to believe, because I was angry—because I was far more manipulative than that, and I would much prefer to 'puppet master' other people to do my violence for me. I am often a magnet for other people's need for violence committed against them, which is interesting. I can sit quietly at a party to this day and people come up to antagonise me. I'll just give an example of the other night. I'm sitting quietly at a party—I don't even like parties—and somebody is getting really spidery and annoying. I merely deflect, which causes him to punch himself. I just merely deflected a spidery embrace, which caused him to hit himself. Then I'm accused of hitting him. Therefore, I hit him, to prove the point. I didn't just hit him, but now I did.

JIM SCLAVUNOS Lydia's personality has always been, she thinks very rapid-fire, and there's maybe just some difficulty in concentrating at times, or she loses her patience, or maybe her enthusiasm for all that life has to offer is so overwhelming that she can't stick with one thing for very long. Whatever the case may be, whatever's behind that, in terms of her personality, one of the results of that has been that she's very much the kind of person that moves from project to project to project. Teenage Jesus & The Jerks actually might have been one of the longest ones, and she said, 'Well, as soon as I'm not a teenager anymore, I'm going to stop this and move on to the next thing.'

JOE BUDENHOLZER That stuff is timeless. The beats and the timing are nuts, the level of complexity for guitar-bass-drums. It's underrated that she's a pioneer of guitar music at age sixteen. What do you do after you've broken the barriers of rock music on your first twenty-minute-long album?

CHAPTER THREE

GIRLS ON FILM

LYDIA RAPIDLY BECOMES AN ICONIC PRESENCE IN THE NO-WAVE CINEMA SCENE, WITH A NUMBER OF KEY FILMMAKERS UTILISING HER FEARLESSNESS IN FRONT OF THE CAMERA.

LYDIA LUNCH We—the aliens, the weirdos, the ones that were escaping family, looking for something else—we were all here. And why it was easy to come together is there were only so many places to go. There were clubs that welcomed our type, and we would go there night after night, so you're going to meet the filmmakers, the painters, the musicians, the photographers, the writers. It was a very accepting time. To me, what was also interesting is there were a lot of women involved—it didn't feel like there was a gender divide. It felt like we were against everything else. People were doing all kinds of things, and we had to do it all now: we had to make the music now, we had to make the films now, we had to take the photos now!

JAMES NARES We had this aesthetic that I believe Eric Mitchell instigated. He would say, 'Just do it.' He was very inspiring to a lot of people, and very antagonistic to some as well. We had this belief in the value of just picking up an instrument and making music, just figuring it out. The attitude was one of making something new and starting from the beginning: three-chord rock became very simple three-roll films—*I'll be in your movie if you do sound for mine*, that kind of thing. The whole production was shared within this amorphous but connected group. We were connected by the feeling of marginalisation—we felt unseen, unappreciated, that the art world and the music world didn't care what we were doing. So, we opened our own theatres to show our own movies, made our own music and played it in lofts, those sorts of things. There was a very strong sense that we were being negative, intentionally iconoclastic, but it was all toward a good end—we felt there was a need to be that way at that time. It was something that was shared by a lot of different people in different disciplines at the same time: dancers, poets, painters, singers. Everyone was fuelled by this same grievance.

VIVIENNE DICK I got to New York in '74, then moved to France for a little while, then I was in England for a period in the mid-70s, then went back to New York and stayed there. There was nothing happening in Ireland, and it was impossible to get any work in England as well. I had been teaching English as a second language in Paris, and it was very boring out in the suburbs, not exactly fun. I was looking for adventure. I don't know what exactly brought me to New York, but it felt like a place where I'd somehow be freer—which turned out to be the case. When I got to America and saw American independent cinema, it was mind-blowing for me. I did not know films could be made like that, by individuals, and on such low budgets— films with Taylor Mead, Jack Smith, Ken Jacobs, Maya Deren, Shirley Clarke. There's a whole history of independent filmmaking centred in New York, and I was enthralled by it.

BETH B I picked up a Super-8 camera and started making films in 1975, not knowing what I was doing, but with one key concern, which was that there had to be content. There was so much going on at that time, politically, that was insane: it was a time of terrorist groups rebelling all over the world, and film was my small way of rebelling, by representing the truth of what was going on in the country. Truth-telling has always really been my concern. I wanted to voice the unheard. What was most important to me was content: looking at the politics of that time and making a controversial commentary on that. No one was talking about disproportionate wealth, what was going on in families, the abuses, the addictions, the dysfunction … no one was talking about any of this. We didn't have a language to verbalise what we were feeling.

My problem with a lot of the experimental films being made was that they were masturbatory, structuralist, about nothing, but going on forever. Are you kidding me? Cut it to ten seconds! I wasn't thinking about length, I was thinking about what needed to go into that film, that statement. Alongside that were all of these 70s radical groups—the Symbionese Liberation Army, the Red Army Faction, the FALN*—who were trying to explode the hierarchy and power structure of that time.

JAMES NARES I went back to England for the first time since I'd arrived in New York and shot *Suicide? No, Murder!* (1977), which was a kind of travelogue that I then fictionalised. The political scene in England was really heavy—there were all these demos and protests, and I filmed these kinds of things, then wove in a sub-narrative. When Andreas Baader of the Baader-Meinhof gang—the Red Army Faction—was found dead in his cell, there was a graffiti on a wall I filmed that read 'Suicide? No, Murder!' and we all believed they'd been killed in their cells. I gave it a double meaning because I was feeling, not exactly suicidal, but I was very self-destructive. I wound a faux-suicide attempt into the narrative, at the point where you don't know what's really real. It was about not killing yourself—kill your enemies instead.

BETH B In the film *G Man* (1978), the first film that Scott and I did together, I felt we were trying to confront that power structure. You had actor Bill Rice playing Max Karl, the police chief, head of the arson and explosives squad. In public, he has a lot of power, and we follow him into his private life, where he wants to dress up in women's clothing and be dominated by a woman. The imbalance of power is what *G Man* was about—that conflicted state that

---

* The Fuerzas Armadas de Liberación Nacional was a Puerto Rican paramilitary organisation. The Red Army Faction was a militant far-left guerrilla group based in West Germany. The group's founders died in their cells in 1976 and 1977. The Symbionese Liberation Army was a left-wing group active in the USA across 1973–75. This was an extraordinary era in which a variety of urban guerrilla groups were active across most Western countries, including the Angry Brigade (UK), the Weather Underground (USA), and the Red Brigades (Italy).

exists in many of us. It was a way of trying to scratch the surface and to talk about the repression of pain, the magnetic attraction to things we know can destroy us, the obsessions we are unable to control. Prior to coming to New York, I didn't have the consciousness to identify the things that were really disturbed within myself, and actually it's taken a lifetime to understand and dissect them, but this was the beginning of an awakening of sorts.

VIVIENNE DICK I would never have made films except for being in New York and because there was a sense of community, of people working in Super-8— filmmakers like Scott and Beth B, like Eric Mitchell, James Nares, a number of others. Around '77, I met Beth, Eric, all the people like that, all in one evening, in a party at someone's house. They were talking about making films, and it was a really exciting moment—I decided I wanted to do that too. It was very important that it was a community of people—that sense that we were somewhat interested in the same things. If you're making something, whatever it is, it's hard to do creative work entirely alone—you need feedback, it's important. Very quickly, I was making *Guerillere Talks* (1978), then *Beauty Becomes The Beast* (1979). It was a very fertile spell—I was just going for it. I had the need to make these films.

JAMES NARES I love that scene in one of Vivienne's films, *Guerillere Talks*, where Lydia is walking around the rooftop, there's all this destruction outside, and she's talking about, 'We got nothing, there's nothing here for us,' and she goes off into this monologue.

VIVIENNE DICK *Guerillere Talks* was the first film I ever made. I approached Lydia on the street, having seen her perform. I wanted her to be in the film because I wanted to talk to her, but I didn't know how to talk to her, so I asked her if she would be in the film. I told her she could do whatever she wanted or say whatever she wanted, and I would just shoot the film for three minutes— that's what we did. In fact, we made two reels of film. I might have been the first person to film her—she was in demand after that. She's very photogenic, she's fantastic in front of the camera; I turned the camera on and she just started, she didn't need a script, she adlibbed. She's a performer.

I wanted to capture this new type of woman that I hadn't encountered before, someone like Lydia, Pat Place, Anya Phillips.* With *Guerillere Talks*, I didn't have the intention of making it into a film, I just wanted to shoot one roll with each person. In retrospect, possibly, I may have been influenced by Warhol's films—the ones where people are just sitting in front of the camera doing nothing. There's something incredibly mysterious and interesting about looking at somebody on film. I wanted to shoot these people doing whatever they wanted to do. It wasn't like I was directing them, even though we might have discussed a location between us. Then I decided to stick all these films together and made it half an hour.

JAMES NARES We were at a club one night, and a friend of mine had a big 60s suburban station wagon—it was like a truck—and we all piled into it at five or six in the morning and went to the beach. Chris Burden was there—he was terrified the cops were going to get us! David McDermott was there too, and he always dressed in Edwardian outfits.† So there are people there with beach towels and swimwear, then we arrive, looking like I don't know what. David starts tiptoeing through the surf and singing old music-hall songs—it was so great, he was so engaging and funny.

Right there and then, I decided to make a Roman movie—which became *Rome '78* (1978). The idea of doing a historical costume drama on the streets of New York appealed to me—it was so crazy, and there was an obvious comparison between Rome and what seemed like the teetering empire of America. We were dragging people in off the streets to act as guards, giving them a helmet and a spear, and saying, 'Stand here!' It was fun, but it was

---

* Place was a co-founder of The Contortions who played in Bush Tetras and on various of Lydia's projects, as well as creating visual art and appearing in Vivienne Dick's films. Phillips co-founded Mudd Club along with Steve Maas and Diego Cortez. She was a major force in no-wave fashion styles, and managed of James Chance. She died of cancer at age twenty-six on June 19, 1981.

† Burden was a major force in performance art from the early 70s, with his work often involving degrees of self-violence. He would later turn to installation art and sculpture. McDermott is a visual artist best known for his enduring collaboration with Peter McGough. From 1980 to 1995, the duo would dress, live, and work as gentleman from the early 1900s and converted their entire home to match (it was lit only by candles, for example).

serious fun. Fun was anathema to the art world—they were almost completely opposed to it—so that made us feel that enjoying ourselves was almost a political statement in opposition to the stance of those who had power in the arts. Vivienne's presentation of Lydia was the most accurate. In my film there are a couple of scenes where it's accurate—a scene where she's talking to Pat Place, the assassin—but there's also a scene where everyone got drunk and she gets giggly and silly. I got the sense she didn't like seeing herself in that film. She also shines in Beth B and Scott B's movies.

VIVIENNE DICK *She Had Her Gun All Ready* (1978), it's about relationship, trying to understand it, and that song '96 Tears' that was used in the film is about that too—but the lyrics are kind of horrifying, if you listen, even though I love that song. Relationship in every sense is a complex thing, and it seems to be that in the history of philosophy, at least up until recently, relationship has been described as a case of one party dominating another: that's what this film was attempting to examine. There's two women in the film, and, in a way, Lydia is made for a certain part: Pat being the more passive party and Lydia the more dominant. There's a sense of one being in thrall to the other, or of someone looking at themselves in a mirror—you can read things in so many different ways. I had a very strong need to make this film, and I'm unwilling to give exact meaning. There are moments of noir in it, moments of melodrama, all these things—and also humour. The ending, the rollercoaster at Coney Island is gone now, but we went on it four times to film it. Lydia loved going on the scary rides, and she'd scream. Lydia is very good at collaborating and working with her on the films. She does trust you; she doesn't question things.

DONITA SPARKS We met Lydia when L7 came through New York in '89, because we were staying at Richard Kern's place. We ended up going to Coney Island together, and we rode the Cyclone, and that was just insanity. I thought we were all gonna die, while Lydia is laughing her ass off and just flailing, practically standing up in the rollercoaster! She was sitting in front of me, and I was just like, *Oh my god, I'm gonna die with Lydia Lunch and Richard Kern! This is going to be fabulous!* But then, *I don't wanna die!*

JIM SCLAVUNOS We used to take acid and go to Coney Island and ride the rides there. We were young and foolish, free-spirited. There was one particularly epic acid trip that she and I shared where all sorts of things went on, everything from throwing TVs out of windows, to throwing hammers through French doors, all culminating in a visit by the police, who were answering a report of a woman screaming. When the police came, they wanted to inspect the premises. 'We got this call, a woman screaming.' We led them to Lydia's room. The door was locked, and I tapped on the door: 'Lydia some policemen are here, they want to see you.' And she said something to the effect of, 'Yeah? Send them in here and tell them to fuck me!' No doubt more eloquent than that, but that was the gist. I don't know what happened, but the police officers were satisfied with what they saw in the room and went on their merry way.

*

LYDIA LUNCH Back when I started doing films—because I'm not an actress, and I don't consider myself one—we just did whatever we wanted to do, in any form of expression we could find a way to do it. There were a lot of women doing films at that point. The first film I did in New York was with Vivienne Dick. I was drawn to her because she was like nobody else I had ever met. She had a great sense of fear yet boldness, and in one film that she wanted me in I was playing somebody that somebody else was stalking because they were frightened of me. Basically, I wasn't acting, I was kind of just playing myself. It was more than just films at that time—we were trying to document a moment of personal insanity or political insanity. People would ask you, 'Do you want to be in a film?' You say, 'Yeah, I'll be in a film, I'm not doing anything tomorrow.' And because it was a new kind of cinema and I really like the idea of short films, that was interesting to me, and that was attractive to me.

BETH B People were feeling a kind of urgency—we didn't know what we were doing, we didn't know at all, but we had this urgency to speak out about the abuses of our times. We didn't have a voice, so we found other people to create a voice with us. It made for a surge of energy and collaboration that, in a way, revolutionised things for a lot of artists and filmmakers. They crossed boundaries that previously had been seen as exclusive. There was no idea of success—it really wasn't on our radar—we just had to do it, against all odds, and nothing else mattered. The first film series I did was shown at Max's Kansas City on a weekly basis. It was booked just like a band. Showing films at a rock club had really never been done. To do it, you had to be as insane and as loud as the rock acts were. The advantage I had was that a lot of people from the scene appeared in the films as actors—that was an attraction to the audiences as well. The clubs could see that there was money to be made from this, and that was the bottom line.

VIVIENNE DICK We were interested in making films centred around what was going on at the time. We supported each other in various ways, showed our films in the same kinds of places, did the same things, like putting up posters—doing what the bands were doing. We bypassed the whole film thing—we showed at music clubs like Max's or Mudd Club. I was invited to show *Beauty Becomes The Beast* at the New Cinema when it opened, the first time it was shown.

BOB BERT Any time one of Beth's films, or Vivienne Dick's films, was on, I used to love going to these little rooms in the East Village on a Tuesday night, watching Lydia Lunch or Pat Place sitting in a kitchen or something like that. I loved the image of these women, I was spellbound, there was nothing else like it. It was this outsider image that was totally unique. Growing up in suburbia, going to a Catholic school, I got fed up with normal people really quickly. I was attracted to the counterculture, to more underground stuff, and Lydia ruled over all of that.

THURSTON MOORE I remember sitting on the floor and seeing the first showing of Beth and Scott B's *Letters To Dad* (1979) and thinking how amazing it was.*

---

* *Letters To Dad* is a short, stark film in which various individuals address the camera, voicing letters that had been written to the cult leader Jim Jones in the run up to the mass suicide/murder of his followers in Jonestown, Guyana, in November 1978.

It was such a new and brutalist kind of film. I just knew that I was kind of where I wanted to be.

BETH B My first memory of Lydia is seeing her onstage. I was blown away. It was so black—but there was something so attractive in that bleakness. I saw her play a number of other times, and when writing the script for *Black Box* (1979), we needed a torturess. I said, 'Lydia!' She was the perfect representation of that. *Black Box*, even though it's in the guise of this government agency arresting this young boy and taking him to be interrogated, it was more metaphorical, more about the emotional and psychological self, hand in hand with the political. It was crucially important for me to cast a woman in that role—it was the opposite of most films made up to that time. It was, in a way, taking that role model of the dominatrix and bringing it into politics. It makes that film so powerful, that it was inverting the norm. What was exciting to me at the time was finding other people who wanted to break these boundaries and who were willing to spew out all this rage and alienation. That's why I identified so much with Lydia, and with Teenage Jesus. I found that band frightening, and I found her equally scary because I had never seen a woman have that much presence and articulation of self—never in my entire life.

PAUL ZONE There were artists, painters, writers, musicians, all hanging out on the cusp of oblivion, and with no hope beyond being put in some little fanzine or playing a show at one of these little clubs—it was the smallest scene ever, until some of the major newspapers started to write about CBGB's, some of the bands, some of the painters. That brought people in from other parts of town because—until then—no one wanted to go to the Bowery, where the bums were laying down on the pavement in front of you.

CHAPTER FOUR

BEIRUT SLUMP

INAUGURATED AT LYDIA'S NINETEENTH
BIRTHDAY IN JUNE 1978, BEIRUT SLUMP
EXIST FOR JUST UNDER A YEAR, PLAYING
JUST FOUR SHOWS BEFORE DISBANDING.

LYDIA LUNCH I had another band, Beirut Slump, which was like horrorcore—the exact opposite sound to Teenage Jesus. I wrote the music, I played the guitar, but Teenage Jesus was short stabs of brutal precision offset with shrieking slide guitar, while Beirut Slump was like a slug over a razor blade, very slow and torturous.

BOBBY SWOPE There was a birthday party for Lydia in her loft, which was on Delancey Street. My sister Liz and I went to the party, met Lydia for the first time, and we clearly hit it off. My sister and I were roommates, and the next day Lydia called on the phone and spoke to Liz and said, 'Oh, I want you to be in my new band.' Liz told her, 'OK, great!' Click. That was it. Two days later, Lydia called back—Liz answered the phone again—and Lydia said, almost as an afterthought, 'I want Bobby to be the singer.'

We just thought, *Why not?* I really didn't give it a second thought. Someone had asked me to do it, and I thought I should try—if it was terrible it just wouldn't go anywhere, and that would be the end of it. I'd had no musical training or anything, but it was interesting! I don't know how it was decided who else would be in the band. Vivienne Dick was an obvious choice, as she was a good friend of ours and of Lydia's; Jim Sclavunos was on the scene and available, so we just got together and started rehearsing.

LIZ SWOPE It was almost like a project, like building a boat with some friends, then maybe you're going to take it out sailing. I was a little intimidated because I couldn't really play an instrument, but I was there as part of the look and the vibe of the band. I became the bass player by default because Lydia was the guitar player, Jim was the drummer, Vivienne played keyboards, and Bobby was the singer, so, by default, bass was the thing that was left.

VIVIENNE DICK Lydia, in certain company, with certain people, would show so many sides of herself: she could be playful, she could be gossipy. After we made *Guerillere Talks* together, she invited me to rehearsals, and, during the rehearsal, asked me if I'd like to be in this band. 'Do you want to be in this band?' Just like that. I had played a little piano and violin at school, and at one point I played some sounds on the violin on one of The Contortions' recordings. It was such a thrill for me to play the keyboard or the violin and just make my own noise. Beirut Slump rehearsed a lot, and rehearsals were really good fun. Bobby wrote the songs, and we had the same set—there'd be a pause and there'd be all this gossiping going on, then we'd start again. The rehearsals were more fun than playing out, though we did do that a few times, which was interesting because people found the noise intolerable!

LIZ SWOPE Joining the band did mean the end of our friendship with Gordon Stevenson. Maybe there was some jealousy—it's hard to know because it seems so silly, looking back, given it wasn't like anything was going very far—but maybe it was the tipping point, because it seemed to be a big thing to him that we were now involved with Lydia.

JIM SCLAVUNOS Around the time that I heard James Chance had just left Teenage Jesus & The Jerks, my first thought was, *I wonder if I could get a gig playing with Lydia as a sax player?* I figured there was a vacancy she was waiting to fill with a suitable racket-maker on saxophone. Turns out she wasn't. She said, 'No, I don't want a saxophone in the band.' Then she said, 'But I'm firing Gordon next week, as soon as the *No New York* recording session is over, and you can replace him after that.' It turns out she was also firing Mirielle Cervenka, who was managing the band at the time—she already had plans in place to replace Mirielle with Anya Phillips. Mirielle was married to Gordon, and they were both going to get the boot in no uncertain terms. And that's what happened.

LIZ SWOPE Bradly [Field] and his boyfriend Kristian [Hoffman] were living in a big apartment on the corner of Grand and Bowery. They had a rehearsal space down in the basement but I don't think we ever rehearsed down there—we always rehearsed up in their bedroom. It was a commercial building so, at five, everyone would leave apart from them, and they had this loft on the top floor. We would just go there once or twice a week and rehearse our five or six songs.

BOBBY SWOPE We rehearsed in a small, windowless, airless room. The rest of the band would be jamming, trying to come up with a song, and there I was, with a few poem fragments in my hands, trying to enter this overwhelming, cacophonous musical hurricane.

LYDIA LUNCH I didn't write the lyrics. They were written by Bobby Swope. They were all quotes from homeless people.

BOBBY SWOPE This is one of the biggest misconceptions: the idea that all the lyrics were taken from street people. Exclusively, in the song 'Try Me', I did use a few phrases I heard a crazy bum shouting on the subway: 'Try me! When you gonna try me? I went down to the river last night, are they gonna catch me?' And finally, 'They tell me to shut up! Shut up with a knife!'

LIZ SWOPE Bradly, who was usually cooking dinner while we rehearsed, commented years later how often he had heard the line, 'Shut up with a knife!'

BOBBY SWOPE The lyrics in all the other songs were written by me. I had, in some moments of loneliness or introspection, written a few short poems, which I brought to rehearsals. One song, 'Staircase', was inspired by once being with Lydia when she was telling me, 'I'm feeling very anxious these days, I don't like going out of the house, I feel like becoming a recluse.' We talked about that and it stuck with me, so I crafted a song about somebody who couldn't go out of the house. That song became 'Staircase', which included the line, 'The door is a carnivore.' You can imagine how intimidating it was to try and sing in a way, and with subject matter, that would be a match to the music. It was a kind of a musical battle between them and me.

PAUL ZONE There was something about Lydia—she had the ability to reach people in a way that they'd never been reached. Who knows where it came from or what put it inside of her brain? She had a gift. Believe me, there were just as many people walking out as those who would stay there, so I'm not saying she had a tremendous audience at first—I'd see people laughing, then getting up to leave. What was completely out of the ordinary is that as soon as you heard that she had a band going, as soon as it was something you might have heard of, you'd learn that she had one or two other bands going at the same time. Hardly anyone did that. It meant if you didn't like what she was doing this week then that was OK, you might like what she was doing next month.

LYDIA LUNCH I had both bands at the same time because I had a musical schizophrenia. We'll say my schizophrenia manifested itself musically because I had various sides and emotions I needed to express but, musically, I'm a conceptualist. I have an idea for a sound then I find the collaborators that can make that sound with me, then I would document it, then I would go on. I never had a band in those days that lasted beyond its necessary means. And the means were, write the songs, find the collaborators, perfect the songs, play or not, record—next!

BOBBY SWOPE The only thing Lydia made clear was that she wanted the music to be very, very slow—which was quite different from what everybody else was doing. Like a funeral dirge, excruciating to listen to, something inducing extreme and agonising discomfort in the listener.*

---

* For anyone seeking to confirm the truth of this description, the eight known studio recordings of Beirut Slump are available on the 2008 compilation *Shut Up And Bleed*.

LIZ SWOPE Lydia told me to play, and I used to joke, if anyone asked me about my participation, I would plead the Nuremberg defence: 'I was only following orders!' She showed me that instead of having a bass line, you could just pluck whenever you felt like it. Vivienne knew piano and she was a good keyboard player, while Jim knew how to drum, so I felt like Lydia wanted me to do this, and maybe the point was that I wasn't an expert. The music was almost like a nightmare—that's what I found interesting. The whole package, not each individual person—what we came up with together. Lydia was very business-like—she knew the sound she wanted and built the band around it.

JIM SCLAVUNOS I found it very easy to work with Lydia. She didn't have to explain very much to me, and her directions have always been rather economical and pretty clear: *Play slower, play faster, play harder.* All the other nuances didn't really have to be gone into because, a lot of times, her instinct for finding people to play with, collaborators, is rather precise. But at the same time rather generous and flexible. She can see that certain people can do certain kinds of things, and she embraces that and she allows them to do that.

BOBBY SWOPE I don't remember how rehearsals would start, but we would try to figure out a song from Lydia's lead. She would tell Jim and Liz pretty much what to play—this very plodding bass line—and they would keep going. I was expected to just jump in when I was ready. That was always a challenge. I remember that at rehearsals I made a point of trying to sing against the tempo of the music and not with it. As far as the music was concerned, Lydia had an intuition about the sound she wanted the band to have, and she winged it. Vivienne was very inspired to add this horror-show organ to the thing. The atmosphere was key to the whole thing—it was really pretty terrifying. It was terrifying to do it, and I'm sure terrifying to listen to it. Maybe it has something to do with the fact that I'm a Gemini, the two sides, the Dr. Jekyll and Mr. Hyde. On the one hand, for the most part I'm a very quiet person, and yet, on the other hand, I can draw on rages inside and bring them out pretty easily. That's what I was doing with

Beirut Slump: accessing part of myself I didn't usually have an occasion to access.

LIZ SWOPE For maybe literally a year, we rehearsed—we didn't play anywhere, we just consistently rehearsed. It got to be kind of funny that we rehearsed but we'd never play, so I guess at some point Lydia decided we were ready.

BOBBY SWOPE I remember one bit of advice Lydia gave us before the first gig: 'Remember that you're up here and they're down there. They're looking at you, so you have the power.'

LIZ SWOPE I remember two shows. There were a few more people there at the Mudd Club as opposed to Max's, but not many. I was a little nervous, so once you get started it's all kind of a blur. We had practised a lot, so there were no huge disasters, but it was a fairly short setlist—we probably didn't play for more than twenty minutes because we just didn't have that many songs.

BOBBY SWOPE There were three live performances: a film benefit in the East Village, the second at Max's Kansas City with my mother from Tennessee in attendance, and the last at Mudd Club. The gig at the film benefit, it was pretty crowded and there wasn't really a stage, there was just an area where we performed—we were all on one level with the audience. And when we started, some street person came right up to me and tried to take the microphone away. He was drunk, he was yelling, I resisted, and then he just drifted back into the crowd. Mudd Club, the place was packed with people right up to the stage, and when we began to play it was like a sonic boom or a stink bomb had exploded. In a huge mass, the audience moved to the back of the club with only a handful of diehard fans ringing the stage. My only real memory is the shock—people were so unprepared for what they heard. I didn't laugh, but it did make me laugh to see this mass of people heading for the exit like it was a fire or something. It was very gratifying as that's what we were really after. That was the thing about Beirut Slump: it was meant to be discomforting, scary, painful. I think it achieved its goal.

LIZ SWOPE Lydia wanted to be in your face, so different to most of the stuff out there—even though all the bands at the time were so different in their own way. For her, even the fact that she wasn't having to sing was probably different. Lydia just stood and played—that was almost confrontational, the way she played.

BOBBY SWOPE Since Lydia already had a recording relationship with Charles Ball at Migraine, it was only natural that we would want to record our output, even though, at that point, we had never played live.* We always knew 'Try Me' was our strongest song, but I can't remember why we chose 'Staircase' for the B-side. I know that Charles—aka Woody Payne—listed himself as the producer of the single, but Lydia always told me that the credit should have gone to Robert Quine. He was a big fan of Beirut Slump. We recorded everything because we knew this was the opportunity to lay it down, so we just did it. We rehearsed so much and we had so few songs that we had polished them to perfection, so when it came time to record them we fell into our places and it was very comfortable. At that point, basically, we had our set of six songs—'Try Me', 'Staircase', 'See Pretty', 'GI Blue', 'Sidewalk', and 'Case #14'.

LIZ SWOPE Jim told me, after we recorded, that Charles Ball asked him to rerecord my bass parts but he declined. I guess Charles just did not get that my 'primitive' playing contributed to the 'slump' in Beirut Slump. Incidentally, the Son Of Sam serial killer was terrorising New York and killing people in cars in summer '77—that was what the gun sight on the cover was about. The guy was called David Berkowitz, so that's where the 'Bobby Berkowitz' name Bobby used in Beirut Slump came about— apparently Berkowitz said his dog was telling him to go out and kill.

---

* The New York–based Migraine Records label released the Teenage Jesus singles 'Orphans' (1978) and 'Baby Doll' (1979), as well as the EP *Teenage Jesus And The Jerks*, colloquially referred to as 'the pink EP'. Charles Ball founded Ork Records, the publishing company Lust/Unlust Music, and various sub-labels that played a significant role in getting the music of the NYC punk and no-wave scenes out into the world. He died in 2012.

BOBBY SWOPE At the time they were selecting the bands to be on *No New York*, Beirut Slump auditioned for Eno to be on that record. Besides the fact that I don't think he wanted Lydia to have two bands on his record, I understood after the fact that he really did not like my singing.

LIZ SWOPE It was more like a loft than a recording studio, and we played a song for him—that was a high point for me, he's an idol! We filed in, and he was sitting there, there wasn't a lot of interaction, but he was in the room as we played.

BOBBY SWOPE After the last live performance, Lydia made it clear that she was moving on, and so Beirut Slump had a gentle demise. I would have liked to play CBGB's, but I remember Lydia thought we would get killed there because we were so unlike the other bands that were performing—she thought it would be disastrous. It was such a special moment that year that, when it ended, everyone just felt we had done what we had to do. It was a band, from the beginning, that didn't have very much longevity built into it.

ABOVE Teenage Jesus & The Jerks line-up #4: Jim Sclavunos, Lydia Lunch, Bradly Field (photo by Godlis). **RIGHT** Four Migraine Records releases from 1978–79: Teenage Jesus's 'Orphans' and 'Baby Doll' singles, plus the *Pre-Teenage Jesus & The Jerks* EP, and the Beirut Slump single 'Try Me'.

OPPOSITE PAGE, FROM TOP Stills from early film roles: *Rome '78* (James Nares, 1978); *Guerrillere Talks* (Vivienne Dick, 1978); *Beauty Becomes The Beast* (Vivienne Dick, 1979); *She Had Her Gun All Ready* (Vivienne Dick, 1978); *Vortex* (Beth B and Scott B, 1982); *Black Box* (Beth B and Scott B, 1978).

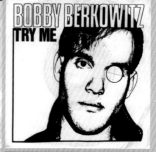

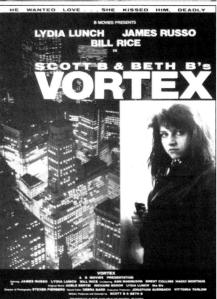

RIGHT *Queen Of Siam* (ZE Records, 1980); 8 Eyed Spy's self-titled half-live/half-studio album (Fetish Records, 1981); the split EP *Drunk On The Pope's Blood / The Agony Is The Ecstasy* (4AD, 1982); *13.13* (Ruby Records, 1982). **BELOW** An undated live shot of 8 Eyed Spy (photographer unknown).

ABOVE Polaroids of Lydia with Henry Rollins and Marc Almond (both photos by Jessamy Calkin). **LEFT** A still from *The Wild World Of Lydia Lunch* (Nick Zedd, 1983).

THIS PAGE A still from *Submit To Me* (Richard Kern, 1985); the album *Honeymoon In Red* and the EP *Stinkfist* with Clint Ruin (both Widowspeak, 1988).

OPPOSITE PAGE Lydia with Sally Ven Yu in *The Right Side Of My Brain* (Richard Kern, 1985); with Marty Nation in *Fingered* (Richard Kern, 1988).

FOLLOWING PAGE Photo by Christina Birrer.

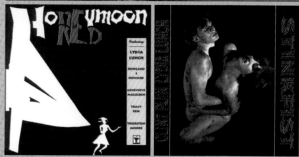

CHAPTER FIVE

QUEEN OF SIAM

*RECORDING SESSIONS FOR LYDIA'S
FIRST SOLO ALBUM TAKE PLACE IN
SEPTEMBER 1979, WITH THE ALBUM
FOLLOWING IN FEBRUARY 1980
VIA ZE RECORDS.*

BOB BLANK By 1979 I was twenty-eight years old and I worked in the music business, which meant I was in the studio all night! I'd never been to any of the punk clubs—I never went anywhere. Then ZE Records came in. One day Michael [Zilkha] calls me up and says he has an artist he'd like me to work with, and he sends over Lydia Lunch.* She shows up at the door; I'm only five-six and she's like five feet, up to my nose. We started talking about the project and how her stuff had always been recorded very quickly and cheaply and loudly—so this time we were going to work with her poetic side. Michael said we should do something really radical. Lydia had a lot of intellect—a lot of those musicians did. While their music might have sounded really simplistic to the average listener, it was coming from a very smart place.

We had worked on other things with Lydia, but *Queen Of Siam* was the first time we would be doing a full Lydia Lunch record. Rock'n'roll records at the time had half-a-million-dollar budgets, then you had rhythm & blues records that had fifty-thousand-dollar budgets—that was the way

---

* Michael Zilkha co-founded ZE Records with Michel Esteban. As well as *Queen Of Siam*, the label released music by Suicide, The Contortions, Aural Exciters, James White & The Blacks, and Lizzy Mercier Descloux.

for anything involving black artists—then with punk they'd get together five hundred bucks and make an album. Michael said they were going to turn that upside down and make the music that these people were doing, but in the best possible circumstances. On *Queen Of Siam*, when we started working, there was no set budget, so I didn't have to sit down and work out how many hours we could spend or anything like that—it was like we could do whatever we wanted. We didn't really spend a lot of money on the album, but there was never any talk of having to rush to get it finished, no issues with timing. ZE Records really thought about the records they were putting out. Look at the album cover for *Queen Of Siam*: nobody sent their artists off to these top fashion photographers to do album covers—this was them saying that they took it seriously, that this was an important artist and an important record.

PAUL ZONE On the cover, the bustier with all the nails sticking out of her breasts, I made that for her! I was doing everything ever since I was thirteen years old, the height of glam. I didn't want to be a designer, though—I thought of it as sculpture, as making a piece of art. I made it with Lydia in mind, but I didn't know she would be making a solo album and would need something to wear. I just gave it to her as a gift one day—that's the way you are with your friends. Next thing I know, she told me she used it for a photo session and that it might be the one for the album. I made a vest first, for myself, then I perfected it for Lydia. I was already going to S&M bars, leather bars, as well as rock'n'roll clubs, being in the back room at Max's Kansas City, hanging out with the Warhol crowd, so I was very young and open to all these ideas.

PAT IRWIN At some point Lydia asked me to work with her on *Queen Of Siam*. We didn't get together to rehearse; we first got together to write the songs. When the songs were in place we then got together at my place on Twenty-Seventh Street, to rehearse what we'd written. George Scott played bass and Dougie Bowne played drums—George had met Dougie on tour with John Cale. But before that happened, Lydia and I would get together and write—she had lyrics and I would give my ideas, and we pulled it together.

DOUGIE BOWNE I spent much of my adult life playing in a band called The Lounge Lizards and ended up playing a whole lot with folks we'd call 'jazz-leaning'. But I didn't play on the big-band tunes, which was kind of a drag because I'm probably the one guy involved in these sessions who would possibly have some connection to that stuff other than irony. Blank Tapes was a relatively inexpensive joint: smaller room, soundproofing on the walls. As I recall, we were in for a few days—not a big thing.

PAT IRWIN We recorded at Blank Tapes—Talking Heads did stuff there, and so did Kid Creole & The Coconuts. I didn't have much experience going into recording studios, so as far as I was concerned that was, *Wow! Amazing!* The studio was behind a club called the Limelight, a few doors down from there on the higher floors of a building. We always recorded at night because you couldn't make noise during the day.

BOB BLANK When I started working with her—my studio is on the eighth floor—we're in the elevator one day and there's a whole bunch of people, then there's a tap on my shoulder, 'Hi Bob!' I turn around and there's this woman there, a little tiny girl, and she says, 'It's me Bob, Lydia? I'm not wearing my makeup.' She looked so young! She looked like any sixteen-year-old girl—she was able to transform, it was amazing. We laughed about it—she looked so cute. She put a lot of time and effort into being Lydia Lunch, but don't get me wrong, it was a moment. It wasn't like she'd go into the bathroom and come out as Lydia Lunch.

If Lydia had personal relationships with people, unlike other artists who would bring in their girlfriends and boyfriends and it was obvious they had other people in their lives, Lydia was very discreet. I would hear stories about her, though, and she would make offhand remarks like, 'Oh, I had to give him a blowjob just to get him to come up here and play!' Who knows what was real!

I remember when Michael [Zilkha] came in, he was a very sweet guy, always wore a grey suit, very polite, very nice. When he came in, she'd berate him and curse at him, and he'd start smiling. Everyone had a role to play! He thought she was great.

PAT IRWIN I played pretty much everything except the bass and drums on one side of the record—I played guitars, piano, clarinet, vibes on 'Spooky', a lot of stuff. We went fast, and Lydia had ideas—we just went for them, we were ready to go. I remember Lydia singing, or evoking the mood she wanted for 'Gloomy Sunday', and we just put that together in an afternoon. Everything was done in two sections: Robert Quine came in and played guitar, there was that stuff, then separately there was the stuff with the big band. Lydia threw her imagination out there and just said that she wanted to sing over a big band and have it sound like a cartoon. We had the tracks for that, then she and I worked together on arrangements for her lyrics, for the singing. It was all her ideas—I was just helpful coming up with how her lyrics could go with the music. 'Atomic Bongos' started from a riff that George had. I started bashing away on guitar, and Dougie Bowne added drums.

BOB BLANK Lydia had the vision to say she had this poetry she had written and that we needed to put it into context. If you're screaming those lyrics, that's one thing, but my resources were people like Billy Ver Planck, who was the orchestrator for *Courageous Cat And Minute Mouse*, which was a 60s cartoon comedy based on spy movies of the 50s. Lydia had written the stuff, she brought in players she'd been working with—known quantities. The orchestra stuff, Lydia sat with Billy—he was a trombone player in the 40s who became this famous arranger—and she gave him ideas of what she wanted and he wrote this music, an album's worth of stuff, and you hear only half of it on the record. She worked with him to make sure it accented things just right.

Those sessions were booked by the hour because musicians were paid by the hour. The music contractor stands there, a guy rolls in a cart piled with sheet music, there's nineteen, twenty musicians in the studio, and all of this happened before she put the vocals on. It was totally different to what she was doing with bands like 8 Eyed Spy, where everyone piles in, you count it off, and everyone starts playing. Those parts had to be written before she could come in, but she was always extremely prepared, and she'd come in with her lyrics. She worked very hard as an artist, and very fast— she gets to the place she wants to be very quickly, she doesn't have to walk around getting into the mood. Part of the reason the record sounds the way it does is, she was in an unfamiliar environment and she's reacting to it. When we put guitars on top of the songs, when Robert Quine came in and played his guitar, you had to hear it in real time and figure out how it would fit in—but she was totally cool. Every time I've worked with her, she would work with the musicians very professionally. The fact that she has so much respect in the world now is because she's always treated the people around her with respect. She always had a gentle demeanour.

BOB BERT The *Queen Of Siam* album was beautiful, almost jazz, a masterpiece as far as I'm concerned.

BARRY ADAMSON I grew up on jazz and Motown, then found all things punk, so the first Ramones record, the first Suicide record—they were like the holy grail of what was happening now in America. We'd all sit around listening to the first two Suicide albums over and over—they'd be playing in the background, then I'd jump in and play something new like ESG and people would be going, 'Oh, what's going on here?' because it was outside of what was the conventional cool. Then, right in the middle of it all, Lydia dropped *Queen Of Siam*. That record joined another set of dots for me because a large part of it was done with a jazz ensemble, but it was still punk as fuck. Some of the arrangements were slick as anything, but she was able to turn it into something that was very current and *now*-sounding. We would sit around listening to tracks like 'Gloomy Sunday', Atomic Bongos', and 'Knives In The Drain', thinking, *This is the coolest!*

LYDIA LUNCH People have very strange memories of *Queen Of Siam*. If you go back and listen to it, there's only actually four big-band songs, the rest is like nursery rhymes. People think of it as this overblown big-band thing, but the whole first side I play guitar, and I love it. It sticks in the memory according to when people heard it—that's interesting. It's like when people come up and say to me, 'Oh I really like your music!' And I say, 'Oh yeah, which music?' I learn a little about them according to what it is they first heard, what era it was, what interests them. You can't just say you like my music—if you like all my music then you're as sick as I am. It's not even easy to hear all of my music—you have to be like a detective!

CATHI UNSWORTH *Queen Of Siam*, the noir-jazz, I love how she sings 'Knives In The Drain' as a fifteen-year-old girl who has seen far too much. That is the essence of noir that I try to capture in my books—that gulf of empathy between a man and a woman, which is what Lydia is singing about on that song. I know that Lydia really loves Hubert Selby Jr, and the character she portrays in that song reminds me of Tralala from *Last Exit To Brooklyn*, a really young woman who has seen too much, and Lydia's voice sounds so young when she sings that—she's so young but she feels so old and worn out. She captures all of that atmosphere in her voice.

JOE BUDENHOLZER When it comes down to it, in some ways, it all comes down to writing, and she's a great writer. You can dress it up in singing, theatre, any kind of performance, but it comes down to writing. Then she decides what's the best way to express it effectively.

PAT IRWIN The way records got played in New York was amazing—there was a real DJ culture. You could hear *Queen Of Siam* at a dance club or the Paradise Garage. You'd hear 'Atomic Bongos', and then the next song would be by Chic, then another real disco record, and then Arthur Russell. It was so eclectic. At the Mudd Club you'd hear Roxy Music then *Queen Of Siam*—it was wide open back then, and full of different worlds colliding.

HARRY HOWARD Around the time that The Birthday Party were getting ready to go to the UK, I started to hear about Lydia. *Queen Of Siam* had come out, and I remember Rowland pinpointing that record, he said it was really, really good—he was serious about it.* That album had such broad scope—there weren't many records being made with that level of support, a properly

---

* Rowland S. Howard, brother to Harry and a stellar musician who played with—among others—The Birthday Party and Crime & The City Solution, founded These Immortal Souls, and was a key collaborator with Lydia in the early 80s and early 90s.

arranged brass section, et cetera, but mixing that up with Richard Hell's guitarist—Robert Quine—then the naïve element from Lydia, it's amazing. It's all realised very well. There's those sickly little nursery rhymes that come from the Teenage Jesus angle, then there's 'Knives In My Drain', which is a really powerful marriage of music and lyrics.

PAT IRWIN The thing about New York at that time was there was a real supportive group of writers—I'm thinking of Robert Palmer in the *New York Times*, there was the *New York Rocker*, the *Soho Weekly News*, the *Village Voice*, the *East Village Eye*. Word got out about 8 Eyed Spy pretty quickly, and the response was positive. So was the response to *Queen Of Siam*, and that shook Lydia up. She was ready to move on. As soon as it looked like the record was getting popular, she was done with it. I don't think I understood that at the time: how could you move on and not want to play *Queen Of Siam*? I would never have said that to her directly because I didn't really care, I just wanted to play in 8 Eyed Spy.

LYDIA LUNCH A lot of things I did were never toured, often because it was impossible—there were no booking agents, it was too expensive. How could I tour *Queen Of Siam*? Who was going to support that, at that period? What kind of band would I have?

BOB BLANK Lydia is very smart. ZE Records remove the funding for a tour because she won't play the songs, she won't just come out and perform 'Knives In The Drain', but it's very smart because it makes the record the only place you can hear the music. It gives it value. Who in their right mind would go on a tour that was being financed by a record company, and, when asked to promote the record, would say no? She was crazy like a fox, and that's why she's had such a long career! Things were very precarious for artists in that era, and, in hindsight, it was very smart of her to not let anyone mould her.

CHAPTER SIX

8 EYED SPY

8 EYED SPY EXIST FOR A SINGLE
YEAR BETWEEN SEPTEMBER 1979
AND AUGUST 1980. THEIR FINAL
SHOW, ON AUGUST 2, 1980, IS NOT
INTENDED TO BE THEIR LAST . . .

BOB BERT 8 Eyed Spy were kind of like a surf-punk band.

JIM SCLAVUNOS I worked with Lydia on a lot of different projects over those years: Teenage Jesus & The Jerks, Beirut Slump, then we had this band called 8 Eyed Spy, which was George Scott and Pat Irwin, Michael Paumgardhen, Lydia, and myself.

PAT IRWIN I came back to New York in '78 and had a couple of different jobs: I worked at a record distributor in Soho; I drove a truck which lasted about a week, maybe two, then I hit a bus, so I walked away; I then got a job working in a restaurant, which was the perfect gig. I got a cheap loft on Twenty-Seventh Street, and one of my roommates knew someone who knew George Scott, and that's how we met. George had gotten kicked out of The Contortions and was looking to start a band. The two of us got together and played in his apartment in the Lower East Side. We started to make cassettes for one another of song ideas and got together every day—once we started we couldn't stop.

Lydia was done with Teenage Jesus. She and George were friends and they wanted to start a band, and it seemed like the time was right. Lydia had a following and they wanted to hear what she was doing. We had a bit of a buzz going on. But the *Queen Of Siam* record put us on hold for a while, and then George went out on the road with John Cale, which delayed things for even longer. Once everyone was in the same place at the same time, fall of '79, we were ready to go.

ROBIN HALL I left Jack Ruby in the summer of '77 and was out of town for about three months. I wasn't going to get involved anymore—I was living in Brooklyn, I wasn't hanging out with anybody, I graduated from college and was working at the record store, and I somehow got tickets to The Knack at Hurrah. When I got there, I bumped into George, and that's how I was reacquainted with Lydia. Between the time I left and the time I got back, Lydia had gone from being a fan and exploring stuff to having had two bands and a third band which was really successful and really good: 8 Eyed Spy was an amazing band.

PAT IRWIN My first impression is going up through these creaking little rooms into a tiny little rehearsal space at Kristian Hoffman and Bradly Field's place and making a bunch of noise. We didn't spend a lot of time plotting it out, and as soon as we started to play the songs came together pretty quickly. George had a dozen ideas about what a rock'n'roll band should sound like. He knew Michael from a record store that he worked at. Lydia and Jim had worked together in Teenage Jesus. Lydia had some lyrics she would fold in and change around a little bit—she'd ask us to make something longer, slow something down, and it came together really quickly. George had influences he was passionate about, and so did Lydia. Everyone brought their own ideas into the band, and I liked that it really was a real band: it wasn't just Lydia and this group, and the sound of 8 Eyed Spy wasn't just Lydia's vision—everyone contributed. She really wanted to be a part of something like this, and, when it clicked, it was awesome.

BOB BERT When I heard this—no-wave music—I just really loved it. I started going to see all the shows, and I bought all the Teenage Jesus singles and the twelve-inch. I just started going to see anybody that was on the *No New York* back cover, any chance I got. By that time, Teenage Jesus was already over with, but I started to go see Lydia with 8 Eyed Spy—saw them a good ten times—and I, as Lydia would refer to her fans, became a *Lydiot*.

PAT IRWIN I remember the first 8 Eyed Spy gig being at Max's Kansas City. We then played the Mudd Club, which was a really great gig. We got offstage and Lydia didn't want to do an encore, she was finished, done, but Steve Maas—the guy who ran the Mudd Club—gave her some more money to do an encore. People really liked it. They were sort of shocked that it was like a real rock band. Listening back, it's certainly not like Blondie or even someone like The Heartbreakers—we were pretty noisy, we made a racket—but you could tell there were elements of song writing in there.

We started to get some press in the *New York Times* and the *Village Voice*. Pretty soon we played the 7th St Entry in Minneapolis, and the 688 Club in Atlanta. We played the 9:30 Club in Washington, DC. But it wasn't like offers were pouring in from around the world or around the country to do gigs that would pay well—it was all pretty fly-by-night.

ROBERT SINGERMAN I started off booking some dates for them, then it morphed into managing them. It was a whole scene of brand-new bands, and there weren't many managers looking to manage completely new bands because it's a 24/7/365 job for an army of people, even if it's just one band just starting off, because there's always more you could be doing. You have people's livelihoods, in collaboration with them, in your hands, and everyone needs to pay rent. I was the person that tried to make that happen.

The clubs where 8 Eyed Spy played—Tier 3, Mudd Club, Hurrah—they all paid guarantees. That's why they didn't play CBGB's. We were friends with the owner of Tier 3, Hilary Jaeger, who paid us a guarantee rather than a door deal. There were only a handful of live venues in New York because it was much cheaper to play some records and get people dancing, so the live music scene had really grown from '78 on, with a few exceptions like Max's Kansas City and CBGB's.

There were a bunch of people over at my house, including my sister's husband—he's a straight shooter, an attorney. He reminded me recently that we were talking to Lydia and all of a sudden she grabbed my package! She just did it to make a point or to be bold, we weren't going out or anything, she was just being outrageous, and he's always remembered it. She would do things like that. She had a bigger-than-life personality, and she could always tone it down when she wanted to, or she could go full-tilt boogie a second later. She was just fun. Her intensity was a good thing—it shook the atoms in any room she was ever in.

THURSTON MOORE 8 Eyed Spy was considered a *supergroup*. There were two supergroups: 8 Eyed Spy and Bush Tetras. It was musicians that came out of The Contortions and Teenage Jesus kind of trading members and creating these two other groups that weren't playing totally atonal no-wave noise. They were actually playing kind of more rock'n'roll, and as soon as anybody plays any semblance of boogie chords, it's over! DNA becomes Ambitious Lovers and Contortions, and Teenage Jesus become Bush Tetras and 8 Eyed Spy. And these bands were great, you know? It was kind of welcoming and the audiences kind of expanded because it was a bit more accessible, but it was still crazy music.

Bush Tetras was really just a rhythm-driven and funky band, while 8 Eyed Spy was all these guys playing really well with this singer who wasn't supposed to be singing! She was a shouter, a screamer, a poet, yelling in a microphone about how life needs to be obliterated now—but instead she was singing cover songs and originals. I will always remember that first gig at Tier 3, the excitement of everyone wanting to see how this would go over was palpable—and they killed it, they were wonderful. There was graffiti on West Broadway that said *Bush Tetras sending love to 8 Eyed Spy*, like it was this huge thing.

ROBIN HALL 8 Eyed Spy played around town a lot. They were almost the house band at Tier 3—a great club that doesn't get memorialised enough. Tier 3 was in the west of Soho, a few blocks from Mudd Club. It was kind of like home—the place we all went to hang out. 8 Eyed Spy were amazing live, and I'm not sure the live recordings ever did them justice, they kicked ass. A lot of times, Bush Tetras would open for them, and that was a great double bill. There also wasn't, at the time, that sense that you could only play out once every two months or something, which is how bands are now—they would play almost every week.

*

ROBERT SINGERMAN 8 Eyed Spy was definitely getting bigger—the ticket prices and the audiences were growing, though it wasn't like they were going to end up rich. It was a real band, and, it may sound immodest, but it did help that they had someone working with them on the business side so that was being properly handled. 8 Eyed Spy was the first band I got over to Europe.

PAT IRWIN By the time we did shows in Italy, doors were opening, but Lydia was already starting to close them. We did some gigs where the people in the audience were responding to the band in ways that I don't think Lydia was comfortable with. For some people it was almost cathartic. We had real energy as a band, and in some ways it was too much like a traditional rock band. She looked out in the crowd and she saw something she didn't want to see: people looking at her like a rock star—I don't think that was ever what she wanted.

LYDIA LUNCH There are many reasons why I was never going to be the big star—I love to suck cock as much as the next woman, but not for corporate whoremongers, let's start there. Second, the truth is not a popular commodity. Third, I'm too instantaneous in my creation to be manipulated into performing the same songs for ten, twenty years just to sell some records. I stopped 8 Eyed Spy because we were becoming too popular and I could see it in people's eyes. My literary heroes, most were not recognised in their lives and some not even in their deaths. Pop culture sucks. I don't think there's any fear of me ever, in my lifetime, achieving the kind of success some of my peers have gone on to achieve because I can't be persuaded to play the same album over and over again.

TOM GARRETSON The basis of Lydia's creativity is forging something herself around her own artistic vision. Lydia's never been particularly interested in building up her career like a pop artist would do—foremost, she's been a writer, a musician, and an artist. What she's about is exploring different aspects of her creativity, and that's not what you'll see in a standard pop or rock act. She finds playing the same songs over and over the death of creativity.

THURSTON MOORE She was never trying to buy into any kind of fame or celebrity. In fact, she thought fame and celebrity was just such a false ideal, just like, *That's for squares.*

ROBERT SINGERMAN Lydia had a bit of reputation, which I'm sure she was fairly proud of because she was already an iconic personality, let's say. She wanted to be known, not in a fame-grabbing sense but in an outrageous way, because she truly wanted to do things differently. She was like no one else I had ever met: alive, riotous, brilliant, caring, devil-may-care—or not—sexual, provocative, challenging, screaming, poetic, memorable on every occasion.

DON BAJEMA What was going on that made her unique was glamour. You'd play music, people would come and see you, you'd be famous or a rock star, you'd be adored. Lydia said, 'Fuck that.' That wasn't what she was doing, or what she wanted. She even wound up doing things to counter it, in terms of mass appeal and mass success—she made everything on her own terms. She's taken art as an opportunity to exercise freedom from abuse and oppression, the manufacturing of a person by society, and to make her case.

TOM GARRETSON Lydia appeals more to an intellectual mindset than she does to popular culture. That's why, if you ask most people on the street who Lydia Lunch is, they'll say they've never heard of her. She's never had a Top 10 hit, but most artists who have had a Top 10 hit no longer have a career. She's always appealed to a more literary mindset, people who read. She thinks of herself first and foremost as a writer—that's what she's always said to me.

*

PAT IRWIN The Raybeats had a photo shoot scheduled with Stephanie Chernikowski, just down the block from where George lived—she was across the Bowery from CBGB's. We were all there, and George didn't show up. I went down to his place as the cops were just getting there. It was such a shock, it was brutal—we all knew something was up and that it probably wasn't good. His death was a horrible surprise to all of us. He had an energy that was unique, personal, and musical—when he died, it was like a giant door closing. It was terrible.*

ROBERT SINGERMAN When George died, everyone was really crushed. It was probably the first friend we lost in that era, a great guy, everyone was devastated. The fun wasn't there, and everyone decided, no, the band couldn't continue with George. He was one of the most giving men I had ever known. A powerful musician, an athletic and strident player, he was really instrumental in a lot of artists' careers. He was a big listener to music and a huge supporter of other bands, even if he wasn't playing in them. A huge loss for a whole lot of people. He brought so much energy to the scene. It made me rethink what I was doing because I was working with quite a lot of people who were dabbling with drugs that were debilitating them, and I was pretty much the same age as most of the people I was working with.

ROBIN HALL When George passed away there was a wake at Donnie Christensen's loft, and I went to that. I hadn't seen Lydia in a bit, Chris Gray had come down from Albany—the only time I saw him after I left Jack Ruby—and at some point, in this crowd of people, Lydia threw an ashtray at me, and I don't even know why!

PAT IRWIN I have mixed feelings about the 8 Eyed Spy record. Everybody was pretty shattered when George died—I don't think any of us knew how to process it. George's death shakes me to this day. We didn't dwell on it, but I do remember wanting to continue 8 Eyed Spy in some way, or, at least, to document it. Lydia had no desire to continue the band without George, but we had an opportunity to record and we went ahead with it. I'm not sure it was the best decision, but we were ready to go. We could play those songs in one or two takes.

---

* George S. Scott was a highly active presence in the New York City music scene as a member of Jack Ruby, The Contortions, James White & The Blacks, The Raybeats, and 8 Eyed Spy. He died of a heroin overdose at age twenty-six on August 5, 1980.

CHAPTER SEVEN

DEVIL DOGS

*PLAYING FOR ONLY A FEW MONTHS,
FROM NOVEMBER 1980 TO FEBRUARY
1981, DEVIL DOGS ARE A ROUGH 'N'
READY BLUES BAND WHO MANAGE
TWO COMPLETELY DISTINCT LINE-UPS
INSIDE THAT TIMEFRAME.*

BOB BERT Right after 8 Eyed Spy, she had this band Devil Dogs that didn't last very long. They were doing, like, blues covers and stuff.

RUDI PROTRUDI Robert Maché worked with my sister at a print company and Robert was playing with Lydia. They needed a bass player so he asked my sister if I'd be interested. I was in a band called Tina Peel, singing and playing guitar, but maybe my sister had told him I'd played bass in cover bands in Pennsylvania before moving to New York—because the only way you would play music in Pennsylvania was if you were in a cover band.

We met at Bradly Field's rehearsal studio, which was a really damp, dark, dungeon sort of a place, in the bottom of a rundown apartment building where The Cramps used to rehearse. We had one rehearsal, I barely spoke to anybody, just ran through the songs once each time, and they said OK and told me they were going to play Georgia. Really, the only reason I did the first show was Lydia offered me two hundred bucks—and I'm a big fan of blues, so when they said it would be blues music, I was into that.

LYDIA LUNCH Devil Dogs was so short-lived—a blues band that Bob Quine suggested all the songs for. It was fun to play a frying pan with a drumstick, and I've always loved doing cover songs, taking songs I've always hated and augmenting them—it's always about the words.*

JIM SCLAVUNOS In terms of her musical tastes, I've never really had a very clear bead on what Lydia likes to listen to. I remember her telling me, when we were in Teenage Jesus & The Jerks, that her favourite song was 'No Milk Today' by Herman's Hermits! I knew she liked some of the local bands, but it wasn't anything that clearly informed the music we were making. She didn't cite any bands that she liked that sounded like us even remotely. Lydia has always been a collector, in terms of her own personal taste, as far as I can tell. She was the one that brought the idea of covering Credence Clearwater Revival in 8 Eyed Spy, doing 'Run Through The Jungle' as a cover song. She also might have been the one that suggested we cover 'White Rabbit' by Jefferson Airplane.

RUDI PROTRUDI In Georgia, there wasn't much intermingling. Lydia gave me the impression that she felt she was very underground and special and really couldn't be bothered talking to me. She wasn't *not* nice, but she'd just gone through something with her boyfriend: they had an argument, she went on tour, and when she came home he'd killed and gutted all of her animals and laid them all out for her with a bloody message on the wall or something. So she wasn't really friendly.

When I got the call for the next gig, I had a recording of the first gig—I just learned the songs from the tape. We recorded that night for what was going to be a live record—or, at least, that's what Lydia told us. Unfortunately, Lydia decided that she had laryngitis and she didn't want the record to come out. It was funny because, when I heard the recording, I didn't know why it was a problem, she was as off-key as always. I refer to Lydia's style as 'bitching the blues': she doesn't sing them, she bitches

---

* Devil Dogs began with Michael Paumgardhen and Jim Sclavunos (both formerly of 8 Eyed Spy) alongside new bassist Stan Adler. After only a month of gigs in November 1980, Lydia reformed the band on the West Coast with Robert Maché, Rudi Protrudi, and Kristian Hoffman, with whom she played a handful of shows in December. A four-date tour of Italy marked the band's demise in February 1981.

them, which has a certain charm if you understand where she's coming from—it makes sense.

A month later, they called me up and asked if I wanted to play a few shows in Italy. It was some kind of international trade situation where, through some performing-arts organisation, the Italians sent over a package deal to America, and we sent one to them. There were four acts playing with us on the bill—and none of them had anything to do with the other. It was very intellectual, except for Devil Dogs. There was a classical pianist and violin player who played together, there was the band Orchestra Luna, then I don't remember the other.

It was a good experience but a little rough, because we would get on the subway and the guys would literally try to lose me—I don't know who they thought would play bass if they lost me, but they really would try to lose me. I wasn't used to this kind of stuff—it was a different sense of humour to what I was used to, like teenage girls trying to ditch an ex friend. When we got onstage, it all gelled really nice, but I can't say I gelled with anyone in the band as people, and I can't even say I really *joined* the band—they just asked me to play some gigs.

We never did end up getting along, and they all seemed very cynical. In Italy, Lydia was really mean—no one spoke to her in Italy. Interviewers would come up to her and she'd snarl, 'Buy me dinner!' and they would, then she'd give an interview where she only gave yes/no answers. It kind of opened my eyes because Lydia is a master con artist, and I learned a lot about dealing with the press and pushy promoters. I never got the impression from Lydia, however, that this was anything other than a filler band to go in between what she had done and what she wanted to do next. She didn't seem to have a vision for it—I have a feeling Lydia just likes blues music and thought it would be fun to do this band for a few minutes.

CHAPTER EIGHT

13.13

THE CYCLE OF ACTIVITY TURNS EVER FASTER WITH LYDIA'S FIFTH BAND, INITIATED IN JUNE 1981, REFORMED IN JULY, RECORDED IN AUGUST, AND DISBANDED IN NOVEMBER— A SPAN OF BARELY SIX MONTHS.

LYDIA LUNCH 13.13 came about when I was performing with 8 Eyed Spy at a club downtown. It was really packed—I had to have my leg on the first person in front of me because it was so crowded. That man happened to be a Wall Street stockbroker and heroin addict who was obsessed with medieval literature, and, somehow, he wanted to finance a record by me.

EXENE CERVENKA California had a completely different vibe, which is why people didn't take the West Coast seriously, compared to New York. Their thing was very dark—hair was black, rooms were black, clothes were black, the music was dark. Our side was crazy, goofy, funny, driving around in cars— the difference was the cars. We could get anywhere we wanted, and we were having a wild and crazy time going from town to town, city to city, to the beach, to the valley. In New York, you had to somehow get your stuff onto the subway, and the weather was a lot worse. We were just as poor but we had sunshine and cars, so that made a difference in our outlook. Sometimes people thought we weren't as serious, but that's why The Cramps relocated to California, and eventually Lydia came to California too. Back then, maybe you'd get a postcard—you couldn't talk on the phone all the time. Sometimes people just turned up at your front door. You just found people somehow—it was a real force of will. When Lydia moved to California, she was right near me in the Mount Washington area, Highland Park. We were the only white people in the area at the time—it was completely Latino, and we loved it.

JIM SCLAVUNOS Lydia had always had a predilection for Manson and his disciples and that whole kind of murderous cult California post-hippie apocalyptic vibe. A thread of it was already there with 8 Eyed Spy: the darker hippie vision, the kind of trashy biker, dirty hippie thing. And naturally, as time goes on, if you're an artist, you're sort of absorbing things around you. Her influences and the things she thought she could apply her talents to became broader, but was not quite what you would expect from someone who was making the kind of music she was known for—that really stripped-down, brooding, brutal music. It was given freer rein in 8 Eyed Spy, and 13.13 started invoking psychedelia as well.

JOHNNY NATION I met Lydia through my brother, Marty Nation, and she knew I played guitar. She was looking to put a group together in LA, and I was young, good looking, and carefree. My charisma might've worked against me in the long run because I might have taken some spotlight away from her. As for the tour, I knew she had a good manager that got her good bookings, so that was on the table from the get-go. I came from a much more rock'n'roll style but adapted to her more psychedelic feel as needed. As far as who the leader was, it was definitely Lydia's thing, top to bottom. As far as rehearsals and the build up to actually playing shows, it went pretty fast. I would come up with a rough arrangement of chords, structures of things I would be jamming on, and Lydia would come up with lyrics. We rehearsed our set and started doing a couple of LA shows.

CLIFF MARTINEZ In 1980, I joined The Weirdos. My first show with them was at the Whisky A Go-Go, and when I saw three people do swan dives off the balcony, I thought to myself, *That beats applause any day*. By 1981, The Weirdos had disbanded, and I honestly can't recall a first encounter with Lydia. Greg Williams facilitated my entrance—he had played in an earlier incarnation of The Weirdos, and I believe he had a vision of 13.13 being composed of all ex-Weirdos—except Lydia, of course. After I expressed interest, Greg brought up the idea of also adding Dix Denney to the group. Dix and I were bandmates in The Weirdos. I thought he was a great guitarist, we worked well together, and now the recipe for 13.13 really began to sound intriguing.*

JOHNNY NATION Greg formed an alliance with Lydia and wanted me out to bring in his friend Dix Denney to play guitar. Dix had better equipment, was a good player, and was not a threat to Lydia at all. I don't know how long the whole thing lasted, but it was a good little run—the shows were always full, and it was good touring and seeing the East Coast.

CLIFF MARTINEZ The previous line-up was performing somewhere in Silver Lake, around the same time that Greg first brought up the idea of me playing drums in the group. The show was sold out, so I couldn't get in. I stood outside and listened to the whole show from the street. My first impression was that it was one of the strangest musical descendants of punk rock I'd ever heard. I assume they were playing the same material that eventually ended up on the album … all reduced to inarticulate woofing due to there being a building between the band and my ears, but the 13.13 blueprint was all there and fully intact—slow, dark, and angry. And the thing that really held my attention was wondering what it all looked like—and I still wonder, as there is no photo or video record of either version of the band, to my knowledge. The sound was distorted and muffled from the street point of view, which probably magnified the weirdness. The experience completely sold me on the band—I only wish that I could have seen them.

RON ATHEY Now, the poor goths have ruined everything by never going away, but when *13.13* came out, that was the most goth album ever, and it was chilling—I was a fan for life. 'Suicide Ocean' and 'Afraid Of Your Company' … a lot of tracks on that album are mind-boggling. I didn't understand until later that each one is about a serial killer that was on the loose in LA at the

---

* 13.13 performed for barely a month in June–July 1981, with Johnny Nation, Greg Williams, and Alex MacNicol (guitar, bass, and drums, respectively), before Nation and MacNicol were replaced by Williams's ex-bandmates from the band The Weirdos, Dix Denney and Cliff Martinez. This line-up would tour sporadically until November 1981.

time. This ability to look into the harshest, most abject thing—the Hillside Strangler, Ted Bundy escaping from prison and on the loose again—and then put it to a romantic mood abstract melody, it's pretty genius.

CLIFF MARTINEZ When I officially entered the new band, it was me, Lydia, Greg, and Dix on day one. Lydia had great leadership instincts. She had a very broad yet very specific vision for the music of 13.13. The songs would be slow and somewhat long, and have no more than two parts. She designed the macro view but otherwise let the three of us out on a long leash. The biggest challenge was trying to put across this very slow, dirge-like music with punk-rock intensity. It came together all too quickly for my taste—the writing, the rehearsals, the recording, all of it. Then again, sometimes great things happen when you don't have the luxury of time. In hindsight, I wish we had more time to prepare the album. I have some live recordings made from our subsequent tour, and the music just got so much more gnarly.

We all thought that 13.13 was great fun. But we were part of a musical milieu where laughing and smiling was frowned upon, so maybe *fun* is not be the best description of it. 13.13 didn't last long enough for many interpersonal conflicts to develop. Dix and I had always worked together smoothly, and Greg and Dix shared a similar effortless chemistry. Lydia was a veteran bandleader of several groups and knew how to manage everyone's potential rock-star ego. Bands are complicated social organisations that ultimately end in a chaotic explosion of animosity, but 13.13 was one of the more well-lubricated and drama-less bands I'd been in.

Meanwhile, Lydia was kind of *normal* in our day-to-day activities but became something different onstage. And that's not to say her stage persona didn't represent the real Lydia, it's just that this ferocious side of her really only emerged in front of an audience. I had gotten a whiff of it from her performances in the studio, but I recall being somewhat flabbergasted the first time I got onstage with her. Lydia once said something to me along the lines of seeing herself as a female W.C. Fields—one of my all-time heroes—and I could never get that image out my head when watching her perform. Onstage, she projected an angry sexuality that was straightforward and easy to recognise. But there was also a dark and dry comedic side that usually slipped past everyone, like the lyric 'A fly in the butter screams my name.' C'mon! That is hysterical! While anger and bombast was the big takeaway from her live performances, offstage Lydia had another side that was the opposite of that; warm, friendly, and, uh, maternal.

SADIE MAE I was seventeen. My great escape to the Lower East Side from Rockland county, New York, was an easy hour drive to step into my ass-kicking boots, chip of a Lemmon 714, followed by any alcohol available. Mudd Club, Pyramid, Max's, Ritz—always something worth the travel, almost worth the car impoundment, busted window, or the tickets. As a vinyl junkie, I came across my first Lydia Lunch album, *13.13*, and I was instantly hypnotised. I was pushing sugar, baking delicious treats at the farm in Pomona—where Mick Jagger and Jerry Hall lived for a while, and, yes, he gave me his autograph because I was sporting a Stooges T-shirt.

I heard Lydia would be doing a show somewhere in Long Island. I smuggled cookies, pies, turnovers, and éclairs out through the back door into my old seven-miles-per-gallon Duster and headed home for my boots. I was too young to be let into the club. A hot polka-dot-dress-wearing, dark sunglasses, Exene Cervenka–looking chick came to the back door. 'Who are you and what do you want?' Hot on meeting Lydia, and with a huge shit-eating grin, I replied, 'I'm Lydia's caterer.' She yelled back to Lydia, 'Your caterer is here!' The witch's voice came back with a bellowing, 'Well? Let her in!' I must admit it was instant attraction. Hell, who wouldn't be intoxicated by that tight dress in heels with an hourglass-shape figure, black hair, red lipstick, and, well … you know the rest. We stayed in touch via old-school postcards and handwritten letters. She liked to bookend the stage with me and another female warrior, Jetta Bara, out front with baseball bats, to handle anyone throwing beer bottles. Befriending Lydia, I was under her wing, lucky to be taken into so many shows that sprung up so quickly.

EXENE CERVENKA While living in LA, Lydia got this offer to write a book for Grove Press, which is a huge thing!* If you consider that '81 is coming off

---

* *Adulterer's Anonymous* by Lydia Lunch and Exene Cervenka (Grove Press, 1982).

the heels of the beatniks, and that imprint was super-important. She asked me if I wanted to do it with her, and I felt very fortunate that she asked me because she didn't have to. Lucky me! We came up with the idea of two different fonts so you could tell who was writing what. You had to do everything by hand or on a typewriter, so it was really tactile.

I remember sitting at the kitchen table, and she said, 'Do you want me to pierce your nose?' We got an ice cube out of the refrigerator and got a needle and Lydia put a little stud in my nose, then we sat down and carried on writing. We did a lot of work just sitting in that kitchen, drinking tea. Her focus was always a lot darker than mine, though: I was writing about baseball and diners and travelling around America in a band—the colloquialisms of what people say. She'd be writing about this more savage and brutal thing. We would take it all and put it together, a lot of pain and misery and suffering, and unfortunately that's what a lot of writing usually is, underneath. We related on that level, but we definitely had a different outlook. I was into mundane Americana, what gets done to people by society, while she was into the dark intrigues of social interaction and what people do to each other. It really worked together.

We were touring a lot, so she wrote a load of stuff and gave it to me or mailed it to me, then I wrote a bunch of stuff and gave it to her. We wrote whatever we felt, and we really laboured over it. Grove Press made some small edits but otherwise it went out as we intended. Lydia is known for her dark, sexual, tortured and shocking tales—but that isn't what our book was about. It was about two girls writing a book about how we felt about things. A lot of *Adulterers Anonymous* was wordplay, alliteration, rhyming sentences—me responding to her, her responding to me—it wasn't so much about big brutal stories of life.

Do you know what 'Dear Abby' is? Someone writes a column and people write in, 'I don't know what to do, my husband this and that, signed Nervous Wife.' There was one about this woman who was cheating on her husband and it was signed 'Adulterer Anonymous', and I thought that'd be great. I would save all sorts of weird things like that—I thought it was a perfect title, and it was before Alcoholics Anonymous really became famous, so it's kind of funny because it's still 'AA' back when nobody knew what that was.

CHAPTER NINE

LONDON AGONY/ BERLIN ECSTASY

LYDIA AND HER NEXT BAND PLAY SEVENTEEN EUROPEAN SHOWS IN LATE 1981. THE NEXT FEW YEARS SEE HER LIVING BETWEEN LONDON, BERLIN, AND NEW YORK, INCREASINGLY COMFORTABLE AS THE FOCAL POINT FOR A VARYING CAST OF COLLABORATORS..

CLIFF MARTINEZ My dim recollection of the breakup of 13.13 was that it was somewhat expected, it was by mutual consent, and it was relatively amicable. Our big plan for world domination hinged on touring Europe. We all flew to New York, played a handful of shows, and waited for tour dates to materialise. They didn't, and you can only sleep on peoples' couches for so long. Greg, Dix, and I wanted to go back to LA, and Lydia wanted to remain in New York. Bands are nearly impossible to maintain without money and forward movement, and as Woody Allen famously said, 'A relationship is like a shark. It has to constantly move forward, or it dies.' What we had on our hands was a dead shark.

MICK HARVEY We met Lydia in '81, on the first American tour by The Birthday Party. We'd been playing in Australia since '77, so we'd been able to develop our stuff in isolation—fortunately. In '81 we started becoming a bit more popular and started meeting all of these people who we had known of for three, four years. It was nice to discover there was almost an automatic connection—an international community grew up as these bands started touring and met each other. Within quite a short space of time, Lydia moved to London. I'm pretty sure it had something to do with us being there.

MURRAY MITCHELL The first time I went to America was with Siouxsie & The Banshees, and the very first night—I was a day later than everyone else—I arrived at the hotel as everyone was leaving. They told me to drop the bags, they were off to the Mudd Club. I'd read about it so I tagged along. Devil Dogs were performing. I ended up in a diner with Siouxsie, Budgie, and Lydia, talking about Alice Cooper. I immediately hit it off with Lydia—she seemed to think I was Siouxsie's boyfriend, so she was interested in me. I was only eighteen at the time. A year later, I was back in America with the Banshees, and 13.13 supported on a couple of shows. We ended up at Studio 54 of all places, and Lydia made a move on me, and, for the next week, she moved into my hotel room. When I headed back to London, she came with me.

We moved into a really sleazy hotel on Westbourne Grove that, for some reason, I've always remembered the name of: the Venus Hotel. She had just abandoned 13.13—at the time, she told me that she didn't want to have to pay to get them to Europe, even though they already had shows booked as support for The Birthday Party and The Cure. I imagine that was supposed to be 13.13 doing the gigs—I can't imagine they meant for 13.13 to break up and Lydia to start an entirely new band to do the gigs! She and Steve Severin had already cooked up what was going to happen. He was somewhat obsessed by Lydia at the time. That led to Lydia asking me to be in the band. I'm guessing it was just convenient because we were shacked up, plus it helped financially. Next thing was, she got Kristian Hoffman to come over, and that was the band: Lydia, Steve, Kristian, and me.

JIM THIRLWELL I moved to London in 1978, and I knew that I wanted to do something involved with music. I come from Melbourne, the same town as The Birthday Party, and eventually I ended up being roommates with Mick Harvey. I was going to see their shows a lot in London, and they asked me to write a couple of their press releases, which were … I wouldn't say whimsical, but they had a few exaggerations in them. Then Lydia came to town. The first time I met her was at this place called the Venue—it might have been a Captain Beefheart show. Not long after, she read the first press release that I had written for The Birthday Party and asked if I would write something for her. This is the first time we actually sat down and had any kind of conversation properly. I got to sit and pick her brain as to what should go into this one-sheet bio-type thing that she wanted to create. I went through the main biographical details, then I concluded with something about her learning to play tuba or something like that.

The London that I moved to was still a post–World War II country. There were huge swathes of it that had still not recovered. It was amazing—empty desolate warehouses and streets that seemed totally deserted.

CHRISTINA BIRRER London was still in the midst of transitioning from a post-war bombsite. There were lots of abandoned buildings and open spaces. I was with a writer, and we had proposed a book project on 80s music, even though it was 1980! Lydia came to my Wapping studio near Brick Lane for portraits for the book, and then with Rowland for 'Some Velvet Morning'.* We knew there was the graveyard nearby that we could use for photographs.

Later, I had a loft studio in an old church school building in Vauxhall. Lydia started staying with me whenever she came back to London. We made lots of photographs together. I tend to do setup portraiture as opposed to documenting because I'm very shy myself. I work with people more in a proper location. I loved Lydia's ideas—she would come to me with projects, and I would work to illustrate whatever the project happened to be, so, for example, I have the photos of Lydia and Nick Cave that we made at a wrecking yard somewhere on the outer edges of Notting Hill Gate. Lydia and I would spend days together on photo series that I guess you could say I 'art directed' for her.

MURRAY MITCHELL Pretty quickly we went into a studio—without Steve—and recorded an atmospheric backing track, me feeding back and playing with a

---

* The first collaboration between Lydia Lunch and Rowland S. Howard was a cover of the Lee Hazlewood/Nancy Sinatra duet.

delay unit, Kristian banging things, sound recordings—just a thirty-minute cassette we'd give to the front-of-house guy to play. That formed the basis for the rest of it, though, bizarrely, that backing track got used at the London Dungeons. Lydia and I went there and they were playing it.

The first The Agony Is The Ecstasy gig in Sheffield, Steve, Kristian, and me—we were all meant to wear these leather gimp masks, but I ended up being the only one wearing one. I was probably the most nervous. It was all totally freeform feedback with Lydia ranting over the top. To say it wasn't well received is an understatement. By the time we got to the Hammersmith Palais there were three thousand people chanting 'Fuck off! Fuck off!' Which I thought was quite wonderful, to get that intensity of dislike. Usually, Lydia was first offstage, then the rest of us would follow, and maybe Kristian would stay, thumping a beat out, but that night I was the last one to leave because it was my home town, and I was really soaking up having this rammed venue all chanting 'Fuck off!'

Steve baled as soon as we'd finished the gigs with The Cure. The thought of going to Europe in the middle of winter wasn't very appealing to him. There wasn't any question we weren't going to do Europe—Lydia was determined to fulfil the obligations that had been booked. We never thought about replacing Steve. We were going to get the money.

It wasn't glamorous touring. I remember being in Sweden, and I'd taken this guitar in its flight-case because I considered it quite a prize possession, but it was quite heavy, so I tied a belt around it so I could drag it through the snow from the station to the guesthouse. Kristian found the whole thing absolutely hilarious—I remember him laughing all the time, especially at me. He would constantly remind me how transient my position would be in everything to do with Lydia. I thought, *Whatever ... fun while it lasts.* In one place, we were barricaded in the dressing room as glass bottles were hitting the door; there were these wooden steps up at the back of the stage, so the door to the dressing room was in full view of the audience but half a level higher. We put the sofa up against it until the promoter came to bang on the door to tell us it was all right. That wasn't an unfamiliar reaction. I don't remember any bottles thrown during the gig, though, because it was only a half-hour thing, the length of the backing cassette.

*

BARRY ADAMSON I remember The Birthday Party first arriving in London, then piling round to my house and never leaving. People would pretty much get together every day or every other day. It was like keeping a party, a connection, ideas going. It was a real community. Lydia lived around the corner, or someone would travel over and stay over, even if you jumped on a train and went to north London to carry on it was all one thing. Everyone was from different places—nobody was from London—so it was like living in one big hotel.

HARRY HOWARD I got to London in '82. There was a show at the Clarendon Ballroom, and Lydia turned up. My sister was in London at that time. Lydia dubbed Rowland 'Rush', me 'Hush', and our sister Angela 'Ash'— we all have the *S* middle initial—and she rolled them off her tongue with her particular New York aplomb. Lydia had drinks at her house, all of The Birthday Party were there, a soiree of some description, and I remember glimpsing through her bedroom door, this tastefully spartan room but with an array of tools, torture instruments, pincers and things, mounted on the wall—nicely done but archaic looking, giving it extra mystery and class.

CHRISTOPH DREHER Nick and Lydia seemed to have some kind of thing going on. I vaguely remember Nick saying that Lydia had a collection of handcuffs and torture equipment in her bedroom. Lydia was calculating, a little bit, this Marquis de Sade connotation. It was part of her dark and seductive— and powerful, dominating—image. She had this really great humour and was so quick, so eloquent and punchy in her talk. It was very impressive. She had this authoritative and playfully aggressive aura. At the same time, she was totally nice.

HARRY HOWARD She called me up sometime after the drinks night and invited me round in this slightly suggestive manner. It was just beyond me, this New York Dame; I didn't have the wherewithal to deal with anything like that—lying to my girlfriend or anything. She was incredibly nice, Lydia. I felt young and basically I was quite shy, and she's got this inner strength that is really obvious to see. Plus, the tools on the wall were flashing through my mind: perhaps I dreamt the whole thing?

BARRY ADAMSON Nick said, 'Why don't you pop round and say hello?' I did, and she was indeed this kickass person from New York, while I was quite naïve at the time and quite shy. I remember being quite reserved because of her feisty vibe, the same as I was around Patti Palladin. I'd been told that I shouldn't fuck around with Lydia because she had a lover who would be in the wardrobe and I'd be being watched, so I shouldn't even look at her in that way. I was totally intimidated because I really did think someone was going to jump out of the wardrobe and throttle me! She was incredibly seductive, but I was terrified someone was going to jump out of the wardrobe, so I just stayed in *yes, I would love another cup of tea* mode, then left, somewhat relieved.

CATHI UNSWORTH The first time I heard her work was *The Agony Is The Ecstasy.** There was an *NME* article, which was the first time I ever saw her: a brilliant picture of her and Nick in a junkyard, sitting in the back of a car that was about to be scrapped. They looked amazing. I grew up in a Harry Crews–equivalent part of the world in Norfolk where it was very isolated and rural. I was quite a socially awkward child and didn't have many friends, but the way you find your friends when you know you're weird is you wind up with all the people no one else likes, and you band together. One reason to stand out at school is by having a brain—you're not supposed to. Seeing that picture of Lydia in the *NME*, she looked brilliant, and I thought I'd really like to know her and to be more like her. When I finally stopped dressing conventionally and started spiking up my hair, finally the horrible beer boys left me alone—so I learnt style techniques as well as enjoying the music.

HARRY HOWARD *NME* was sea-freighted to Australia, so we'd get it six weeks late, but it was really important to get that missive about what was going on

---

* *Drunk On The Pope's Blood / The Agony Is The Ecstasy* was a split twelve-inch EP with The Birthday Party on side A and 'The Agony Is The Ecstasy' on side B. Note that the latter was credited to Lydia Lunch, with 'The Agony Is The Ecstasy' featuring as the track title rather than the band name.

in the world. There was a photo of Lydia and a quarter-page interview with a quote of her saying, 'Anyone can be intelligent, I want to be beautiful.' That really grabbed me. I turned it over in my mind, wondering what she meant, the implications. It was an interesting thing to say, as she was clearly very intelligent, but she was choosing to credit something else. She was clever with words. I thought of her as a Dorothy Parker—another New York girl with a dark bob, a wisecracking and witty person.

LYDIA LUNCH Nick and I never agreed on anything from the moment we met— Rowland S. Howard and I agreed on everything. But Nick had an idea for one-page plays so we wrote together. Later on, we released some of them as a comic book with Mike Matthews,* a great illustrator who was so paranoid that witches were after him that he eventually threw himself into the Thames … or was murdered by witches.

JESSAMY CALKIN The fifty one-page plays project was basically Lydia trying to get together with Nick. That's what she would do: she'd come up with a project so she could work with someone, then try to seduce them. The plays were all really interesting, dark or sexy stories.

CATHI UNSWORTH I've always been curious that there are so many words lavished on the greatness of artists like Nick Cave or Tom Waits, yet Lydia has an equally impressive body of work and hasn't received anything like the attention or adulation. It's basically because she's female—I genuinely feel that's it, unfortunately. Probably because she is so beautiful as well. It's too threatening to the male ego to have someone brilliant, brainy, beautiful, and hilariously funny all at once. As Ginger Rogers once so memorably said, 'Everything Fred does I had to do backward and in high heels.' That still applies!

CHRISTINA BIRRER I connected with Lydia's work, the unforgiving upfront gaze. I'm always interested in 'the gaze'—I'd rather make images than take

---

* The one-off *as.fix.e8*, published by Last Gasp in 1993.

images, and my slow cameras enforced that. With the large format, a four-by-five plate camera, it took a fair amount of posing and then waiting—one has to focus, set up the lens, close the lens, instigate the lens, put the film slide in, pull out the dark slide, and only then press the shutter. The portraits and series that we made were intimate and sometimes confrontational, playing with stereotypes of 'woman' and 'sexuality', communicating directly, bringing it into the mainstream consciousness, helping open up those borders on how a woman could portray her body.

If you look at my work with Linda Sterling, *She-She* was an EP for her group Ludus, and it was all about a woman being bound and suffocated by one's communication and ability to express oneself. The focus was how mainstream commodification of our bodies constrains and creates false narratives. I also worked with Cosey Fanni Tutti—she's another woman artist who was using her body in a way that some people at the time considered transgressive, but it totally influenced what her art was. I saw her stripping around the corner in Vauxhall at a working men's club while I was taking portraits of her and Chris.* These women were each tackling these topics but all from completely unique and individual perspectives.

HARRY HOWARD Rowland had an interesting character. He had a very sensitive side, and he was impractical about a lot of things in life. We had a father who was a very difficult man with a lot of problems, we all had massive confrontations with him growing up, and they left all of us with difficulties about confrontation. Rowland didn't like any confrontation, which made him pull back from a lot of the things you face in life. But, on the other hand, he was so strong about how he knew what he liked—he was really unshakeable and really creative. He'd reinvented himself at an early age as a creative person. People such as Nick say that Rowland arrived fully formed. He didn't, but I can see what Nick was saying, because Rowland started at a really young age. He'd had this idea of performing for a very long time, not

---

* Cosey Fanni Tutti was a founding member of the performance-art group COUM Transmissions, which evolved in Throbbing Gristle. Chris Carter joined the latter group and, after they disbanded in 1981, formed a duo with Cosey under the name Chris & Cosey.

like kids wanting attention when they're five—he was really refining a style. He was really good at recognising what was good and what was interesting—he didn't have any confusion about that. He could be quite forceful about music. If someone disagreed with him, it was hard to get anywhere with him.

BARRY ADAMSON 'Some Velvet Morning'—somebody had been talking about doing that record for ages. People were all over Lee Hazlewood. I remember feeling envious that Rowland was going to do it with Lydia because I thought I was going to do it myself one day, but I was happy to be included because I could emulate something of the characteristics of the original. I played the upright bass so I could add that sound. What Lee Hazlewood used to do was to have the bass played on an upright bass and an electric bass at the same time, then he'd amalgamate the two so you had that natural earthy sound of the acoustic bass, then the modern electric sound as well—I was fascinated by that. We all knew the song, so we just put it together. It was just this afternoon of working away, then hearing the playback.

MICK HARVEY The connection with Lydia was growing: she obviously got on very well with Rowland and liked his sensibility, and she thought Nick was a brilliant writer, so they had a strong bond there. The 'Some Velvet Morning' single was not particularly spontaneous: Rowland wanted a vehicle because he wasn't getting to sing in The Birthday Party, and his songwriting was difficult because Nick had to sing his lyrics. He was happy to hook up with Lydia and use that as a platform for him. Myself and Barry and Genevieve going in was organised as part of working out how to do that.*

BARRY ADAMSON This was an interesting period of time in music—there was real diversity, and the extreme was extremely alternative to the mainstream. There was a definite distinction between what was seen as hip or the mainstream and … not. Things were very much chart-driven, with the

---

* Genevieve McGuckin was a longtime friend, sometime domestic partner, and regular collaborator of Rowland S. Howard who joined The Birthday Party in moving to Europe and went onto co-found These Immortal Souls alongside Rowland, Harry, and Epic Soundtracks.

occasional thing poking through into the mainstream. The whole punk scene threw things in the washing machine, shook things up a bit. People in the know were questioning: *Oh, is this OK?* And that meant there was an opening people could use to find all these different worlds. In the UK—and I saw the same thing in New York too—there was a subterranean scene going on with people like Nick and The Birthday Party—then it shifted to Berlin, which was like the same scene but times twenty.

CHRISTOPH DREHER West Berlin was very empty at that time, and few people wanted to visit, because it was considered very poor, very rough—nothing that normal people would want to go to. The people who came there were mainly young men who wanted to escape the army, because Berlin had special status and you couldn't be conscripted; also artists, because rents were incredibly cheap, even if you were starting out you could live very well without having a day job. For years, I didn't have much money, but I didn't need any: I paid little rent, I didn't eat much; I went to a couple of bars where all the people from the underground scene went, so we drank for free and we saw lots of bands play, also for free. My then-girlfriend, Gudrun Gut, formed Malaria!, and we were living together in Dresdener Strasse, where all of The Birthday Party would live for a little while.

MICK HARVEY In late '81, we went through Berlin having met this all-girl group on tour in the US called Malaria! When we got to Berlin they were there, and we felt we'd met more people and made more friends in twenty-four hours than we had in the year-and-a-half before that in London. We drove out of Berlin heading to Amsterdam for the next show, and everyone was thinking, *Why don't we just move there?*

Berlin was less of a music city in terms of having a scene based in big business—music business—while London, New York, and LA were big music-business centres, and there was a lot of mainstream stuff going on in those places. London had really established itself through punk and new wave as the new centre, alongside New York, while Berlin was an alternative cultural centre—it was such a strange place, with this stateless feel about it. You were in Germany but not really in Germany; you were in a

German city disconnected from its own country. People from all over went there because they didn't like their own countries—it had an entire parallel world going on. There was a really healthy music scene there, but it wasn't an industry scene. The underground was quite well connected, though.

BOB BERT I'm with Sonic Youth, and we go over to England and someone shows us a videotape of this new band from Berlin called Einstürzende Neubauten, and we're blown away. Then I look into them, and Lydia is already recording with them.* Then she did the same thing with The Birthday Party. Meanwhile, she took Rowland S. Howard from The Birthday Party and she put out a great version of 'Some Velvet Morning' by Lee Hazlewood and Nancy Sinatra, with the flipside of 'I Fell In Love With A Ghost'. She's the ultimate collaborator.

MURRAY MITCHELL A couple of months after *The Agony Is The Ecstasy*, off we went to Berlin, and the *Honeymoon In Red* album came out of that, years later. The owner of the studio had gone away for a summer, and the engineer, trying to make a bit of pocket money, rented it out to this rich guy who wanted to make a record with Lydia—he definitely had some money because Lydia, myself, and The Birthday Party, we all had hotels to stay in, with this guy financing it. The studio was really inappropriate—its main revenue was recording jingles for TV ads. We were there a couple of days when Lydia, out wandering the streets, met Blixa Bargeld and was somewhat fascinated by this stick insect of a bloke in a rubber suit with animal hair stapled to it. She came back to the studio having told this bloke to get his band into the studio, and a couple of hours later, Einstürzende Neubauten turn up with this old truck and start dragging all these rusty steel springs and other metal junk in over this perfectly polished wooden floor. The engineer was having a meltdown!

CHRISTOPH DREHER Die Haut started around 1978–79. In 1982, we were rerecording an album because, the first time, we had been stuck with a very

---

* Resulting in the 'Thirsty Animal' twelve-inch, released in 1982.

anal German engineer who didn't understand what we were doing. We now recorded in England. Nick Cave was around, so he performed with us, and then there was 'Der Karibische Western', which Lydia sang on. Lydia was living in London, so it was very easy to get her to join us. I had a band by the end of the 60s, then a long pause to Die Haut, so I wasn't an experienced musician or skilled at writing songs. That was something I then cultivated, but I didn't know about writing lyrics and how you do it and how long it takes. It was great, and surprising, that you only had to talk to Lydia for five minutes about what you're up to: *We have this instrumental called 'Die Karibische Western'*. It was called that because it described the two elements in the music, a western-type guitar line and a surf-influenced guitar line, then Lydia came up with these lyrics for it that totally relate to the themes. She did that really quickly and sang it quickly too. It was really refreshing and loose.

MICK HARVEY Rowland and Lydia did the opening spot on the tour we did in Germany. They'd go out onstage and do this noisy thing related to what she did on *The Agony Is The Ecstasy*—a similar type of thing for twenty minutes. I used to be terrible before we went onstage, I couldn't talk to anyone, so I couldn't watch them, it was too much for me—but I heard them some nights, and it sounded pretty … confrontational, in a good way. I remember watching from side of stage in Munich, Rowland making a lot of racket, Lydia doing Lydia.

CHRISTOPH DREHER Lydia had her duo with Rowland S. Howard—they toured with The Birthday Party, and so did we. I remember we were playing Batschkapp, this famous venue in Frankfurt, and, after we had played, The Birthday Party went onstage, climbing up this ladder, which was under the stage, from backstage, and Tracy Pew was wearing these leather shorts he wore at the time, and she reached up between his legs and squeezed his balls in a friendly and encouraging way. It was like saying *break a leg* or something like that! That was so typical—she's capable of being so open, not shying away from talking sex or making jokes and gestures like that. She was often the only woman around, and she dealt with that in a very sober way. She was very respected for that—she was so independent and in control, without having to significantly lay any stress on that.

In the 80s, you had a couple of female bands, but it was still a minority thing. You had The Raincoats and The Slits in the UK; we had Malaria! in Berlin, but things were still very male-dominated in the underground scene. It was striking that Lydia was surrounded by all these male musicians who were heavily into drugs, and she was in the middle of all this but she wasn't into that at all. And she wasn't particularly into the nightlife, either: she would go to her room early while we were on tour. She was so productive because she was so disciplined.

*

MICK HARVEY *Honeymoon In Red* was originally conceived as a band, which was Lydia, Rowland, myself, and Genevieve—that's what it was meant to be. When we co-opted Nick into singing on one song, Tracy to play on a couple of others, it was just because we'd got to a certain point and Lydia liked the idea of having other people involved. It was fine with me, but maybe it was less comfortable for Rowland, having Nick coming in to sing a duet, given it was meant to be his platform outside of the band—a springboard to somewhere he could project himself, outside of The Birthday Party. It was OK with me, we were having fun and—at the time—it was all very friendly and cool.

For Lydia, it was probably just whatever was coming along, but we really did conceive of it as a unit. The four of us recorded almost everything on the album, then we did 'Done Dun' with Tracy and Nick very late in the session, once they'd arrived in town. We'd already recorded ninety percent of it, and, for me, I was looser about it, but Rowland and Genevieve probably preferred it to remain a simpler band that recorded. The band name was literally going to be Honeymoon In Red—that was the idea.

LYDIA LUNCH For *Honeymoon In Red*, Rowland wrote most of the songs, I wrote some songs, Nick and I have two songs on it, some of The Birthday Party played on it. Then it was lost for many years before I got it back, and we brought Thurston in to play on it and Jim mixed it. It's kind of an oddball record: it's not really a concept, it's kind of disjointed.

MURRAY MITCHELL What I remember is that when the recording for *Honeymoon In Red* finished in Berlin, nothing was entirely finished—the guy who was financing it had run out of money—so I remember getting thrown out of the hotel, and I went to stay with some strange girl I'd met while Lydia went off and did some gigs with The Birthday Party. I spent most of the time shoplifting with Rowland S. Howard's girlfriend, Genevieve, who was incredibly adept at it—and it was rather easy in Kreuzberg at the time.

MICK HARVEY The *Honeymoon In Red* thing went really weird. The album never came out and sometime in the mid-80s Lydia managed to get the tapes, all of the multitracks bar one, and took them to New York and reworked the whole thing. We heard what she'd done with Jim Thirlwell and a couple of other people, and I couldn't even recognise what we had recorded. I said to Lydia that it wasn't the album we made and I didn't really like what they'd done—so I asked for my name to be removed. I felt that the recording wasn't anything to do with me.

I thought it was fair enough—maybe she took it a little bit badly, but it really wasn't what we'd played together. Nick had no reason to take his name off because the one song he was a part of was one of the songs that was unchanged, because Lydia didn't have the multitrack—but he decided he didn't want his name on the record either. I suppose from Lydia's perspective it must have been a really incredible insult, and it must have been quite hurtful for him to do that—it was a very direct rejection. Now, when I look back, I don't even know why he did that, or what the background was for that decision. So when she wrote the liner notes, with this thinly veiled abuse of the two of us, it was definitely about us taking our names off.

I would argue in hindsight that I had a perfectly reasonable reason, no insult to Lydia, while Nick had no reason at all. I thought it was a bit crap, of course—if you've got problems with people then you don't air them publicly. I never said anything critical or defamatory about her because I have no reason to—I've always liked her! We did get into an argument backstage at a show sometime afterward, in Berlin—a big benefit night with twenty different acts on. I just said whatever it was I felt about it. People around us looked terrified, but my bark's worse than my bite—hers too. It took me a while to realise she was justifiably upset by what Nick did—but, as a consequence, we didn't talk for thirty years! It's turned around now, and we saw each other recently and got along fine, which was really nice.

LYDIA LUNCH My participation with Nick Cave wasn't that elaborate, and, I mean, there was a lot of prejudice against me because I wasn't a heroin addict. Not only in London but in New York too, people held it against me that I was never a heroin addict. Bizarre! Like, *Don't trust the straight one ...*

*

JIM THIRLWELL She had been invited by Danceteria to make a show for Halloween in '83. She had a concept, which she proposed to myself, Nick Cave, and Marc Almond. We proceeded to create backing tracks and to decide what we wanted to do for this concert, which Lydia dubbed The Immaculate Consumptive. It was around this time that Lydia and I became romantically involved. Mick Harvey, Barry Adamson, Blixa Bargeld, Annie Hogan, and Nick all played on the backing tracks. We did two shows at Danceteria and one at the 9:30 Club in Washington, DC, and that was the entirety of our performing career.

TOM GARRETSON I saw the gigs Lydia did with The Immaculate Consumptive— they were absolutely amazing. It's the closest thing I've seen to the hysteria and frivolity of what Berlin cabaret was in Weimar Berlin, but with a more no-wave attitude onstage. Each of them did separate songs, alone or in duo, and a few with three singers. At one point, in one of the shows, I remember Nick came out and was going to do a solo song on the piano, and he told the audience, 'We borrowed this piano from Brian Eno.' He started playing and the piano broke, so he couldn't complete the song, so he started telling jokes to the audience to smooth out the situation. I remember Jim falling off the stage once and getting the barrier bar between his legs—you could see how much pain he was in, the poor guy! But he didn't miss a beat, and, like a true trooper, the show did go on.

CARLO MCCORMICK It was a moment where all of them were trying to stretch out as artists, outside the context of the milieu from which they came, doing something really sleazy, really bringing it down to something more psychosexual than purely transgressive. A lot of women, especially in rock, had played with tropes of sexuality before, but Lydia's was so much more psychological. It was not a nurturing kind of affection—it was desire that could be self-abnegating at the same time. We had had some angry women, but we'd never had anyone channel it into something that wasn't just vitriolic feminism. Here we had an artist manifesting it in a way that was really engaging.

TOM GARRETSON In late 1983, I decided to move back to New York, and in the second week I was there, I went to Danceteria. I was by myself, and I ordered a gin and tonic—a scared little creature standing in the shadows. I looked across the room, and on the other side of the room there's Lydia standing with Marc Almond and Jim Thirlwell. I'm not a celebrity hound, so I just glanced over, thought, *Oh, that's cool*, and looked away. Suddenly, Lydia materialises right in front of me, as if by magic, and she looks into my eyes and she says, 'I need to know you, I don't know why, I'm too fucked-up to talk right now so here's my number. Call me tomorrow.'

I took the number and I called her the next day. She's like, 'Why are you calling me?' And I said, 'I dunno, you told me to call you!' 'Well I've never given anybody my phone number before.' 'Well I don't know why you gave it to me, you wanted me to call you!' I thought she was trying to pick me up—I'm gay, I thought it might be a problem. This went back-and-forth on the phone, and then she just decided to invite me to every one of her shows. I went to everything she did, all the film premieres, all the shows she did in New York or New Jersey—she would demand that I go and always put me on the guest list. Fate is very weird in life at times, I'm still trying to figure it out, and sometimes today we talk about it.

*

NICK ZEDD In 1981, I got Lydia's address in LA and wrote her a letter, which I guess moved her to plan on meeting me one day in the future. She didn't write me back, but when I premiered a feature film in 1983, at Danceteria, she walked up to me and handed me a piece of paper with her phone number on it. A few days later, we met up at my place on East Eleventh Street, where she aggressively attempted to seduce me. I agreed to meet her later at her place. I knew we were going to have a very intense sexual relationship that would change my life.

Later that night, I met her in a coffee shop on First Avenue, in the twenties. As we sat at a table, she had a big grin on her face. She was staring at me and smiling the whole time. That surprised me. After that we went to an apartment she was staying in on some upper floor of a residential building. The soundtrack music to *Last Tango In Paris* was playing in the other room while we fucked on the floor. I knew immediately that I was in love with her. We started seeing each other for sex. Soon after that, I moved out of my apartment and moved in with her. I went with her to a performance she did at some place called White Columns in Tribeca, and she did a gig with Thurston Moore and Norman Westberg in a one-shot band they threw together.* We also wrote a short performance piece called 'She', which she later performed on television in Sweden or Holland.

After living with Lydia for a month, she left for London. I figured out a way to raise the airfare to meet up with Lydia a month later. She was living with some English guy named Murray in an open relationship, so I'd go visit her in their apartment, then she arranged for me to stay in Thomas Dolby's empty apartment. London was expensive—nobody I met could afford to go out to nightclubs—and the tube trains shut down too early to go anywhere. The vibe was nothing. We went together to Ireland, staying with Vivienne Dick. First, we wanted to shoot a Super-8 film with Lydia and Rowland S. Howard acting together, but he would never leave his apartment, and we were both broke. I was determined to shoot a movie with her anyway and had stolen Super-8 film cassettes from some counter in Heathrow Airport. So we just had to borrow Vivienne Dick's camera to start shooting in Ireland.

The footage we shot in London before that was with some other borrowed

---

* May 5, 1983, was the second day of the Speed Trials festival at the White Columns Gallery art space. Lydia played with Jim Thirlwell and three members of Swans. The only known song from the set is 'Main Kelly And Me On A Blender', essentially an eight-minute improvised blues tune.

camera. *The Wild World Of Lydia Lunch* (1983) was shot spontaneously. No plotting. The guy on the bike on the bridge was a happy accident, along with the dog. It was all unplanned. It was several hours of travelling, then filming. Almost nothing was edited. I wanted to contradict the threatening public persona and convey the simple beauty of Lydia's charisma in whatever environments were available to us. The burned-out buildings in Ireland were also something different to the mundane tenement buildings of NYC. There's a visual romanticism that emerges in the film. Lydia's self-love was maybe behind her involvement, but I did make her look good most of the time.

VIVIENNE DICK That film that Nick Zedd made with Lydia? I hadn't realised that was made partly in Dublin, in Phoenix Park, when she stayed with me. We went over to Connemara and made a little film there, *Like Dawn To Dust* (1983). She's generous, and she trusts you as a collaborator. She gave me music for it too. It's just a short poetic film, about eight or nine minutes.

NICK ZEDD I remember when we were driving around in a car in Ireland with Vivienne and her boyfriend, then we stopped somewhere and Lydia tried to convince me to shoplift candies from some convenience store for the ride. I refused. I figured she could steal her own candy. Maybe she was hoping I'd get caught and deported? Who knows!

When I returned to NYC, after two months in England and Ireland, I discovered the cassette tape of the letter Lydia had dictated to me and realised it would work perfectly as the soundtrack. It all fell into place. She knew there would be a film. We shot it together. She trusted that I would complete it. The cassette tape, she had sent it to my mail box. She recited it alone in a room in London. I didn't hear it until after we had broken up and I was back in the USA, but it was not a kiss-off—the tone of her voice had nothing to do with me. The film seems to convey ambivalence thanks to unfortunate circumstances and resentment on her part at some unreliable people she had been hoping to get money from to do a more explicit film with me. She was hoping to make something like what she ended up doing with Kern.

CHAPTER TEN

IN LIMBO

*DURING A BRIEF RETURN TO NEW YORK
CITY IN LATE 1982, LYDIA SETS UP A NEW
BAND. THEY PLAY HALF A DOZEN SHOWS
AND RECORD AN EP IN NOVEMBER.*

BOBBY SWOPE If Lydia liked you then she was really nice to be around. She was supportive, funny, and sweet. If she didn't like you then she was brutal. I remember being in front of CBGB's one night, after some bands had played, and Lydia and Anya Phillips—they were kind of the two queens of the scene—they were sitting on the hood of a car parked in front. Every guy who would walk in front of them, they would shred his ego—they were so hilarious, so funny, and so mean. When those two were together they really enjoyed bringing down straight men.

BETH B When I first met her, on the streets she'd be like, 'Fuck you!' when guys were saying shit to her. For me, I was like, *OK, I'll look like a boy so they don't come anywhere near me.* She was like, *OK, you want to pull out your dick, right? Go on and do it!* She was one-upping them, being even more aggressive than the aggressor, more abusive than the abuser.

RICHARD KERN Walking around with her was always a trip, because if a guy said something to her, she would turn around and say, 'Well come on then! Fuck me right now. C'mon. Stick it in!' She didn't care who they were—there was nothing that she was afraid of.

RON ATHEY That's strong. Why should you be the girl walking down the street with your head down while everyone's talking about your ass or your tits? Why not be willing to have a fistfight right there? You learn, nine times out of ten, it won't come to that—they'll back off of you because you're a crazy bitch and they never thought you would stand up for yourself. That creates an evolution in a bigger population than yourself.

Confronting sexual harassers is genius—then not being sentimental about it either, that's like the nugget for me. Not to pull out the violin afterward, like, *It's so hard for us ladies!* It's not her thing. It's just another *fuck you* and move on, be productive about it.

JARBOE When I met her, of course I knew who Lydia Lunch was—I had *Queen Of Siam* and everything. It was exciting, and she met all my expectations: she's such a star, such a bright light, a stunning personality. Meeting Lydia and Jim Thirlwell together, it was enough to fill up an entire arena with their light—so powerful as artists, incredible charisma. Lydia would wear these black leotards with stiletto heels—a strong image.

I remember Michael [Gira] and Lydia and me walking through the neighbourhood and I was learning my own skillset for not getting killed—and I watched her very carefully, to see how she kept from being mugged on those dangerous streets. How you did it was to seamlessly—without giving a pause—have radar working all the time, all around your head. You see a group of guys hanging on the sidewalk and they're not your friends so you don't stop, and—as Lydia did that night in her leotards and high heels—you seamlessly walk to the other side of the street, or you walk right down the middle of the street and keep going.

*

THURSTON MOORE I met her when she came back from England. I would see her in the Laundromat on Thirteenth Street, and she would look at me—I was this tall, skinny kid coming in with short hair—and I knew that was her and she didn't know who I was, and she would look at me, and I felt, like, caught in her stare. But what was I going to say? So I was introduced to her through Richard Edson, who was playing drums on the first Sonic Youth EP. He started working on soundtrack music for the film *Vortex* by

Beth B and Scott B, and he asked me if I would play on it. Lydia Lunch was sort of involved—she was the female lead in the film—so that's when I met her.

Richard brought me over to where she was staying, on Rivington Street—she was just crashing in a room. We immediately got on. Lydia's completely welcoming, and we just became really good friends. We would call each other up, we'd go see movies together, and she saw Sonic Youth really early on. I was really into hardcore bands in '80 to '82, Minor Threat and Black Flag and all these kinds of things. I would play her cassettes and she was like, 'Nah, it's horrible, it's too fast, where's the poetry? I like slow music.'

BETH B The early films that I made were coming directly out of the desire to have women front and centre in the story. Even putting women into roles that had previously been dominated by men was very important to me. In *Vortex*, Lydia plays this iconic figure, usually cast as a man: the 'hard-boiled investigator'. James Russo plays the corporate underling, white male lead, representing the power of the hierarchy. Lydia is there to bring down that structure, but, at the same time, she's seduced by it. That's often the dynamic in power relationships: you have a dance of power, between the dominant and the submissive. They are inextricably merged. The film talks about that kind of dynamic and the two characters—Lydia and James—flip that power back and forth. The film has a real detective-noir sensibility, while still being subversive.

Vortex was the first film where there was actually funding, but by funding I mean fifty thousand dollars, which is still not very much. Trying to make a 16mm film on that budget was difficult, and it meant a lot of people working for free. It was made on a more professional level, but it was still fairly experimental and inaccessible, in terms of telling a story. It was more about mood and style than it was about writing a script that would be commercial. It was the last film I collaborated on with Scott too. We made films together for five years, then the relationship de-integrated, the work dissolved, then I have to say, gratefully, for the rest of my career, I have been making films with a solo vision. I really wanted to have that voice, my own voice, and that departure was a great liberation. *Vortex* was pivotal for me; it was the end of an era.*

RICHARD EDSON I knew Lydia, but not too well. She was around, I was around. She was like the queen of the East Village. She had such an attitude, she held herself with this cocky negativity—it was very charismatic. She'd seen me in Sonic Youth, so she knew how I played. We ran into each other, and she asked me if I wanted to be in her band. I said yes, I was into any kind of experimental situation, and it seemed like a perfect situation: she was talking about two gigs and a record—it seemed like no commitment, just a great project. She asked me if I knew a bass player who might want to do it. I suggested, 'Yeah, why not ask Thurston?' She came back and said that he would do it. She had Pat Place on guitar already, then she got Jim Sclavunos to play saxophone—he's a great drummer but I was already on drums.

THURSTON MOORE For me, that was just like Heaven on Earth! I'm playing with all these musicians that I've always been fascinated by in my neighbourhood. Lydia kind of ruled the roost as far as the downtown no-wave scene at that point, but a lot of people had dispersed, and I wasn't trying to attain any kind of notice or celebrity—I just really wanted to play some music with her. We started rehearsing in Bradly Field's basement, where Bradly and Kristian lived upstairs. She started showing me these song ideas, like, *I want it to go like this, like a funeral march*, and in my mind I'm hearing Minor Threat! It was a bit of a challenge. And I was just like, *I'll play slow if I must.*

RICHARD EDSON My only regret is that I was so committed to the idea of the groove that I tried to pull the band more in my direction, rather than just committing fully to what Lydia was hearing. I'm happy, it's a great album, but I know I could do more. Lydia heard what I was doing and said, 'No, that's not what I want.' So I did what she wanted, this really primitive tom-tom, when I was more into riding the hi-hat or the ride cymbal. She had no sympathy with that—she liked that simple bottom tribal drumming. We did

---

* Lydia would also perform on a number of songs for the soundtrack to *Vortex*.

two rehearsals, then we went down to Washington, DC, to play a gig, came back and played a gig, then we went into studio. It was very painless and a lot of fun. Lydia, despite being such a tough individual, she wasn't a slave-master, she didn't crack the whip. She was clear what she wanted and very easy to work with.

THURSTON MOORE We played at Peppermint Lounge, and Joe Strummer was in the audience. I can only hope that he was inebriated: he was just standing in the back going, 'Buttocks! Buttocks!' while we were singing slow songs about death and misery.*

JIM THIRLWELL In the spring of '84, Lydia was going to do some shows in Sweden, playing some of the material that was on the *In Limbo* album. It was going to be Rowland S. Howard on sax, Jessamy Calkin playing percussion—she had these champagne glasses that she would smash rhythmically—and Lydia on vocals. For some reason, Rowland couldn't do it, and she found out that I played sax, so she invited me. We did two, three shows with Lydia, Jessamy, and my friend John, John 'Tex' Tottenham, an English poet and a good friend of mine still—Lydia and John were romantically involved at that point. We did these shows, and I got to know Lydia better, then we started writing material together. We had this idea for a project called Hard Diamond Drill; we were swapping lyrics and I was coming up with ideas for arrangements. We would get together now and then and brainstorm.

Each of our musical collaborations is very different. One of the things that I really enjoyed was that she was very open to what I brought to the table and almost hands-off with that. *Stinkfist* is a thing unto itself—a percussive rhythmic chant—and Lydia had the idea of taking the beat from Alice Cooper's 'Black Juju', expanding it, and using it as a sort of sexual mantra. It's very repetitive but it swells and goes through a whole lot of different avenues. We actually expanded that idea and made some other pieces, which Norman Westberg from Swans played on, then that expanded into a project called Swelter, which we did live a few times with Lydia,

---

* Weasel Walter suggests that Strummer was more likely shouting, 'Bollocks!'

myself, and Cliff Martinez from 13.13.* We did it at Danceteria once, then
LA, Portland, and two shows in San Francisco. We would find 'found
percussion' like forty-four-gallon drums, and we'd have a few drums on the
rider. I expanded the *Stinkfist* EP by adding the 'Meltdown Oratorio', and
we did a couple of singles … I mixed the *Honeymoon In Red* album, then
we also did the *Don't Fear The Reaper* EP, which was a cover of the Blue
Öyster Cult track and a couple of originals.†

ROB KENNEDY The Workdogs were the revenge of the rhythm section—a
drummer and a bass player with a bad attitude toward guitar players and
frontmen. Scott [Jarvis] came out of Th' Cigaretz from North Carolina, and
I had been in Da Chumps from Washington, DC. My first impression of
Lydia was she was an extremely hot, angry, punk-rocker, which I dug—I'm
married to one.

What happened was, Lydia and Jim Thirlwell needed some carpentry
done at their loft in Brooklyn. Scott and I did the work in exchange for
getting their contributions to *Workdogs In Hell*. All they had to do was
give us cassettes. The album was based on the idea that we could mix our
jamming ethos with elements of 'mail art' to create a collaboration where
we didn't actually have to meet the player in person. We mailed cassettes to
people we wanted to work with and crafted a record based on *The Divine
Comedy*, specifically the Lower East Side's resemblance to Hades.

Lydia was working on a lot of the same ideas and she would have been

---

* As well as being Lydia's domestic partner for lengthy period, Jim Thirlwell was her
primary musical collaborator throughout the mid-80s to early 90s. The 'Swelter' piece was
toured—the Danceteria show was on November 10, 1983; the others were on November 23
and December 2, 3, and 4, respectively—but never documented. It apparently forms the DNA
of the song 'Stinkfist', recorded in 1986–87.

† The remixed *Honeymoon In Red* album was released in 1987, the *Stinkfist* EP in 1988,
along with the single 'The Crumb' (featuring Thurston Moore). The *Don't Fear The Reaper*
EP and 'Twisted'/'Past Glas' single (featuring Z'Ev) came out in 1991. Thirlwell was also the
engineer on *The Drowning Of Lucy Hamilton* (1985), reprocessed the tapes for the *Hysterie*
compilation (1986), remastered Emilio Cubeiro's *The Death Of An Asshole* (1989), and
engineered various pieces on the *Our Fathers Who Aren't In Heaven* compilation (1990)—all
three of which were released on Lydia's Widowspeak imprint. He would then produce 1991's
Shotgun Wedding album.

perfect to play the Devil, but I let the contributions dictate the final content. For Lydia to have been the Devil we would have had to tell her what to do, and you do not mansplain to Lydia Lunch. The track with Lydia is called '*'. The verbal translation of that symbol is 'Star Circle'. The reason is that we rat-fucked all the 'big names' onto that ring of Hell.

LYDIA LUNCH When did I become the voice of justice for all? I don't know. My first subject matter was the authoritarian abuse within the family. Then it went to the authoritarian abuse from my father, then to the father of our country, then God the father. That was the triad I was attacking, and I acted as resistance against the tyranny and oppression of the patriarchy, of male domination. It's always a war. We share something in our bloodlines, the persecuted and the persecutor—there's molecular memory of the horrors of history. We cannot just sit quietly and la-di-da-di-da.

Look: I want to be the last sound heard in the apocalypse but, in the meantime, I've got a lot of complaining to do. It was never about my wound. From the time that I was young, I knew that these were universal traumas, and that's what gives me the strength to continue talking. It's not my war, it's never been my war, there's just no choice, because if I don't, who will? Trust me. I wish women had stepped up to take my place.

ROB KENNEDY My favourite Lydia memories are taking Lydia and Jim to the rodeo at Cowtown, New Jersey. I was telling them that rodeo was the only thing I knew that was stupider than playing rock'n'roll. The paycheque in rodeo is based on 'entry fees' that the contestants pay. It's like paying to play at a club, then, instead of having a good/bad/OK show, you have an animal kick the shit out of you. We always laughed at PETA's complaints because rodeo animals are treated like royalty and the cowboys like trash. They got interested, so my wife and I took them to Cowtown, the oldest continuously run rodeo in the USA.

*

JIM SCLAVUNOS After we'd done *In Limbo*—I had finally got my saxophone wish with Lydia!—Lydia told me, 'Well, Sonic Youth are looking for a drummer, why don't you do that? They're a really good band, you should try out.'

THURSTON MOORE Lydia comes into Sonic Youth's lives when we're recording *Confusion Is Sex* in Wharton Tiers's basement. Wharton was the drummer who played in Theoretical Girls—there was sort of a bit of no-wave continuance going on there, and also there's a song on that album called 'She's In A Bad Mood' that's about Lydia. She came to see Sonic Youth and she's like, 'OK, you guys are it! You are the proper extension of what we were doing in '77, '78. Thank you.' Then she saw Swans and Live Skull, these compatriot bands of ours—she loved Swans, she loved Live Skull. And this thing was happening at this club that was way lower east in this really dangerous, drug-infested street on, like, East Fifth Street. The club was called SIN Club—S-I-N: Safety In Numbers—and you couldn't go there alone, you had to go with two or three people or otherwise you were anyone's casualty. She would come there and see us play, these bands, and that became our hangout: the horror zone of New York City.

LYDIA LUNCH Everything was different. Someone paid for Teenage Jesus to be recorded. *Queen Of Siam* was sponsored by ZE Records. I sponsored *In Limbo* because I don't imagine anyone would have paid for that in advance. It all depended. I had the ability to have my own label and then license them out whenever people wanted to do something—because I might have only been selling five hundred to a thousand records—then I'd take that money to record something else. I don't go into the studio to piddle around, honestly. And I've rarely had backing. A lot of those mid-80s records were self-financed, and they'd each have a different method of getting done. Whatever it took. I was always insistent that everything be documented, even if it was just a live recording—I'm certainly glad I did that. I always felt I was shitting in the face of history, and it needed to be in a time capsule eventually.*

---

* The recordings of *In Limbo* were finally released in 1984 by a British label. The money allowed Lydia to move permanently back to New York City in the spring of '84.

BOB BERT When I auditioned for Sonic Youth, they were asking me, 'What records are you into now?' I said *13.13*, and Thurston said, 'Well, I'm working with Lydia Lunch on this project called *In Limbo*.' I played that first show, and it was a complete thrill for me in the first place to be on the CBGB's stage. Lydia Lunch and Arto Lindsay were two of the probably twenty or thirty people that were there. I was floored that Lydia came backstage and complimented me, and we started chatting. And, like, here I was, meeting someone that I was such a big fan of, looked up to, and admired so much, and she turned out to be so cool, and we've been friends ever since.

In 1984, Kim Gordon and Thurston Moore got married, and I was in charge of driving Lydia and Jim Thirlwell to the wedding, up in Connecticut. It was a really scorching August day, and I borrowed my mother's air-conditioned big boat of a Buick. We cruised up there, and Jim was playing the Foetus recordings, which, in the car, were blowing my mind. We were having a good time, smoking a million joints, and we were late to the wedding. It was almost like a Norman Rockwell scene in this little quaint church in Connecticut, a pretty traditional kind of wedding, and we walk in: Lydia has got her flowery dress, no underwear, her hair's all crazy, and Thirlwell's wearing leather pants and a wife-beater. The whole church turned and looked at us. It was hysterical.

THURSTON MOORE Lydia and I went to WKCR at Columbia University because she had to do an interview. I went with her because she wanted me to sit with her in the interview. The DJ didn't know who I was, so I just had to be there, answering questions with her, as her musical friend. And then we took a bus back downtown, and taking a bus down from Columbia University is about a three-hour trip. On the way, I was telling her how I was really fascinated reading these books on Charles Manson: Vincent Bugliosi's *Helter Skelter*, then *The Family* by Ed Sanders. She had read the books as well, so we started bantering about lyrical ideas, and I showed her the lyrics for a song called 'Death Valley '69'. I have this chorus—'Now-now-now!'—which is sort of like a Manson Family chant, and she wrote out a lot of the lines that became the verse. By the time we got downtown, I had this page of lyrics. And I had this riff that I was playing around with that was more rockist that anything Sonic Youth had done up to that point.

BOB BERT We were playing a show at Danceteria, and it was a triple bill of Sonic Youth, Swans, and Lydia was performing upstairs. Lydia had arranged the whole thing, and she came down and sang 'Death Valley '69' with us. At the end of the night, Ruth Polsky was drunk, and we had a $1,500 guarantee—which, back in those days, was a lot of money. Ruth paid Lydia twice.*

THURSTON MOORE Ruth would never book Sonic Youth—we weren't really her thing. But Lydia told her, 'No, you book this band, and I'll sing with them.' So, she comes out onstage and sang 'Death Valley '69' with us. And I always remember that because, all of a sudden, the audience was like, *Oh. Wow.* It was sort of like Lydia Lunch was passing the baton to us.

One of the first times we palled around, she called up and she's like, 'Hey, let's go to this bar.' I met her and we just walked around, and it was sort of just one of those things where you're kind of young and you don't have any money and you're walking around with a friend, and you're just talking and talking. We went to a bar; we went to a Chinese restaurant and had some tea. I was sort of like, *I'm gonna go home.* We were walking back. We sort of lived near each other: I was on Eldridge, between Hester and Grand, and she was over on Rivington. I didn't know her that well—we had just kind of started hanging out—and she goes, 'I really, really, really have to pee.' And I was like, 'Well, you can use my toilet,' but she was like, 'No, I really have to pee now.'

We were on the Bowery and Grand, and there was this one doorway of this building, right around the corner from A-Space, which was Arlene Schloss's performance space—that whole area was these cheap spaces and

---

* Polsky booked the bands for Hurrah and then Danceteria and was responsible for bringing numerous bands to New York City, as well as helping break local artists to wider audiences. She died tragically in 1986 when she was hit by a runaway taxi that left her pinned against the front of the Limelight club. She was thirty-one years old.

people doing weird art.* Lydia kicked the door open and she said, 'Be my watch-out.' And I said OK ... and I just sort of held the door open. Maybe some homeless man would walk by, and she just went up to the middle of the stairwell, lifted her whatever up, pulled her whatever down, and just peed for, like, five minutes. And I was just, *Oh my god.* And I was just kind of looking into the street, then I would look at her, and she was just laughing. It wasn't disturbing, but I was watching somebody just completely owning and embracing their environment, themselves, everything. And me. Every mask was off. And that's when I was sort of just like, *Oh, I don't know anyone like you, and I probably never will.*

---

* Schloss established A Space, a multimedia arts venue, in a New York City loft. Having already established a reputation as a performance artist, she went on to create sound poetry and a variety of other visual, video, and performance works.

CHAPTER ELEVEN

THE RIGHT SIDE OF MY BRAIN

LYDIA SPENDS AUGUST 1984 WORKING WITH LUCY HAMILTON ON AN INSTRUMENTAL RECORD, WHILE ALSO COMMENCING A PRODUCTIVE ARTISTIC RELATIONSHIP WITH FILMMAKER RICHARD KERN.

LUCY HAMILTON For *The Drowning Of Lucy Hamilton*, Lydia and I created the album with Jim Thirlwell, who did an amazing job in Roli Mosimann's loft.* Lydia then took what we recorded and put it into Richard Kern's film, *The Right Side Of My Brain*, which I wasn't a part of. Beyond the sounds on *The Drowning*, they had other tracks we recorded that they used for the film. My friend Sarah lived around the corner and had a piano in her apartment and offered that we could practice there. I don't know if Lydia played the piano before we played together, but she's a natural. We would meet in the afternoons and compose different pieces—I was on bass clarinet, she was on piano, so we sought to understand how these two instruments could work together as we arranged different tropes. I then brought an amplifier over so we could play electric guitar. We knew each other's guitar style really well—we already understood how that would work.

LYDIA LUNCH I have my styles of guitar playing—slide, slow motion, or

---

* Mosimann is best known for is work as drummer for Swans in the early 80s. He went on to a significant career as a music producer and engineer.

brutally precision fascist rhythms—but I only do it when it's mandatory, when I don't think anyone else can do it. I love when metal guitar players come to me and bow to Teenage Jesus—I find that hilarious.

PAT IRWIN I loved the way Lydia played guitar—I've always wished she played more of it, but as early as when she started 8 Eyed Spy, she didn't want anything to do with a guitar anymore.

LUCY HAMILTON The music felt readymade for a soundtrack. We weren't envisaging taking the music out on a concert tour! We played together because we wanted to work together, and Lydia had the vision that we could create an album, then it was her idea for it to be used in the Kern film. The album was recorded in August, and the production continued into the fall. Lydia is very quick; she's great at first takes, so it's either in or it's out. Roli's loft was wonderful; I loved the reverb they added to my bass clarinet up front. I'd gotten accustomed to conflicts with sound engineers. They'd argue that they'll add reverb post-production and not understand that my playing develops through the reverb. Jim and Roli set up all the reverb one could want in the world, and I played in the bathroom, which was particularly resonant. Lydia was in the main part of the loft, playing piano. It was the best recording experience of my life!

*

CARLO MCCORMICK The notion that Lydia Lunch is a persona, rather than a person, only really dawned on me later. When she was living up in Harlem, she'd cook a really nice meal; it was a really domestic situation, and it would be this really polite thing, and, at the end, she kind of had to say, 'Now get out of here, you fucking asshole!' Because she'd have to go back to being Lydia Lunch. It occurred to me, *Wow, if it's ever tough to hang out with Lydia, how tough must it be to have to be Lydia all the time.* Even if she's totally honest and totally herself all the time, Lydia Lunch is also a persona that she had to create. She's this larger-than-life figure, then, when you start looking at the art, you can see all the different nuanced parts of who she is as a human being.

JIM THIRLWELL Lydia's onstage persona in the 80s, and what she would do when she started doing spoken word, that's not what she was like domestically, and we lived together for six, seven years. We had quite a domestic life—she's very sweet, a great cook, a fastidious housekeeper, and a very organised person.

LYDIA LUNCH In the past I was just a character, maybe—or not—based upon part of my personality, in other people's films. When I met Richard Kern, after I'd begun doing spoken word, I was more into public psychotherapy. I needed to make a film, *The Right Side Of My Brain*, which—to me— was like a homage to Polanski's *Repulsion*, which I thought was a very important film about female paranoia and disgust. I needed to explain it, first to myself. I felt I wasn't alone in my obsession, this search for something more, forever or never enough, pushing people to take everything further. I just felt there had never been a film that really talked about that, or even literature that I could find that really talked about that.

RICHARD KERN As a teenager, I was real into communism and all that shit. It was also the time of the Symbionese Liberation Army—that was huge to me. That was a time period where people would say something and they'd actually go and do something super-violent, like a negative. When you're young, you have these fantasies that you can actually change something, and I guess you do, but my whole thing was *Destroy everything!* Specifically, I really wanted to destroy the way people thought about sex. I felt everything was run by sex. I felt like destroying someone's sexual feelings, or the way they look at sex, was a way to really fuck them up. All this stuff, all the relationships, the love, the way it was portrayed in the movies and stuff—it was all a big lie. And a lot of stuff was a lie. You wake up and everything's a fucking lie. You just want to destroy everything possible. But, of course, that's a young man's fantasy. I just had these meagre fantasies, and, when I met Lydia, I met someone I'd say all this fucked up shit to and she'd just go, 'Yeah, that's right!'

LYDIA LUNCH The films that I did with Richard were autobiographical, and that was important to me too. *Right Side Of My Brain* was more about me trying to get over my obsession with the need for more, my forever unsatisfied cycling through a series of men, none of them able to really satisfy my unquenchable hunger, which is why at times I'd need six of them, not necessarily at the same time but in the same frame of time.

My book *Paradoxia! A Predator's Diary* really talks about this. I was never a typical junkie—I was never addicted to any drug or to alcohol because I was addicted to adrenaline, which is naturally manufactured in the body. There was a point where I needed to feed on this, which is why I needed an accelerated romantic life, sexual life. And there came a point where you just reach a limit that is pretty much beyond the beyond, or you're really going to make yourself sick, or something's going to take you out. I had to pull away. I had to really go inside and say, *Where is this vacuum coming from? Where is this absence? What is it? What is not fulfilled when I can do everything I want with whoever I want musically, sexually, where I have no limitations on myself? Nobody can tell me what to do—and, trust me, they cannot, because I will do exactly what I want to do every moment as I feel everybody should.*

RICHARD KERN When I met Lydia she was living with Jim, one block over from me on Twelfth Street. We quickly got into a rhythm, talking about filmmaking, DIY filmmaking, underground filmmaking, photography, or whatever. Lydia is like, *I have this fantasy I'd like to do with a person, so I think I'll make a film about it.** The basic premise was: Lydia had these cute guys, hot guys, that she wanted to mess around with. There was no written script, no narrative, nothing. Norman Westberg was in *The Right Side Of My Brain*, and we borrowed a shotgun from Nick Zedd, because Lydia wanted to do something with a guy who pulls a gun on her, and she has sex with him and he slaps her around. Brian Moran was this muscly dancer she also did something with, where he's slapping her around too. A lot of it was just showing men treating women badly, but her surviving it and basically telling them to fuck off after. Henry Rollins, we shot a scene with him that

---

* Filming took place across August–October 1984.

was upstate, and he's this guy who comes in and slams her around some. Jim Thirlwell plays this greasy, slimy guy in a filthy basement, and she comes down and gives him a blowjob, and he just slams her away when he's done with her. Then the last scene has a woman, Sally Ven Yu Berg—it's Lydia making out with her. Lydia shows these scenes where the men were just assholes and scumbags, and then she finds some kind of solace in a woman. But, usually, she starts messing with a woman then she discards her too. So, we had these five or six little pieces, and I came up with the idea of making this into a dream: *Lydia, we'll just shoot stuff of you rolling around like you're asleep, and this'll be your dreams.*

JIM THIRLWELL It was this story of the fantasies of a girl who she described to me as sexually insane. A lot of it was projections of these fantasies, or maybe things she wanted to do and get filmed doing.

CARLO McCORMICK Lydia's insistence on pleasure, or demand for it, is different from the way most people perceive what women are looking for in a relationship. Lydia is looking for an orgasm, or she's looking for something to satisfy her needs, and her demons, and not to care so much about the guy beyond his utility. *The Right Side Of My Brain*, what was so haunting about it is how much of it actually was in the head, the fantasy of letting loose. The movie's really hallucinatory in that way.

RICHARD KERN Lydia said she could do a voiceover, so she wrote this incredible narration, and that just strung everything together. The best part of the movie is just her talking this dream talk, and I was really fortunate in that Jim was her boyfriend, and Jim is this fucking genius in the studio, so he says, 'Oh, I can make the soundtrack.' And he has a million cassettes of different sounds that he's collected over the years. The way you had to do Super-8 in the old days is two tracks of sound, so you had to record it and it's all fucked up because it's not in sync, or you can just lay it over. We set up a projector in the booth, we set a mic on Lydia, Jim has an array of cassette players all over the place, Lydia's watching the movie and just reading her thing, and Jim is watching the movie at the same time, just doing cassettes, making loops and playing different soundtracks. The whole soundtrack was done live, basically. When I think about it now, I just can't fucking believe it! It was a one-take soundtrack—pretty amazing.

I've always wondered, the scene where she gives Jim a blowjob, and I'm thinking, *Was this just that she wanted to blow him while I was watching?* We had to shoot that scene twice. The first time we were in the basement in my building, and all the power blew out for the whole building when I plugged in a light.

JIM THIRLWELL For me, it was acting, you know? It was a film, and it wasn't the era of reality television—this was a film. So, this is what happened in the film, and I was required to perform the best as I could … with some difficulty! It's not something that I do in public every day. It's been immortalised on T-shirts, from what I hear.

LYDIA LUNCH What was missing was a part of myself. I was always my biggest fan, I always loved myself, and what makes me different than most people that have suffered trauma or abuse is that I never turn the knife inward, I always turn the knife outward. From the very young age of nine, I was having homicidal dreams, I never had suicidal dreams, and this is very unlike most—especially female—victims.

Part of it could be because I was born with a dead brother: there was death before, after, and with me. My mother had eleven brothers and sisters; three lived to adulthood. I was always surrounded by death. My grandmother died in bed with me when I was six. My mother had a miscarriage before and after, and I had a dead twin brother. I asked my mother once, *Did I kill him? Did I consume him?* Sometimes I wonder if a lot of the physical pain I have is him beating the shit out of me from the inside. Whether I consumed him or not, I embody a lot of him because I feel as much male as I do female. I think part of that is what gives me my stamina. I'll always be the last man standing—it's just the way it is.

This other side of me really defines who I am anyway, because I feel as much male as female. It's interesting I never had abandonment issues or neglect. I was always the one to leave, to move to the next thing. Was this a reversal of the neglect I was forced to feel in the womb? Was this some kind of perverse twist? Because I never felt neglected. *Neglect me! Leave me alone!* So, really, what that absence was—it becomes very Zen, in a way—is then you just have to remove everything. You have to stop it all, and you have to get back to appreciating the smallest thing, because if you've done everything, or done everyone, or gone everywhere … as a child, the thought of appreciation was wiped out.

KATHLEEN FOX When women are sexually abused or involved in sexually violent relationships at a young age, it's most likely that that's going to be the relationship model for them their whole lives. Being lucky enough to be introduced to Lydia and Lydia's work at a very young age allowed me to see it in a different way and allowed her to be my voice until I could find my own voice and never be a victim again. And I will make someone else a victim before I will become a victim in my life ever again. And that is a direct influence of learning about Lydia Lunch at a very young age, which I don't think many kids back then did.

LYDIA LUNCH In the trauma zone, you're not appreciating anything; you can't smell the flowers, you don't see the light falling on a wall. I had to go back and learn what that was. I had to literally detox from myself, put myself into forced segregation, lock myself away. I had to decide to replace them—want, need, desire—with myself. I had to become my own lover. Literally, I would walk around and talk to myself like I was on a date with myself. Then you strip the bullshit away, and then what are you left with? You're left with a pretty open slate.

RICHARD KERN The first screening of *Right Side Of My Brain* was at the Kitchen in 1985. And J. Hoberman just eviscerated it, if that's the word. He just shredded it. Like, misogyny up and down: *Misogyny, misogyny, misogyny!* I was sitting there thinking, *This is Lydia's story.* I guess she could be a misogynist—anybody can. I was getting the misogyny … but I'm telling Lydia's story! Everything in there, pretty much, was Lydia's idea! After seeing the way we were getting attacked, Lydia and I got together,

I remember vividly, and she said, 'They think this is bad? Fuck them! We're gonna make something that's really offensive. They're gonna think this is nothing.'

CARLO MCCORMICK All these people were basically saying this was pornography, it was anti-women—they're calling it all this stuff. It gets this big backlash from a world that's meant to be pretty tolerant, though we know, in fact, that there were a lot of orthodoxies and intolerance built in. They get these accusations that they're being artless, exploitative, sexist—all these different responses. Lydia and Richard were basically like, *They think that? Let's show them what that looks like!* No Vaseline on the lens.

CHAPTER TWELVE

FINGERED

FOLLOWING 1985'S SUBMIT TO ME, RICHARD KERN AND LYDIA FILM THEIR THIRD WORK, FINGERED, IN MARCH–APRIL 1986. THE CYCLE IS COMPLETED WITH SUBMIT TO ME NOW IN 1987.

RICHARD KERN Lydia said we'd make this film about this phone sex operator who goes to meet one of her customers and they go on a rampage. I was watching a lot of horror movies, and I remember seeing the previews for *The Gates Of Hell*—it kept saying 'The Gates of Hell!' and then they would show something really bad from the movie. I realised, by the end of the preview, I knew everything that was in the movie. So, I said, well, let's not make the whole movie. We'll just make a trailer and we'll say, 'Coming Soon,' and we'll never have to make the movie! We set it up, and the whole idea was they're going go around killing people, and they're gonna pick up this girl and rape her. There's going to be no redeeming value, nothing. No artistic trappings, it's just gonna be this hillbilly movie, because we were both fans of Russ Meyer, people like that.

Lydia said we could pay for the movie by going on tour and saving up some of that money. We did a few cities, I did the performance-art shit, she would speak, and Jim would play. It was unusual for a three-act thing to show up at a venue and there's only three people. They'd say to Jim, 'Where's your band?' And he'd say, 'Here it is!' And he'd hold up an 8-track tape. So, we had a bit of money to use in LA to make the movie. Lydia said, 'Well, I know this guy that I used to sleep with, or fuck, or whatever, way back when …'

I had a girlfriend at the time who I brought as the slate girl, and there's a scene where Marty [Nation] has to jerk off. He's on the phone to this phone sex operator, so he's got his dick out, he's jerking off, I'm sitting there filming. And then Lydia, who likes girls, boys—she doesn't give a fuck, you know?—I hear her and the girl, on the ground. I can hear Lydia, like, 'Come on baby,' and she's feeling her up, molesting her and making out with her. I can hear that's happening over there so Marty can get off. And I was like, *What the ... oh, OK.* I've noticed over the years that there's nothing Lydia's better at than being in some town—I don't care where it is, she finds the cutest eighteen-year-old boy/girl, or girl/boy, and they're in her lap at the end of the show, and she's making out with them. They worship her and she just loves them.

CARLO MCCORMICK *Fingered* strips away the poetics of Lydia's narrative in *The Right Side Of My Brain*. It makes everything way more, intentionally, artless.

RICHARD KERN There was one point where I thought, *This is too much.* I have to tell you about Lung Leg. She was this really photogenic character. When Lydia said they were going to rape this girl at the end, I told her, 'I have just the girl for this.' I realised later that Lung actually did have some mental issues, but, at the time, I just thought how everyone is trying to be quirky, like, *Hey, I'm crazy!* She also took tons of drugs.

I flew her out to LA, and Lydia said we shouldn't let Lung meet Marty, we don't want her to be friendly with him—that way it'll look real. We left Lung in a warehouse, and she just stayed there doing acid the whole time we're shooting the rest of the movie. When her day comes, she comes out, and her eyes are spinning. The scenes where they pick her up in the car and she's all crazy-eyed, I mean, she was terrified. I'm not writing lines for her, she's saying, 'I just want to go home! I just want to get away from these people! I hate these people!' And she's talking about us.

The scene is, they pick her up, drive her to this remote location, then Marty is just slapping her around and ripping her clothes off. I'm standing on top of a trailer, looking down, with my Super-8 camera shooting, thinking, *Man, he's really beating her up*. He's knocking the shit out of her, ripping her clothes off—she's really upset—slamming her head against a wall, and after that, Marty asks, 'Think we should do another take?' I was like, 'No … we got it, man, that's all we need.'

LYDIA LUNCH Even though a lot of the instances in *Fingered* were based on real-life experiences that I had, our first priority was to make a drive-in exploitation trailer, because we both grew up on drive-in films, and films that were specially made for the drive-in were so outrageous—you could get away with anything. The priority was black-and-white, Super-8, very fast paced, based on some of my experience—but the punch line was, victim becomes victimiser. And a lot of people overlook that what's interesting about *Fingered* is that people think of it as the ultimate feminist statement and the ultimate misogynist statement. It would be the prize at frat parties, and then we would have someone like Karen Finley walking out of a cab almost vomiting.* I never did any kind of art, especially the films, thinking I was going to get a reaction. I never thought anything I did was shocking. I'm telling the truth here, for the most part. With *Fingered*, we're pushing it. If you can't take it for twenty minutes, you try to live in it for twenty or forty years.

THURSTON MOORE When I first saw *Fingered*, I was like, *Whoa, that is shocking. Good for you*. I understood the reference of it—I didn't know what to take from it, but I certainly didn't take anything personal from it. I thought she was an even braver artist than I already thought. I was like, *You're on a tear. You've always been on a tear*.

CARLO MCCORMICK I worked the door for the premiere of *Fingered*. It was one of those double bills that made the owner of the club really unhappy. It was hard to see that guy upset about a sold-out room.

---

* Finley is a major American artist whose work as an activist has dwelt significantly, and in various forms, on sexuality, trauma, and exclusion from power. Her work spans music, the written and spoken word, film, live performance, and the visual arts.

RICHARD KERN Honestly, I am so naïve. I make *Fingered*, and it's as offensive as possible, then we showed it, and I'm like, *Why are you all upset? What's the big deal?* I couldn't understand. Lydia had no qualms about it.

LYDIA LUNCH I don't think I've done anything shocking. My art is not meant to be shocking. It's meant to be real! It *is* real! I never set out to shock. What's shocking? *Oh, small woman, big mouth! Oh my god, panic!*

BETH B I totally relate to it. We were living in a bubble. To us, even the perversions, the submission, the domination, all these sexualised things— we'd experienced them, so, in a sense, it gave them a sense of normality. People do not want to see, or hear, or have these hidden disturbances exposed.

RICHARD KERN I will say that when I was working with Lydia, we were living in Lydia's world. It was all her people. After *Fingered*, Robert L. Williams, the painter, was going to work with us on a feature. Lydia told me that Robert said, 'All these people say, *Don't get involved with these people! They're devil worshippers, they're Satanists, they're evil. They do bad shit, they're criminals!*' And I'm looking around, I was selling drugs, so everything seemed normal. In the East Village, you're in your own world, you create this world, and they're the people around you.

RICHARD METZGER There was a guy I worked with, and he had friends coming in from out of town for the Fourth of July weekend. He wanted to make sure they had a completely freaked-out experience in New York—it was their first time—so they'd go home to Pittsburgh and tell other people. He needed an expert so he came to me. I didn't have to think very long because I already knew what I was doing that weekend: I was seeing the premiere of *Fingered* at Cat Club. Perfect!

I got these guys really stoned, then I took them to Forty-Second Street, which was still at the height of its sleaziness. As you go westward, it got more and more intense, until you get to Show World and places like that, where you had live sex shows and booth girls going on. I took them to Show World and straight to the basement, which was called Tranny Island. There were, like, forty transsexuals working, glomming onto these all-American guys. Then we went to the Cat Club. I wasn't even old enough to be in there, and they weren't either. Everyone was just sitting around on the floor drinking beer, smoking, just waiting.

It started off with Lydia coming onstage—she gave one of her typical high-powered performances, ten-minutes that wound the audience up for *Fingered*. The film was projected, and a lot of jaws hit the floor. Imagine being subjected to something like that for the first time. Almost immediately after the film ended, the screen came down, and Wiseblood started.* Thirlwell was banging on the floor with a chair, smashing it onto the stage over and over as he was singing. I've seen hundreds of gigs in my life, and that had to be one of the most insane rock'n'roll moments I've ever witnessed—it was so far-out and ultraviolent. The audience were just pulverised by what they'd seen.

On the way out, I turned to the guys and said, 'So, what do you think?' One of them looked at me, annoyed, and said, 'I thought I was going to die.' Then he gestured to our mutual friend and asked, 'He put you up to this, didn't he?'

RON ATHEY Over and over again, you see Lydia expressing herself through nudity, through sex, through eroticism, though fantasy, in a brutal and unapologetic way that was still sexy. It's not abject—well, maybe some people would think guns and things are abject, but to me it wasn't, and within the context it wasn't. I don't think Lydia ever had any interest in staying in that realm, meaning that sexuality would be her primary mode of expressing herself. It was almost an aside: *Yeah, I'm naked, getting fucked, what about it?* Expressing the female predator has been key. It's taboo for women, but it wasn't taboo for her.

RICHARD KERN Lydia told me that she and Marty went out in the desert on a trip by themselves after that, and he almost tried to kill her, pulled a knife on

---

* Wiseblood was the duo of Jim Thirlwell and Roli Mosimann. They released one album and a number of EPs and singles featuring a range of collaborators and guests.

her and everything, because in the movie, it's a love story. And these two, I would say, 'OK, tomorrow we're gonna shoot this scene, this is gonna happen.' Lydia and Marty would go home and just come up with the most hateful dialogue they could with each other. 'You're a fucking asshole!' 'You're a fucking cunt!' That stuff back and forth, but more poetic. And the tension at the end, she said that Marty just freaked out. Being around Lydia, two weeks of her in your face, insulting you, it would probably drive anyone crazy. I don't see how some of her boyfriends did it!

LYDIA LUNCH What's interesting is, I never felt guilt. I always knew, from a very early age, that I am not alone in what's going on here. I realised it at probably the age of nine, that this kind of trauma, familial abuse, in whatever format it takes, whether physical or psychological, is something that doesn't start there—it has a history, it has a tradition, it's a sickness that goes on and on. By the age of nine, I knew I was going to have to do something about it, and I started writing in journals. I knew I was going to deal with it. I was going to talk about it. I was going to express it. And I was going to try to not carry it on.

There's a lot of emotions I don't have, and I feel that they're cancer-causing emotions, like … I've never felt shame. I never knew humiliation. I never felt insecure for one minute in my life. I felt fear for twenty seconds at one point, from being alone in a desert with a maniac who was kneeling on my chest and holding a Buck knife to my throat, who loved me. But when I realised once more I had the power over the situation, the fear dissipated, 'cause I told him I loved him. And I did. And I knew he loved me.

CHAPTER THIRTEEN

THE WORD

LYDIA'S WRITING—HER ABILITY WITH WORDS, HER SHARP INTELLECT—HAS ALWAYS BEEN THE CORE OF HER WORK. FROM 1982 ONWARD, SPOKEN WORD BECOMES HER PRIMARY MODE OF ARTISTIC EXPRESSION.

LYDIA LUNCH One day, soon after I first met Thurston [Moore], I asked him to go for a walk with me, and I told him a horrible story, a made-up story—I write fiction very rarely, most of my stuff is true—and he just kept saying, 'Oh my god, really? Oh, I can't believe that. That's terrible.' And I said, 'Well, we're doing that as a show tomorrow night at a small café, and you're doing it with me.' It was un-mic'd, so it's like Chinese whispers, and we're walking around telling the story, and people are only hearing snatches of it. He played the straight man to my horrible story.

I brought quite a few people to the spoken-word stage for the first time: Nick Cave, Vincent Gallo, Ken Stringfellow of The Posies. I'm the cattle-prodder. I came originally to New York in '76 to do spoken word, but it didn't really exist at that point. It was post-Beats; Patti Smith was doing rock poetry. Spoken word only really came about when myself, Jello Biafra, and Henry Rollins all seemed to start doing it at the same time.

EXENE CERVENKA We did a lot of readings and toured a lot. Back then, if you went out on the road, you did it yourself—there wasn't any money to get in a van, there wasn't any money to get on a plane. What I liked about it, though, was it meant that anything you made was yours. I was doing poetry as a teenager, then there was a big renaissance in the late 70s and early 80s, so what we were doing together was really timely. There were a lot of avenues, and people wanted to see readings, so we did pretty good.

CARLO MCCORMICK Clubs were really important because it's where all the different disciplines met, and things were much more fluid then—it was all cross-pollinating. Clubs created a vernacular of address that was entirely different from a movie theatre, or a concert hall, or any kind of theatre experience. We were all very much involved in the Pyramid Club, and Lydia was getting these people to do fake blood and gore onstage, fights put on in the audience that were way too real—she was always doing these things.

LYDIA LUNCH Most writers write the same book over and over, but as a musician I've usually contradicted the sound that came before. But the themes remain the same. The themes are always the imbalance of power—they're always dystopic, they're always about discomfort, aggravation, agony, the pains of love, lust, greed, need, or murderous intentions. I'm always trying to find a different soundtrack to the same obsessions. The subjects basically remain the same, as with most writers. They need to write it out to try to make sense of themselves. It's like my obsessions, my disease, I knew from a very early age was not only mine. That's what gave me the leeway of just going for it, straight off the bat, with 'Daddy Dearest'.*

KEMBRA PFAHLER One reason that Lydia's plays and performances and spoken-word pieces were so powerful was because she didn't do it because she wanted to be more popular or to monetise this subject: it was a subject that needed to be addressed for survival. There's so much shame around incest and abuse—a lot of women remain silent because so many of us, I think we feel like it's going to harm our careers, it's going to harm our relationships,

---

* 'Daddy Dearest' was first performed in November 1982, at Lydia's debut as a spoken-word artist. The piece is a graphic description of abuse at the hands of her father. A studio recording was made in October 1984 and features on *The Uncensored Lydia Lunch* (1985) and the compilations *The Uncensored/Oral Fixation* (1989) and *Crimes Against Nature* (1994.) The text is available in Lydia's book *Incriminating Evidence* (1992).

it's going to harm our survival if you are perceived as someone who has any kind of issue whatsoever. Now, in the year 2019, people feel safe to speak about it—not because they're fearless, but because it's been monetised. YouTube, social media, the media itself, film, television realises that there's money to be made by addressing these subjects. Incest, feminism, female empowerment—there's a blush of popularity around it, and that's why people are speaking about it now. But Lydia spoke about it when it wasn't popular, when there was no material gain around addressing this subject. It was a subject that needed to be addressed for us all to survive, and we needed, we still need, that permission.

LYDIA LUNCH My first story was 'Daddy Dearest'. It helped because it was what was obsessing me most, and I had to address that and get it out. A lot of people were horrified, or related, or cried, or couldn't believe I would admit that. It had to be told! I came back to New York from London and started booking shows at the Pyramid, curating shows. Nobody was dealing with trauma at that time, or abuse. To me, I didn't feel it was only my story. I mean, OK, I'm giving you details that are specific to me, but it wasn't the worst story. I needed to be the voice for that. I needed to find some reason or—not even retribution, but I just needed to get it out of my system. Because my targets of attack have always been the father, the father of our country, and then God The Father, it was not long after I began doing very personal spoken-word pieces that I went into the political, and that was under Ronald Reagan.

CARLO MCCORMICK No one was talking about daddy diddling with daughter, or the ways that women were systematically beaten down in our culture. Lydia, she addressed that, but she upped the ante on a number of things that we kind of take for granted now.

EXENE CERVENKA I had started out in Venice, California, doing poetry, doing spoken word, so, in 1981, that was probably newer to Lydia than it was to me. She's a voice, a total voice—whether it's spoken word or music, you want to hear what she has to say.

LYDIA LUNCH I was in LA, and somebody said, 'You have to go see Rollins!' What he was doing was this really hardcore spoken word, like 'Family Man'. It was wonderfully terrifying, as my spoken word was hysterical and terrifying. I approached him, and what was interesting about that period is that we were all doing music; there wasn't really a vehicle to do spoken word, and we all—at the same time—decided to do spoken word. For me, it always started with the word—the music was just the vehicle to get the words out.

SADIE MAE I recall a spoken-word performance with her and Henry Rollins in a blackened basement where a bouncer would drop you off the street through delivery doors. Inside, one would encounter the deafening sound of Henry on a jackhammer, sporadically interjecting acoustic spoken word. It was an in-your-face kind of show. People would be tossed out, stunned and enlightened, having been victimised again. Scenes like this became more and more scarce as corporations moved in, Starbucks invaded, and seventy-five-cent-a-cup Bustillo bodegas went under.

BOB BERT I remember one performance at the Pyramid Club: she was performing while Jim Thirlwell was dancing on the bar, and she asked me to participate. So I went to a butcher shop and I got this gigantic bone of something, and I put it in bleach and got all the rot off it. And while they were performing I just took this bone out of a bag and started smashing it against the bar.

ROBIN HALL Do you know about Lydia's poetry-reading night at Mudd Club in '83? Lydia called me out of the blue and asked me if I wanted to do it and if I'd help with the flyers—I said sure. She took me to some bar east of Avenue A and we sat on cardboard boxes and drank rotgut vodka, and I got totally shitfaced. I don't even know if they had a liquor license—it was definitely old school East Village. It was Lydia, Bill Rice, myself, a guy called Steve Barth, and Thurston Moore. Nick Cave was on the bill but he didn't show up. What was crazy was, I had been interviewing for a job with Steve Maas, who was the owner of the Mudd Club, and all of a sudden a guy came in and said, 'There's a fire!' so we had to stop the interview—a hole was burned in the floor.

The next time I was in there was at this gig, and what had been the VIP room was now stadium seating, and there's this big hole, and below it was the stage—we were performing down in this hole. The place was packed because everyone thought it was Lydia so it'd be great rock'n'roll, but it was poetry and readings, and the audience was really pissed and booing. That's the last time I saw Lydia—a pretty memorable way to end things.

KEMBRA PFAHLER There was something in Tribeca I remember that she participated in with Carlo McCormick, and essentially she upbraided the audience, spoke to the political climate and gentrification that was happening at the time, and stormed out as part of the performance. I hadn't developed my own artistic muscles so much, and I was really intimidated by her. I was terrified every time, affected viscerally; my heart pounded, I got stomach aches. I was so taken aback because it rang of so much truth and the information she was sharing was so necessary. The things that I learned from listening to her have been part of an ethic, and a methodology, and pointed me in a direction that has been part of my own work. What I took was simply to strive toward originality in your own work and to behave in a contrarian fashion and invent a new vocabulary, no matter what. The standard that she set was so high. I always felt like if I didn't create really good work, I'd be chased down by Lydia and beat up. She's very confrontational about the way she interacts with other artists—she'll call you out—and she just pushed everyone to work harder and to come out with some teeth and muscle.

JIM SCLAVUNOS It's always a lot easier to look back and realise that something is groundbreaking or innovative or unprecedented than it is to understand it at that time. A lot of what Lydia was singing about in her lyrics—for example, about abuse, about psychosexual scenarios—she presented herself as a strong woman, but not a strong woman in the Gloria Steinem model. It was a very different kind of strong woman. She was a strong woman that would not just have a very conspicuous sexual personality but also really played around with ideas about rape and sadomasochism, and made it part of her imagery and the source material and that kind of range, from the more abstract invocations of it in Teenage Jesus & The Jerks and 8 Eyed Spy to more directly addressing it in her spoken word. I took a lot of what she said for granted—I didn't take it as a radical rethinking of feminism. But she was quite conspicuously expressing that stuff. And, by the same token, not presenting herself, per se, as any kind of feminist. She had dalliances with the idea of some sort of broader and idiosyncratic vision of feminism, like her *Conspiracy Of Women* thing. But I don't think she ever saw herself as, strictly speaking, a women's liberationist.

BETH B It was a whole new concept of what feminism could be. I mean, for me, it was. It was like, *OK, that's trash—trash that!* We don't want to be *those* feminists. It was just a totally different way of being able to be liberated in the world as a woman.

ZOE HANSEN She's respected because of her work, but she's not an angry feminist; she's got a lot of rage in her, but it's not directed against men, it's against abusers in all forms. I was attracted to her, though, because, as far as I'm concerned, she's just the coolest fucking woman in the world. That's it.

DONITA SPARKS There have been amazing women all through history, totally pushed to the side, even in the 60s. The hard work done in the early 70s by the hardcore activist feminists was paying off for the gals who were college aged by the end of the 70s.

BOB BERT All the Riot Grrls of the 90s and everywhere else should bow down to her. She was outspoken about every little thing. She was always in the underground, never went anywhere near the mainstream, didn't give a fuck. She's happy performing to three people or five hundred, and it doesn't matter to her. It's just mind-blowing to this day what she has achieved.

CATHI UNSWORTH Spoken word, it's about timing, it's about rhythm, and Lydia gets into a trance-state when she does her readings. Lydia helped me to get more courage and confidence, less fear in the face of a room full of people. When Lydia does her spoken word, it sounds like fiction, because she speaks so well—it has the feel of a poem or a novel—but it's from truth. It's the compassion she puts into it.

LYDIA LUNCH *Conspiracy Of Women*, it's funny because I was going back to look at some of my earlier political speeches, and there wasn't the internet then, so we had newspapers and we had books, and we had to make sense between all the lies we were told. I was called an exaggerator—as if you can exaggerate what war is, as if you can exaggerate what inequality, or injustice, or the imbalance of power is. I use the enemy's language in such an aggressive way, because how else can you retaliate against this? I mean, I couldn't deliver casually these thoughts about what I knew was going on and which has forever gone on and is still going on. That alienated a lot of people because they couldn't take it.

EXENE CERVENKA What killed that scene was that it gradually became this hybridised poetry/rap MTV thing with art and music: *I'm a victim; listen to my victimisation.* When Lydia started out, she was so different; she was saying things people wouldn't normally say, and that people wouldn't normally hear at a poetry reading. She didn't have to perform, she just had to talk, and it was compelling and shocking and new.

*

BETH B So that's where we come to *Salvation!* (1987). It is very hard, working hand-to-mouth, for so many years. I wanted a film that would reach out beyond the inner circle of our downtown group—how much longer did I want to preach to the converted? I felt the issues and concerns that *Salvation!* addressed were very much in line with what I had been doing. It was inspired by a trip I took to Lynchburg, Virginia, where I attended a massive—and frightening—convention at Reverend Jerry Falwell's church. I found myself on my knees in church, surrounded by all of these Christians who were in fear of what someone like me, or Lydia, might bring to their God-fearing world. They were showing slides of aborted babies, drug addicts, homeless people—what they called the 'scourge of America' that they needed to obliterate. The manipulation and seduction in that environment were so palpable that I was frightened, and felt I needed to make a film about it, but I wanted to seduce the audience and bring out the horrific humour rather than smash them over the head, which had been my modus operandi before that.

LYDIA LUNCH When individuals don't feel strong enough, then they are made weaker by this false sense of community, which is patriarchy. And patriarchy is one of those things that drives lots of wars. But if the individuals are strong enough in themselves, then the community is stronger. And I think this is also what leads to religious fanaticism, when people have to look for something greater than themselves. Which becomes, *My god is bigger than your god*. Or, *My country is bigger than your country*. This is one of the problems of endless war. If people were strong enough in themselves, nobody would stand up for the kind of abuse this country exports to every other country. If they understood that it was each individual's right to live a life without oppression, and repression, or persecution, we would have far more compassion and less tolerance for the bullshit that goes down in this country and is exported everywhere else.

MERRILL ALDIGHIERI I was working on *The Muppet Show* when the Cinema Of Transgression was at its height, then I was working in nightclubs as a VJ.* I made three documentaries in the vein of parallel storytelling: one was called *Borders*, with Robert Anton Wilson as well as Steve Buscemi; and I won an Emmy for *Metaphoria*, with Doctor John Lilly. I made *The Kissing Booth*, and the main person was Quentin Crisp. He's very polite, and his

---

* In 1985, Nick Zedd published 'The Cinema Of Transgression Manifesto' in his zine *The Underground Film Bulletin*. The manifesto challenged the prevailing approach of academic filmmaking, aspects of the avant-garde, film schools, and their students. It demanded films that would 'go beyond all limits set or prescribed by taste, morality or any other traditional value system shackling the minds of men'. The phrase has been used in relation to Zedd's work and that of filmmakers such as Richard Kern, Manuel DeLanda, Tessa Hughes-Freeland, Jeri Cain Rossi, Richard Kleeman, Tommy Turner, and others.

voice was hard to listen to after a while, so I started looking for other voices. Lydia seemed like an ideal contrapuntal voice; I wanted someone vocal and fearless. I made the movie *The Gun Is Loaded* with her in 1989. When I saw Lydia's show, I was really moved by her work. *The Gun Is Loaded* is a tirade against the death culture in America, and I was an anti-war pacifist, so that worked.

CATHI UNSWORTH One of my favourite things Lydia has done is the war rant: 'Women And Children First'. She's saying that the images of all these men on TV waving guns, that she knows the women are left at home just clearing up the mess caused by this constant desire for war, that they should just give their guns to the women and let them sort it out. She sees the angry priapic men and what she thinks of is the women trying to keep society together, despite the half of society that is trying to trample them underfoot. How can you not be angry about that? Lydia doesn't rant and rave about it, she puts the images into your head so you can feel how it's impacting people—that's a writer's job, to put you into the shoes of the person you're writing about. I enjoy her spoken word—it's an area she really pioneered, and she's the only person I've met who can speak in complete paragraphs that don't need any subbing, in the way she can put across her thoughts so concisely. There's also an amazing rhythmic quality to her voice, like she's seducing you into a trance so that her words go in properly.

MERRILL ALDIGHIERI I really hated theatre. I had been to a Broadway show when I was a kid and sat behind a pillar. I had seen a couple of experimental theatre pieces before Lydia, but I wasn't really excited by filming her show … but when I finally saw it, it blew me away. I hated the traditional way of recording theatre pieces like a surveillance video. I didn't want to make just a blank record of it—I didn't think that would do the experience of Lydia justice. I had done a fair amount of music video work, and I had this way of picking some things where I would do overlapping: repeating certain bits in different locations, in case I wanted to change in the editing. The text, beginning to end, is exactly her text, but we picked the best takes. We did some editing and pacing changes, but not too much.

Sometimes, Lydia would get tuckered out and would slightly lose the punch of the scene, so we would change it so she was fresh, then we would change angles. In the actual theatre piece, Lydia had quite sophisticated lighting and staging, so it was just a question of having good control over how it was filmed and edited, so it wasn't so static. There was a certain amount of intuition and a certain amount of planning. I looked at Lydia's text, which was broken up into vignettes, so I wanted to create a different look for each of them by picking different locations and coming up with ways of filming them. For the restaurant scene, featuring Michael Buscemi and others, I really wanted the visual joke of having Lydia Lunch on the menu—I made that graphic myself. It spurred on the idea of doing it at a diner, a chilli restaurant. That's the piece that strayed the most from her theatre performance. I went to the location beforehand, did a storyboard, sketched out the location and where everyone would be—that was the most choreographed sequence.

We submitted the film to TV stations. There was a TV series called *New Television*, an eclectic showcase for new directors, so I hoped I could get it in there, but the show went off the air. I tried to submit it to general programmers and didn't get any responses. We found a distributor for the VHS tape, and, once that went out, that was it—I was on to the next thing.

CHAPTER FOURTEEN

SOUTH OF YOUR BORDER

IN THE MID-80S, LYDIA BRANCHES OUT INTO THEATRE, WRITING, DIRECTING, AND PERFORMING WITH EMILIO CUBEIRO IN TWO LARGE-SCALE PRODUCTIONS.

LYDIA LUNCH When I came back to New York with Jim Thirlwell, I asked around for anybody doing short violent acts, and somebody mentioned Emilio Cubeiro. Emilio had come out of the Theatre Of The Ridiculous with Charles Ludlam, which was a queer West Village theatre troupe that did all the Greek tragedies. I went to the Pyramid Club, and Emilio was performing maybe something like 'The Death Of An Asshole'—which is also the title of the album I produced by him. It was one of the most rude, raucous, dirty things I'd ever seen, and I immediately went up to him and said we had to work together. I used to put him on at my shows, and people would always ask, 'Why do you have that creep on?' He looked like a sleazy, moustachioed, queer serial killer. He terrorised and terrified people because he wasn't, by their standards, 'cool'—but to me he was the coolest person I'd ever met. He'd been to sixty-nine countries, lived by doing other people's taxes, barely left his house, except for when he would perform—absolutely hateful. The last performance that Emilio did was his poem 'The Death Of An Asshole', which ends when he blows a gun up his ass, blowing shit all over the stage— that showed them what art really was! He was amazing.

Emilio said we had to do a play, and he suggested *South Of Your Border*. I wasn't against doing a play, but I didn't even memorise my own lyrics.

'Memorising an hour and a half? I'm not sure I can do it!' And he goes, 'Of course you can. You just gotta fucking do it!' I let Emilio listen to recordings of my father talking because one of the themes of *South Of Your Border* is the various forms of oppression that I had encountered as an artist and as a female. It was another part of my public psychotherapy, showing the connective tissue—in the same way as my written work has done—between god, the patriarchy, politicians, the military, censorship, male oppression, and the rebellion against it.

RICHARD METZGER There were posters for *South of Your Border* fly-papered up around the East Village, so word had gotten out about it—maybe there was a small ad in the *Village Voice* also. The theatre was on Fourth Street and used for off-off-off-Broadway productions. A small theatre, fairly moth-eaten. The first scene was her being interrogated by Emilio Cubeiro, and, basically, he played the assholes. He represented all of the assholes in her life—like her father—or in government, or the script would be flipped and she'd be the one interrogating him and he's the oppressed one, he's the john to a dominatrix, or he's her father who crawls into bed with her. He was very good at playing a sleazy asshole—he was an absolute exemplar at that kind of acting. There was a scene with Lydia and her dad. He was listening to the radio and getting drunk, ranting about the race riots. She was in bed, playing herself as a child, with the covers over her, afraid of what he's going to do next. Then she's in therapy and she's on a couch, speaking to an unseen psychotherapist: the voice of Karen Finley. As she's doing that scene, she's drinking a lot of beer—it's the kind of detail you only notice in retrospect.

LYDIA LUNCH The play opens and I'm strapped to a scaffold, screaming as people are filing in: 'Let me outta here! I'm innocent!' And Emilio comes from the back of the audience dressed like a South American soldier, 'Pendejo American asshole! You're not innocent!' Accusing me of coming to his great South American Catholic country to pollute the youth with my immoral AIDS, my filthy body. It still happens now for journalists in North Korea, China, Russia, America, and the UK to some degree—Julian Assange. The second scene is Emilio onstage in a leather hood and a trench coat, no pants, and I come out in a nurse's outfit with a blonde wig, then change into a black wig and a leather coat. It's a scene of psychodrama: I'm accusing him of being a murderer, that I know where he has the panties of little girls; I'm going to turn him into the police. The third scene, Emilio's an FBI agent and he has me in there to interrogate me about my 'anarchist associates' and how it's not art I do, it's pornography, and they have the footage to prove it.

This is where it really turns into Emilio's ridiculous horror. This Christian FBI agent is constantly washing his hands, just like Donald Trump. Emilio pulls down this screen and he says you can tell if someone is going to be a welfare recipient by how clean their assholes are—this is total Emilio. There are blow-ups of six assholes, ours included, and he points out which ones are potential deviants—absurd!

The next scene, Karen Finley does the voiceover, because after seeing *Fingered* she ran out, almost puking—she couldn't take it and didn't get the point of it—and, once, she asked me, 'Where is the love? You're just carrying on the cycle of abuse!' I thought we had to use her in this. It's a split stage, Emilio is playing my father—he's in a lawn chair in his underwear, rubbing himself. I'm in a black bra, panties, fishnets. Karen Finley is the psychologist interrogating me, 'You're just carrying on the cycle of abuse,' I'm like, 'Fuck you! I'm doing what I want to do.' And then I tell this outrageous tale of a beer-bottle fuck scene at Club 82 with blood-spattered walls that I was kicked out of—true story, of course—and then she's outraged and starts talking to my father. He's like, 'I gave her everything! Everything she ever wanted.'

The next scene is, I'm a child, there's a bed at the front of the stage, I'm sleeping. Emilio, as my father, is listening to the racing results; 'How High Is The Water Momma' is playing, and Roy Orbison as well. He's cursing at the radio that the fucking horses are against him, then he jerks off, throws the tissues at the audience.

RICHARD METZGER Then the lights go down on that scene, pitch black, there's a Thirlwellian musical interlude, then the lights go back up and suddenly Lydia's completely naked, trussed to a huge X hovering above the stage. Not a cross, it was a big chunky black X. You heard her taped voiceover on the PA system, over the music, saying something like, 'So that's what it's all about. Lydia the oppressed. Lydia the fucked over. Lydia the ...' And suddenly buckets of blood start pouring on her—I don't mean a little bit, I mean a *lot*. She's covered in blood. The volume is going up and up to this almost painful intensity, and I'm thinking, *How could this get any weirder?*

LYDIA LUNCH The last scene, I'm crucified on this giant black rubber cross. Pete Shore of Unsane was my 'blood boy'—he had to climb up and put blood hoses under my wig. I'm naked, bleeding, and Emilio—from the back of the stage—comes with every costume on—South American border guard, john, FBI agent, my father—and he eventually strips down, and there's a poem Emilio wrote about how it's all desert now, that there was a time when a poet's words meant something, but now it's been eviscerated ...

RICHARD METZGER There's this explosion, a loud door opens—BOOM!—the whole audience jumps out of its skin. It was a really intense moment. Emilio comes from the back of the theatre and he's got a leather death-mask on, like what a gimp would wear in S&M. He's holding a gun and pointing it at her with both hands, and he's going toward the stage. His garb was from all the various roles he'd played, except that he didn't have any pants on, he just had his underwear—like Lydia's father, sitting drunk in his chair, before he goes to molest her.

He runs up the left aisle of the theatre and he gets to her and he lays down on an ottoman or bench or something directly under her, and all of a sudden she lets loose with just this massive stream of piss all over him. She baptises him as this collective procession of assholes, all represented by just this one composite character now. She pisses all over him—not a tinkle, not a little bit, this was a waterfall! This was the kind of piss you could only take after you'd drunk an entire six-pack. The audience was stunned. It was an authentic Theatre Of Cruelty–type experience.

That play only ran for ten performances, so not that many people could have seen it—I can't imagine the theatre seating more than seventy-five to one hundred people. Every single person who saw it was a conduit of that legend; they all told people about it.

KRISTIAN   LYDIA
FEB 28TH 1990

PREVIOUS PAGE Lydia and Emilio Cubeiro in *South Of Your Border* (photo by Michael Lavine).

ABOVE Kim Gordon and Lydia as Harry Crews at the Ritz, Stockholm, September 1988 (photo by Ken Andersson).
RIGHT Lydia with Jim Thirlwell, enjoying a night at the rodeo in Cowtown, New Jersey (photo by Caki Kallas Kennedy); with Kristian Hoffman in 1990 (courtesy of Kristian Hoffman).

ABOVE Lydia and David Knight, Universal Infiltrators, 1994 (photo by Ruth Bayer). **LEFT** Lydia's book *Incriminating Evidence*, with illustrations by Kristian Hoffman (Last Gasp, 1992); a poster for the 1991 Shotgun Wedding tour of Europe. **BELOW** Shotgun Wedding USA '94: Spencer P. Jones, Harry Howard, Craig Williamson, Lydia Lunch (photo by Ursula Collie).

ABOVE Lydia and Kamil Kruta, down among the dead at Sedlec Ossuary in the Czech Republic, 1997 (photo by Tracy Reinstein). **RIGHT** *Matrikamantra* (Crippled Dick Hot Wax, 1998); *The Desperate Ones* EP with Glyn Styler (Atavistic, 1997).

OPPOSITE PAGE An original artwork by Lydia entitled 'Blow Me Away' (courtesy of Lydia Lunch).

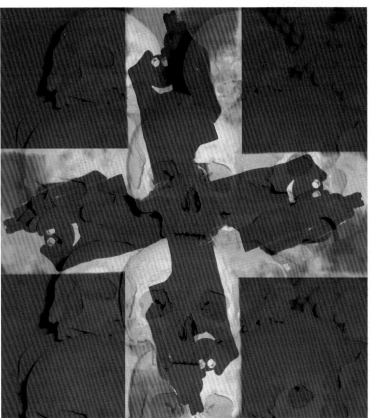

PARADOXIA
a predator's diary
LYDIA LUNCH

OPPOSITE PAGE Lydia's artworks 'Daddy Loves You Too Much' and 'Retribution' (both courtesy of Lydia Lunch).

ABOVE 'My Amerikkka' (courtesy of Lydia Lunch). **LEFT** Lydia in New Orleans (photo by Link Wreckage); *Paradoxia: A Predator's Diary* (Creation Books, 1997).

ABOVE The Anubian Lights—Tommy Grenas, Lydia, Len Del Rio—in 2002 (photo by Angie Garcia).
RIGHT The *Champagne, Cocaine, And Nicotine Stains* EP (Crippled Dick Hot Wax, 2002); *Smoke In The Shadows* (Atavistic, 2004).

JOE BUDENHOLZER I also saw the nightmarish *South Of Your Border*. Emilio was playing some kind of sick paedophile serial-killer character; he had a bondage mask on, a trench coat. Lydia was crucified, naked, on a leather bondage cross. Strobe lights, smoke machines, industrial music, Emilio lays down on the ground and Lydia literally pees on him off the cross. The Cinema Of Transgression was around, Karen Finley was there of course, Annie Sprinkle, Ron Athey, but there was nothing quite like that, or something so technically sophisticated—the cross alone was a huge construction. Characteristically of Lydia, they decided to push it that much further, toward the limits. It wasn't unusual to see people peeing and pooping onstage in those days, but Lydia and Emilio created a spectacular theatrical visual as well.

LYDIA LUNCH We produced it ourselves and put it on ourselves in a freezing cold theatre—no hot water. About the ninth night in, one of my eyes had turned blood red, and I thought, *Oh my god, I've got pigs' blood under the mucus of my eye*. I had to go to the eye clinic. 'What have you been doing?' They asked. 'Bathing in pigs' blood for the last nine nights,' I tell them, then they tell me I've washed my eye too much—it's fine.

The play was a pretty elaborate presentation, outrageous and successful. People came. It was pretty immense for two people to pull off. It took us around six months to organise it. There were stage sets, scaffold, this huge cross—every scene had a set. We had two or three rehearsals in the theatre, so when it came time for staging we knew exactly what we were doing.

Everything I do—all the bands—it's rehearsed until we're ready to do it, and once we're ready there's no need to practice it again. It was the same way with the play: we wrote it, we rehearsed it at his house, then, when it was time to do it, the rehearsals were like doing a soundcheck, and then we did it.

RICHARD METZGER Twenty years ago, I met Lydia in San Francisco, and I asked if anybody videotaped that performance. She said, 'Oh no! I wanted people to talk about it but not be able to see it.' That's a really potent kind of art!

KEMBRA PFAHLER I remember seeing photographs of Lydia's body in *South Of Your Border*, her naked body, her beautiful body that she has so explicitly splayed out for the whole world to see onstage. And I thought to myself, *How could somebody make a huge poster of their asshole that is the most extremely beautiful picture I've ever seen in my life?* She has a most beautiful body. Cookie Mueller said if you ever showed your vagina or your tushy or your body down below your belly button, your life was ruined forever—and that's not true.* All of the gestures that Lydia made that were so extreme really gave me the strength to say, 'This is my body.' It helped me to learn how to not hate myself completely. Lydia's physique is not traditional by any means. There's only one Lydia Lunch, and she's just a beautiful individual. And that's just given room to all of us who existed to, not to sound corny, but to just not hate our own guts so much.

LYDIA LUNCH One thing about my body: I love my body. One of my pieces, 'Psychic Anthropology', is about how we've got to get the poison out of the body—get it out of the body! You have to love your body—every new imperfection is a new delicacy. I love my body, but perhaps I love it so much that it retaliates against me occasionally: it beats the shit out of me, so I rebel with pleasure! From the age of three, I've been in chronic pain. Spinal taps, lymph nodes removed, my appendix burst, e-coli, ectopic pregnancy that burst, on and on and on again. But pain is weakness leaving the body. It's why I'm so incredibly strong. 'Pain is weakness leaving the body': somebody said that, it wasn't me.†

*

LYDIA LUNCH Theatre was such an obvious extension of what I was doing with music, spoken word, photography, film—just taking it to another level. I vacillate between all of these worlds.

---

* Mueller was an American film actress, writer, and journalist. She appeared in various works by John Waters and was a significant figure in the downtown scene. She also wrote the 'Ask Dr. Mueller' column in the *East Village Eye*. She died of AIDS-related complications in 1989.

† A US Marine Corps recruiting office slogan attributed to Lewis Burwell 'Chesty' Puller.

Emilio and I were asked to do a performance for the Dance Theatre Workshop's tenth anniversary, so we did *Smell Of Guilt*. The theme is very de Sadian: we're chained together, he's a priest, I'm a worker at a boys' school. We're both going to be executed: him for abusing boys at the altar when he was just trying to purify them with his priestly tongue, and I was just murdering the born criminals and doing the world a favour. Then you hear the sound of people being executed offstage, and, of course, we're next up for the firing squad or the guillotine. It took us maybe six weeks to get that together—it was short.

DON BAJEMA She wasn't scared, and that's what gave her freedom. The role of the artist onstage is to express, and, through that, to express the suppressed self in the audience. But some people in an audience would be scared by what was being expressed, or what they were suppressing, or by the graphic nature of what Lydia was presenting. It had a cathartic effect, either consciously or unconsciously—that made her a great artist.

LYDIA LUNCH I understand the monster that I am, or the puppet master I've been. This is why people get into the same kind of relationship over and over. A lot of damaged people come together because they have the simpatico understanding, this chemical reaction to each. It's great and it's intense and it's borderline psychotic.

RON ATHEY I started making performance art in 1981, with Rozz Williams, my boyfriend and the front person of Christian Death. We started making noise, automatic writing, cut-up writing, then these images which were initially inspired by Johanna Went. She gigged with Black Flag, with The Germs, and to see this 'witch-doctor performance lady' tear up a punk crowd was quite phenomenal. At that time, when I started doing performance art, nobody wanted performance artists: *Whatever, just do it in a night club for $50 dollars and shut up*. Now, it's taught at every university. You can get a degree in performance art. We have a flood of work from the academy, and, with this dedicated audience of fellow students, you can be as boring as fuck and everyone's like, *Oh that's devastating!*

CARLO MCCORMICK It was an interesting moment for performance art that kind of gets forgotten, because performance artists, performance art, went back into this sanctified space where it's all very frontal, very polite, everyone is sitting down applauding at the right moments. That moment when everything happened in the clubs was way more dynamic, unpredictable, chaotic. You had to deal with the fact there were drunken people who just wanted to get laid that night and were going to talk over you, so you had to command the room in a really tough way. Lydia was one of the best at it. I'm sure she'd love a nice sweet college gig where she gets paid a big chunk of money and all the students love her, but she still does best in a dank little subterranean hellhole where people are used to having their ears blasted out with music and she's going to try to tell them a story.

RON ATHEY I used to curate an event called *Visions Of Excess* based on this collection of essays by Georges Bataille.* I did it with Vaginal Davis†—we used this forty-room sex motel in Hollywood, a different artist in every room and a stage over the pool. The year Emilio Cubeiro died, Lydia said, 'I have all of Emilio's things, I wanna do an Emilio room.' There were a lot of inside jokes; a cat box that shitted fake cat turds with Tootsie Roll; and Emilio said he took a picture of his butthole every day of his life, so we showed his computer with the butthole slideshow going. There's something really intense about looking at someone's sexuality on the brink of death, or even post-death, and this was in that category. It was such a strong room.

---

* Bataille was a French author and philosopher whose work focused on issues surrounding transgressive behaviour and art, eroticism, and surrealism.
† Davis is a genderqueer artist who helped found the queercore punk scene and has spent more than four decades in the world of performance, music, and visual art.

CHAPTER FIFTEEN

HARRY CREWS

LYDIA'S FIRST FULL BAND SINCE 1983–84 IS A ONE-OFF PROJECT INTENDED TO LAST FOR A SINGLE TOUR OF EUROPE IN THE AUTUMN OF 1988 . . .

LYDIA LUNCH I wanted to do a band based around the books of Harry Crews. It was fun to do live, a great concept, but not very well executed, and the recording doesn't sound very good. But 'Gospel Singer' came out of it—it's a great song. That was just a couple of months, that one tour, and there was no need for us to go into a studio as we did the live recording, and that was it. Nobody even knew who Harry Crews was, which was the great thing about it!

SADIE MAE Harry Crews was another sporadic project Lydia put together. We would open for Jim Thirlwell, another genius. Lydia put me in charge as her bodyguard while dropping ecstasy one night in Greece. Wish I had a camera for that! I stepped out of the club at 4am to see her sprawled out on the hood of a car with a group of young kids with their hands all over her.

CATHI UNSWORTH I share Lydia's admiration for the writer Harry Crews, and I love the song, 'Gospel Singer', that she did inspired by his writings. That Deep South swamp-gothic, swamp-witch stuff, she's the mistress of that. Harry Crews sadly passed away a few years ago, but he was an inspiring writer. I came to him via my friend Geoff Cox, who had a publishing imprint called Gorse: he was the first British publisher to track down Harry and publish his work here. Harry was not very well known in the

US, either—I don't think he kept one publisher for any length of time. Geoff published a compendium called *Classic Crews*, which included his autobiography, *Childhood: The Biography Of A Place*, about how he grew up on a sharecroppers' farm in Bacon County, Georgia.

Everything that becomes a part of his writing is there in his childhood— he's dirt-poor white trash, his best friend is this little black guy, and they have one book between them, which is the Sears-Roebuck catalogue, and they'd make up little stories through looking at this catalogue, all of which find their way into his work. It doesn't seem that long ago, but it seems so many worlds away from our world—he conjures all of this up, this almost biblical world of beliefs and spirits. He ended his life as a teacher of writing at the University Of Florida.

SADIE MAE Pat Place, Kim Gordon, Lydia, and myself went into Alphabet City studios for two weeks and put the songs together. We were recording on cassette in the studio, raw. I don't remember talk about an album release until we were back in the States. Like I said, it was a very impromptu project Lydia spat out. It was only ever meant to be that. Pat was dismissed for personal reasons, which left the three of us travelling in a van from London's Mean Fiddler venue through Germany, Holland, Copenhagen, Athens, for a full month. Fuelled by the swampy underbelly writings of Harry Crews, we were all driven. No breaks for sightseeing, except for Hitler's sculptor's house and gardens. It went very fast, shows back-to-back.

MURRAY MITCHELL I ended up tour-managing Harry Crews. I can't remember how Lydia got back in touch, but I was tour manager, driver, roadie. That instantly got bizarre because we lasted about one night into this month-long European tour before we were fucking again. It was like going back seven years, just really good fun. Right near the end of the tour, somewhere in Germany, her boyfriend turned up, and she pretended she wasn't sleeping with me.

SADIE MAE It was my first tour and my first time playing outside of the US. I was terrified the first night and given a push out onto the stage by Lydia. I mostly played bass then but had started playing around on the drums, playing here and there. I liked hiding behind them because I was in no shape or form a front person. As for the leader, hands down it was Lydia. There was a lot of unspoken drama from Kim pertaining to Lydia and Thurston's relationship—whatever that was—so it became like three bulls in a ring.

MURRAY MITCHELL It was a crazy tour but a really good one, driving these three fairly eccentric and intriguing women around in a minibus. Lydia wouldn't go onstage until she had the cash in her handbag, and she'd go onstage with the bag. In Athens, this guy hadn't paid her, so I had to go with this completely drunk Greek guy, on his moped, to his apartment on the other side of the city to get the cash. Then I got back to the hotel and go to give Lydia the money, and she opens the hotel door completely naked: 'Well done. You got the cash.' And that was us in the hotel room for another night.

SADIE MAE What I remember most is crossing paths with the Butthole Surfers in Copenhagen, in a hotel where all of them were tripping on acid, Gibby Haynes creepy-crawling and defecating on their tour manager, who was passed out in the next room. The Henry Rollins band were just a show ahead of us in many venues as well. Nick Cave was with Anita Lane, who was sporting a black eye and peeking out behind his shoulder—wish I had taken a camera. That night we played in a circus tent, Lydia and Nick rolling in the dirt behind the tent.

MURRAY MITCHELL I remember meeting Lydia's family in the US. Her mum met us at the airport, took one look at me, and the first words out of her mouth were, 'Got any money, limey?' Lydia hadn't been home in quite some time, her dad was still alive, and it was like something out of a John Waters movie—proper white trash.

I remember this proper beat-up bungalow with a broken-down car on the lawn. I wasn't fully aware of things between her and her dad—I'm not sure I would have agreed to go otherwise. Maybe it was cathartic for her, part of her playing something out, to take me home with her and then try to fuck as loudly as possible in the next room to her parents. She'd make sure the window was open and be as loud as possible.

CHAPTER SIXTEEN

OUR FATHERS WHO AREN'T IN HEAVEN

LYDIA USES HER WIDOWSPEAK LABEL TO LICENSE HER OWN RECORDINGS, AND ALSO TO GIVE A SHOWCASE TO ARTISTS SHE ADMIRES. MEANWHILE, SHE GUESTS ON AN EVER-WIDER RANGE OF OTHER ARTISTS' WORK.

DON BAJEMA I was doing confrontational performance pieces around San Francisco because I was so pissed off politically. Some people wanted to take the early AIDS scare and quarantine people who were diagnosed. That frightened me a lot and made me pretty pissed because I've never liked the idea of concentration camps or any of that ugly horror, and I saw it coming. I did a piece with my daughter, who was nine, where she answered letters from an American writing suggesting that the government wasn't planning to imprison little girls, that her father was paranoid; that if this was happening, someone decent would be doing something, that America would be doing something! And, sure, there were these people who weren't well, and we were putting them in camps, but that was for their benefit.

Bill Graham had been a survivor of the Holocaust—his sister carried him over the Pyrenees—and he sent a message to come to his office: 'Anything you want, anytime, let me know. By the way, Sunday afternoons are open at my night club, I think you should use it.' So I started a thing called Feral

Theatre. Lydia wasn't there but we were communicating, so she suggested getting Henry Rollins to perform, and she introduced me to him.

KID CONGO POWERS Even when I first met her, Lydia was already formidable. She is not a monster, she's defending her art, and no one can dictate the work that she is doing. Telling the truth shouldn't be so amazing, but it is because so few people really do it, and it's amazing because of how she tells it. When she's performing, people are laughing, gasping, getting offended, or screaming 'Hallelujah!' She's up with the greatest of artists who have stuck to their path. I remember someone asking her, 'How do you keep going and doing all these things?' And she said, 'I know my place within my culture.' I thought that was amazing.

DON BAJEMA The next thing Henry asked was if I wanted to go to Europe. I thought that'd be fun, hell yes! I freaked out in Frankfurt, coming off the plane—I was terrified. I'm this unknown guy opening for these two icons, in front of punk audiences—I thought I was going to get eaten alive. Lydia took me into a café and she laid it out. 'Don, you know you're not really fulfilled. You've had that past as an athlete now you're coasting along not feeling all that much, now here's what's going to happen. Every night the audience is going to love you. You're going to get so much love you won't know what to do with it. So! Instead of being concerned about what's going down here, your big problem is how to deal with all that love.' And off we went to do that first show that night.

The three of us were riding around in a limousine from then on, and every day was magic. In France, we walked in front of Notre Dame singing 'Ode To Billie Joe' one morning, because Lydia tipped me off that the best thing about touring was that if the car wasn't leaving too early then you could hit the museums. The car was filled with music and conversation, and by the time we would hit the stage each night we were three people in high gear. After every show, someone would take us all out; we'd be sitting around some old table in an ancient city, there'd be a Czechoslovakian dirt-bike champion, children from the hoi polloi, other talented people. One bit of advice Lydia gave me was, 'Chronicle everything. Don't let a single thing slip through your fingers.' I'm sure she did. I didn't. Lydia had a tremendous sense of her own worth without ever having to say it.

TOM GARRETSON The Lydia Lunch persona is a very different being than the private one. This is something a lot of people don't understand. She can turn on the persona when needed, use it like a switchblade to poke and probe at people, get under their surface and discover their hidden selves. It's her paintbrush. This confrontational element is what scares the shit out of some people. No one unmasks bullshit quicker than Lydia, and woe to the bullshitter in her presence. The private Lydia is different—she's one of the most loving, kindest, and funniest people I know. I love her like my spiritual sister, my true family, and have always felt a responsibility to protect her.

JIM THIRLWELL She's a performer—that's what she's learned, and that's her mode of expression. And a lot of her mode of expression is that she uses her mind and body and voice as her weapon. It's the bullet and it's the gun— and the gun is loaded. And that's what she's chosen to do. And, as time goes by, she's done it more, and she's honed it, or it's maybe she has more ammunition. But that's her paintbrush.

DON BAJEMA Sometimes, people would try to compete with her or to smart off to her. Most of Lydia's work was confrontational, and some people wanted to try and take a bite, say things to Lydia ... and Jesus Christ! She was formidable! Lydia would just slam them. Not in some crass way—she'd look right in their face and then start reading them a programme about themselves, right there, right now. That's if they made her mad. These big brass people, big beauties—*I'm the shit* kind of individuals—would eat it so badly. Sometimes, if they had brains, they'd throw their hands up and laugh and surrender, at which point Lydia would cut them slack. If they weren't smart, well, I remember this one guy ... the audience was getting scared because she was reading at him so intently and with such intensity. The audience around the guy were making sure to point: *He was the one, he was the one!* The guy had to shrink out the back door.

MERRILL ALDIGHIERI Lydia did two readings in Paris, and, in the first, I had a really bad experience with the audience—it's in the film *Road Rant*. This guy was really obnoxious, he was attacking me, and Lydia wound up using it in her show. He was yelling at me about where I was standing, that he didn't buy a ticket to watch me. I wasn't blocking him but I was definitely in his field of vision. Lydia just lit into him after he grabbed me—I was happy she did. Later on, I spoke to friends of mine who knew her in the beginning, and they said she would orchestrate things like that, pick somebody and booby-trap them. I didn't know if she set them up or if she was just really good at triggering them. She can come up with a performance just out of that. She wasn't calling him a shithead, she had a whole performance that worked almost seamlessly with what she was reading—but it happened spontaneously.

DON BAJEMA Around the same time, Henry tells me that he and Lydia are going to put together an album featuring the two of them, Hubert Selby Jr, and myself. Lydia named it *Our Fathers Who Aren't In Heaven*, and that got some attention. There was an avant-garde agitating art group in San Francisco called Commotion—they did food drives, support for the Sandinistas, hid political fugitives, and they had a theatre they rented. I mentioned to a lady who worked there that I needed to get Henry some tapes, and she said she could do it, so it was just her and me in a little recording room, and I read the pieces to her. I wrote the piece 'Shakespeare' for it.

'Dog Party' I used to do on the road—that was the story of a kid in my neighbourhood who used to drown dogs then rescue them to make them dependent on him, because the last thing they would remember is the boy saving them—they wouldn't remember why they were in a barrel being held down with a broomstick. He had a whole trail of dogs following him around all summer. I used it as a metaphor for America and its treatment of have-not nations: *Here. Here's your corn. We don't want this corn—it's not even good for feed. Now tell us thank you.* 'Dog Party' is racism expressed through American foreign policy after the nation couldn't do it on our own soil anymore; once the plantations were gone, we just transplanted them abroad.

LYDIA LUNCH What about war? The endless war? It's the endless war. It just goes round and round, it doesn't matter. The war is never over. You know, that's my mantra. It's never over. America has been at war every year of its existence except for ten, and I don't even know which ten those are! War. It's a man's world—they can have it. It's how they want the world to be. It ain't gonna change. When is it gonna change? We've come this far, we have come this far in science, history, intelligence, technology, and we're still killing. Well, *we're* not, but they are.

I'm war-obsessed. I am obsessed with the big picture, the mania of homicide, genocide, forever, unending. There are no bombs dropping in my backyard, and why am I so obsessed with this? Because, as much as I hate the war, it does give me great joy to know that men are as outrageous as they are, that they are fulfilling the thoughts I always knew about them. Is it just a pre-programmed, genetic, chemical malfunction in the male psyche that allows them to feel that killing hundreds or thousands of people every year is valid? Bombing whole cities to rubble is valid?

I've never experienced war—I'm a privileged white artist. Why can't I shut up about it? None of my friends really talk about it. They don't want to hear about it. They don't care. I want the numbers, I want the statistics, I want to know how many are dead and dying! I want to know how many cities are bombed, where the military bases are, why? I have no idea why I'm obsessed with that shit. Maybe it just makes the war inside seem so much easier to deal with.

BETH B I did a film with ZDF Television called *Breathe In, Breathe Out* (2001), which was about intergenerational trauma from war. I took three Vietnam veterans in their fifties and their twenty-ish sons or daughters, and I brought them all back to Vietnam and looked at what they had suffered there and how their children growing up had been affected by their trauma. It wasn't something people discussed much—the idea that war doesn't just affect the people who were there, but they bring it back and they bring their disturbance to their children.

CARLA BOZULICH I have a song called 'Bells Ring Fire', and it's about an arsonist, this guy that nobody notices at all. They just go to work, they go

get on the bus, they go home, the same routine every day, nobody's fucking
with him, they don't know his name, and one day he just burns down a huge
part of the city, and he's like, *Now you know my name, you motherfuckers.*
Lydia is one of the few people I know that completely gets that—the fact
that a lot of this is a male phenomenon first, that there's a sickness that is
so dark and black; it's blood like tar running through their veins, and it
needs something bigger than medicine because medicine can't fix it. I feel
a kinship with Lydia in our proximity to that which compels people to do
certain kinds of acts: epic destruction amounting to starvation; for glory,
however short-lived; or something that happens in the dark with a hand over
a mouth and a sharp piercing and whatnot.

These tiny-minded compulsions are a dime a dozen and so easy to dip
into—flip a switch and narc out the motherfucker by simply feeling the same
thing and making it rock or writing it down to scream at you, later. Turn
their sad failure into a work of art—preferably something that pays. The
perpetrators are usually men, but I do understand. I understand both roles.
It's sexual and cerebral and somewhat awful and ecstatic. It's a good fuse.
I do feel those 'man feelings' when I'm weak or bored or just turning my
head to vomit out the balance of putrid domination and satisfying control.
My suspicion is that's Lydia's giving the gift of the fucking world because
she is ripping people open, people that are closed, they're comfortable, and
they're going to be entertained that night. They show up and they get ripped
the fuck open. She just lets them bleed, and that is a gift.

*

MATT SCHULTZ Lab Report was, initially, an improvisational, dark, ambient
sound project. I used to say in interviews, 'We are expressing the collective
unconsciousness of American culture.' We were radicals who dropped acid
regularly, and the project was raw and horrific, conceptually and technically,
a cathartic purge, a 'Heyoka shadow' practice.* Martin Atkins asked me to

---

* The Heyoka is a figure in the stories of the Lakota Native Americans. The character acts as
the direct opposite of those around them in terms of their speech, movement, and reactions.
The purpose of such behaviour is to refuse to conform to the status quo, therefore showing
that change is possible—that alternatives exist—and awakening observers to that potential.

be in Pigface, and my contribution was to play the instrument I invented called the 'Anti-Tank Guitar' or ATG. He also signed Lab Report, and, on tour in 1993, we were opening for Pigface.*

Martin came to us at the Metro in Chicago and told us Lydia and Genesis Breyer P-Orridge were going to play with Pigface. We were setting up when they arrived, and both of them stayed to listen to the entire soundcheck. When we finished, Genesis said, 'You sound like early Throbbing Gristle, and I would like to play with you as well as Pigface.' Then Lydia announced she would only play with Lab Report—quite an honour, and it worked out perfectly. Lydia delivered the intensity I thought we needed. It was so fast: she came out and sang over what we were doing, it was totally improvisational, she literally came out onstage with no preparation and began ranting.

CHRISTOPH DREHER Die Haut were always, basically, an instrumental band. We never found a permanent singer but we decided that was a nice thing—that we could have different singers for different projects or tours. For the *Head On* album, we assembled singers we had worked with before, and a few others. It was easy to get in touch with people like Kim Gordon, because she was a long-time friend; Jeffrey Lee Pierce, we knew him through Kid Congo Powers; Kid and Blixa Bargeld and Lydia were old friends; we even had Debbie Harry, who came to Martin Bisi's studio in New York City, and she recorded a vocal for us to use. We had one person in mind for each song, an intuitive thing. In the main, with exceptions, we had the instrumentals fully recorded, so we could send things around for people to add to.

Lydia hadn't changed much as a person. She's one of these people who are strongly formed at a young age; even when young, the main characteristics were fully formed. But Lydia certainly developed artistically, and through her spoken-word performances—I closely followed her work. Originally, it was this ultra-pornographic rant, then it became ever more sophisticated. She certainly didn't ride one horse to death, or get herself stuck in one position; she developed herself and had new perspectives.

---

* Atkins is an English musician best known for his work with Public Image Ltd, Nine Inch Nails, Ministry, and Killing Joke. He is also the founder of the Invisible Records label.

CATHI UNSWORTH I was working for *Melody Maker*, and I got one of Lydia's singles to review: 'Unearthly Delights'. I was mesmerised by it. I'd heard her work before, but there was something that really struck a chord with me: she was saying we were destroying the planet, but that the planet will survive and will be laughing at us long after we're gone. That's basically what I wrote in the review, and Lydia liked it—she got her PR to get in touch. I did an interview with her, and we got on really well. I was also working for a new magazine called *Purr* with my friend Billy Chainsaw—he knew Lydia very well. Lydia had a book coming out—*Incriminating Evidence*—and she kindly gave us a chapter from the book to run in the magazine. Lydia is such an amazing force of nature, but she's also exceedingly generous with her time and energy—this was an example.*

DAVID KNIGHT I first crossed paths with Lydia at an ICA Rock Week, where I was playing with Shock Headed Peters.† Lydia was in the crowd, and she said afterward that we were godlike, but Karl Blake seems to think she means that *he* was godlike—I've never asked her which it was, and, to be fair, he does look like a mythological god with his beard. Later, Karl met up with her, and he was going to do some work with her and Rowland S. Howard—they'd gotten together in London and talked about their mutual liking for Blue Öyster Cult.

Karl got in touch with Lydia because we had some songs we had released in the 80s, but we wanted to remake/remodel them and give them something extra—we never thought we had done them justice. Karl got in touch with Lydia to help add that other element. She came over to Danielle Dax's flat in Brixton. Danielle had signed to Sire, and with part of the advance she got a 24-track reel-to-reel Tascam with a big mixing desk, which was stuck in Danielle's spare bedroom, so we were doing the *Fear Engine II* album

---

* 'Unearthly Delights' was released as a limited-edition single in February 1993. Given *Incriminating Evidence* was released in 1992, it's likely that UK import copies were only available in early 1993, or that press copies of the single went out in late 1992.

† Shock Headed Peters were a UK post-punk band formed by Karl Blake. They disbanded in 1987, but in 1990 Blake and David Knight decided to recommence performing and recording under the name.

there. We had a couple of songs we had earmarked for Lydia, plus extra songs to fall back on if something wasn't working out. 'Evil Hearted You' reminds me of Black Sabbath slash Alice Cooper—it has that Bob Ezrin sound to it, and Lydia doing her best Alice. 'Suicide Ocean', that's a duet between Karl and Lydia, while on 'Head, Thorax, Abdomen' they're singing alternate lines, like Lee Hazlewood and Nancy Sinatra.* She was very fast and intuitive—she more or less got everything in one take, so we'd move on and try the next one. It was that quick—everything worked, and we used the lot. A productive evening.

A bit later, she got in touch with him about live work, the *Unearthly Delights / Universal Infiltrators* spoken-word tour.† Karl couldn't do it, so he suggested me. We met at Kings Cross Station and discussed what we'd be doing for that night's gig on the train journey. I had thirty cassettes with me, two cassette decks, and a tiny mini-mixer, and I would just follow where she was going with the text. It's fascinating the way that her narratives menacingly roam around then come back at you with a sting in the tail. I'd work out which loops fit underneath her narrative, I'd crossfade, pull and push with the levels. We didn't have samplers capable of it, and computers weren't yet reliable enough. It was great! Lydia puts her trust in you that you can come up with the goods, which gives you the confidence, and it works. Obviously you know she could carry the whole thing alone—she can hold the audience—so anything you do just adds to it, which is reassuring. You already know it'll be good.

We were really pleased with how the *Universal Infiltrators* tour went, so we put out a recording—recorded on Lydia's birthday, incidentally, June 2. We were in Newcastle, and I remember, for her birthday, all she wanted was a decent cappuccino. We went all the way round Newcastle trying to find one—this was before you got Starbucks and Caffé Nero over here—but we couldn't find one anywhere. How times change.

---

* 'Suicide Ocean' originally appeared on the *13.13* album.
† A five-date UK tour that ran from June 1 to 5, 1994.

CHAPTER SEVENTEEN

SHOTGUN WEDDING

LYDIA LEAVES NEW YORK CITY IN LATE 1990 AND SETTLES IN NEW ORLEANS. THE SHOTGUN WEDDING BAND RECORD AN ALBUM IN MAY, THEN TOUR IN NOVEMBER AND DECEMBER 1991.

THURSTON MOORE I feel like every culture, every city, every time period has these characters who express and move the culture in different ways, and she's that person in New York from the mid-70s until forever. She gets out of here in the early 90s, and she's like, *It's over.* And it was like the end of the city—it really was. It was the last time artists could come here without having to work to live so much. You can't do that at all anymore. Back then, it was all about the city: you either go here or to LA, or to Berlin, or to London—but the cities were all crumbling. The idea of moneying cities so that they could become habitable made a lot of sense. I mean, when you start getting yuppie culture, it's just so reprehensible, but it kind of had to happen. But I'm glad to have been there at that time because it was the last time in New York that had that history of being a place where artists could be in a community that's so intensified.

LYDIA LUNCH I left New York for good in 1990, when the gentrification had begun. There's still great people there, but it's not what it was. There are many artistic cycles either when a place is completely bankrupt or decrepit, or when a war has just happened or is about to happen. We could talk about

Paris in the 20s; Germany in the early 30s; Chicago in the 40s; Memphis in the 50s; Haight-Ashbury in the 60s; LA, New York, and London in the late 70s; Berlin for a while in the 80s. Artistic movements—they're never movements at the time, they're just things that happen, usually coming together for economic reasons, and technology has blown that out of the water now.

BETH B In the 90s, filmmaking just kept getting more and more difficult. I kept believing it was going to get easier, but it never did. That's my idealism at work! *Vortex* was 1982, *Salvation!* was 1987, *Two Small Bodies* was 1993—that's how long it took to get a film off the ground. The concept of Independent filmmaking was hijacked by Hollywood taking the label and making what they called 'independent films', but they were all monitored and constructed by corporate studios and subsidiaries. I couldn't find any financing at all in the United States. But as I moved from super-8 to 16mm, the costs became prohibitive. Then *Two Small Bodies* was 35mm. No job I ever had would support that, so I really was looking for financing. There were strong relationships with, and strong possibilities of, co-production funds from Europe. I ended up sending it to a producer who worked with German television, Brigitta Kramer, and she read it and wrote me a letter, pages long, saying how phenomenal she thought the script was and that they wanted to finance it. They then said we had to have a German producer, and then they said they wanted the entire film to be filmed in Germany because they wanted all of the money to be spent there.

That created some conflicts in terms of what I considered a very American story, but it also made me re-evaluate the premise and realise this was more of a universal story. It had to do with these very ingrained roles between men and women and this bizarre dance of domination and submission that occurs between an investigator and a housewife-mother-cocktail hostess who is accused of killing her two children when they disappear. It definitely challenged me in terms of working with an almost all-German crew with language barriers, and bringing my American actors over to make the film.

I had read Neal Bell's play, which the film was based on, and I said, 'I have to make a film of this.' It's a two-character piece with an investigator coming to investigate a mother who, in his eyes, is a 'scarlet woman', and whose two young children have disappeared. I was impassioned by this story, but it wasn't until years later that I understood this was really about my own mother. I was trying to work out the power relationship of my household growing up. It allowed me to mourn my family, to come to terms with the struggle that I had, and it took many years to work out why I was choosing to be with the people I was around in a dance of drama, destruction, and despair.

*

GLYN STYLER When Lydia moved to New Orleans, she was trying to get a band together with Rowland S. Howard.* She found a bass player but couldn't find a suitable drummer. I'd played as a touring drummer with Panther Burns and Green On Red, though I'm not really a drummer, so I reluctantly ended up on the drum-stool—it turned out to be a blast! The first time we met, she picked me up in a cab. I climbed into the back seat with her and said, 'Wow, you look great!' To which she replied, 'I always look great.' I told her that she had looked heavier, weight-wise, in the Kern films. She then pinched me on the cheek, rather hard, and said, 'That was baby fat.' I loved her immediately.

The first time I visited her house, on Spain Street, I knocked on the door and waited. She finally opened the door in a smart little leather miniskirt with a riding crop in her hand. She sat me down, went to the kitchen to make us tea … and, suddenly, a shirtless teenage boy appeared in her bedroom doorway, walked briskly across the room, and out the front door without speaking. When I asked who he was, she said, 'I was just showing him the ropes,' with a mischievous little snicker.

LINK WRECKAGE We were in New Orleans for a while and Lydia soaked up a lot of the ambience, the vibe of the place, and filtered it through her cycle so it

---

* Lydia left New York in December 1990. By March 1991, she was living in New Orleans working on *Shotgun Wedding*. Howard had written to Lydia asking if she wanted to make a record together. The project began under the name Gashouse.

was this different spin, so it was her vision. As much as New Orleans, at that time, was known as a party town, Lydia was not about partying. I was a little surprised because I didn't know her all that well, and she had a reputation—people would think she's this wild person, but I saw how business-like she was when it came to her work. Lydia was leading a very healthy lifestyle, she was biking a lot, she was in great physical shape. So we weren't going out partying, and we didn't have the money to go out partying—her head was in a really good place to conjure up this dark but accessible vision of what New Orleans was about, in sound.

When we did the track 'Black Juju' live, there were moments where I thought Lydia was speaking in tongues—she was channelling this Southern gothic mystical thing that she'd touched on with the Harry Crews project. We did 'Gospel Singer' live—I loved that track, and it might have been me who asked her if we could do it on tour. Lydia played the shit out of the guitar on that track! People don't realise how good a guitar player she is, and she's a good singer too. Rowland could really see that Lydia could sing. He liked that about her, how good she was. But she's never wanted to be just a rock singer, so she's never really gone there—that commercial, commodified singing like Courtney Love saying she's like 'Lydia Lunch meets Madonna,' and Lydia says, 'Fuck that!'

GLYN STYLER Lydia introduced me to a very strange alcoholic beverage called Cisco. It was sickeningly sweet, and she said the orange flavour was best. Turns out it had formalin in it, which I assume was related to formaldehyde. It got us very fucked up. She served it at her many gatherings and barbeques. We drank it all through the recording of *Shotgun Wedding*. I remember laying on the floor in a recording booth in Memphis with Lydia and Jim [Thirlwell], recording the backing vocals for 'Burning Skulls', laughing our fucking heads off. Cisco was taken off the market soon after.

Around that same time, my single, 'The Desperate Ones', came about because Lydia and I were both signed to the Atavistic label. Part of my deal was that they wanted me to collaborate with Lydia, and, of course, I was happy to do so. We recorded two tracks in one evening with no rehearsals. I wrote the little spoken part in 'Casket Made For Two' with Lydia in mind.

LINK WRECKAGE When I arrived, Joe [Drake] was already the bass player, and he was the funniest guy I ever met—he had this very dry sense of humour. After the album was done, he was cut loose—he wasn't invited on the tour—so I know he had a few hard feelings about that. It was clear he wasn't going to survive the record, though. We were a pretty tough group of people, and there was an element of economics behind it. Harry was Rowland's brother, so it was pretty clear pretty quick that he was going to play—he's a class act, so I'm glad that worked out.

HARRY HOWARD You really have to credit Rowland for writing the musical style of the *Shotgun Wedding* album, and he did it really quickly too, drew it together really quickly. He contacted me while I was in Melbourne—I think he was a bit concerned that I'd just stay there too long and it'd make things difficult for These Immortal Souls—and told me I had to come on this tour.

Rowland was 'in character' on that tour. He'd be hilariously comical all day, then in the evening he'd become more deadly. He referred to Lydia as 'Lunchy', just to say the most inappropriately flippant name he could think of—it was so incongruous with Lydia's personality, nothing nasty about it, it was just ridiculous and funny. He had a lot of respect for Lydia. We barely had a night off. As a general experience, things warmed up as they went along. We started with about four rehearsals in London. 'How are they hanging, Harry?' jeered Lydia, as she sashayed in. Any attempted reply on my part was drowned out by the band's laughter. Good rehearsals, though.

LINK WRECKAGE In New Orleans, we had this big Chevy Impala. Lydia was in the back and Rowland would always ride shotgun next to me—I was the driver—and Glyn got in the car and said something really salty to Lydia. She just stared at him—it rolled right off her. That was great. Glyn didn't care who Lydia or Rowland might have been—he was his own person and a really good musician.

GLYN STYLER In New Orleans, I noticed Lydia could be very *domestic*. Once, I popped in unannounced and caught her vacuuming the house in super-high black stiletto heels. She also enjoyed cooking and served some really wonderful dinners. When she found out I was subsisting on mostly fast food, she gave me a few—mandatory—cooking lessons. She'd say, in conclusion, 'Now, how difficult was that?' It was maternal, the way she treated me.

LINK WRECKAGE Glyn didn't want to tour, which is why he didn't come with us. He was a singer and a guitar player—he didn't want to be playing drums, he had his own thing going on in New Orleans. So Jim Sclavunos joined us on drums, and he was my roommate on tour.

HARRY HOWARD There was a lot of banter. Lydia was calling Jim 'Jim Skull-Voodoo', which I twisted into 'Skull-Furnace', which Rowland used as ammunition. Jim and Rowland started this kind of ongoing, good-humoured war of words, which was pretty hilarious on both parts. It ended suddenly one night when Jim and Link invaded our hotel room and Jim picked Rowland up and turned him upside-down. During that process, Rowland's head hit the floor and he hurt his neck: 'Why didn't Link defend me?' I hadn't defended him either—it was a crazed combination of hilarity and revenge on Jim's part. Rowland was quite sensitive about anything even mildly violent, and he was a bit upset. The 'Skull-Furnace' wars quietened down at this point.

LINK WRECKAGE We weren't writing new music on tour, really, which is in line with how Lydia was at the time when it came to music: she liked 'one and done'. There was no indication we were ever going to do more after the tour. Plus, it isn't that easy to write on tour, so we needed to fill up the setlist—European audiences would demand encore after encore, which meant we needed to have material ready. We did 'Run Through The Jungle', a Creedence Clearwater Revival song that Lydia had done a great version of. We did things like that where we knew them, and Lydia had the lyrics—there just wasn't much time to create more new music. Lydia doesn't really like hanging out with rock bands, so that's why there weren't many 'band projects' around that time, but it's good she got some mileage out of the material.

HARRY HOWARD Everyone in the band knew what they were doing on that European tour, and Lydia provided this focus. She was a good bandleader—the head of the project. She had high expectations but she was encouraging as well. She made sure everyone was focused where they needed to be somehow—she provided that. Rowland was backing her up, making sure the musical details were right, and he was inspiring—together it worked very well. When you were playing, you would get that sense of how good it was, because the audience would be so quiet while you were playing, then so loud when you stopped.

CATHI UNSWORTH The record she did with Rowland S. Howard, I saw them perform live—*Shotgun Wedding*—it was the aural equivalent of a Sam Peckinpah movie or a Jim Thompson novel. They told such brilliant stories together, and everything they did carried this air of mystery, but you could really imagine these fantastic landscapes unfolding.

LINK WRECKAGE One thing Rowland liked to do was, he liked to slow the music down a lot—I remember him saying, 'Let's play really fucking slow tonight and torture the audience.' He liked fucking with the audience—he says somewhere how he was accused of writing songs that were way too long and way, way too slow. Lydia was looking chic all tour, wearing these little black dresses, and we all had a good look going. It wasn't like we talked about style, it was just what we liked—we thought audiences were coming to see something, so it was on us to honour them by looking sharp. Not formal, just a certain aesthetic. Of course, then there were the grunge bands coming out, so as the tour went on we probably looked decrepit and depraved.

HARRY HOWARD During the tour, as it was going so well, there'd be talk about other possibilities for this project. Lydia was a bit hesitant—she was against touring America because she didn't want to be stuck in a van with a band getting no sleep. Who could blame her? But it's a shame, it could have been incredibly good, because that band had so much potential—her and Rowland working together was such a good feature. Also, Rowland felt like he needed to pay some attention to These Immortal Souls, but the money aspect probably played a large role.

LINK WRECKAGE Lydia did *Shotgun Wedding* because she really wanted to pull Rowland out of something. He really admired the idea of immortality in music, and that can lead you to some dark places. He had his demons, but Lydia loved Rowland, and she loved his guitar playing—she wanted him to be working. Lydia is a worker—she's always working—and she felt she could help jumpstart Rowland. Plus she wanted to work with him—who wouldn't?

When the tour was winding down, I felt like we were settling into the material. We wanted to keep going. Jim and I were joking, 'What's Alice Cooper doing? We should be his band, not whatever heavy-metal band he's got playing with him!' The irony is that I got back to New York and was at a party at a friend's house, and Alice Cooper's manager was at the party. It was typical of Lydia, though, that she just wanted it to be this one-time thing.

CHAPTER EIGHTEEN

MATRIKAMANTRA

WITH MATRIKAMANTRA, LYDIA MERGES HER INTERESTS IN LITERATURE, SPOKEN WORD, AND MUSIC INTO AN EVER-SHIFTING ENTITY THAT TOURS AND RECORDS DURING 1997–99. MEANWHILE, A FRESH GENERATION OF ARTISTS BEGIN SEEKING HER OUT ...

TOM GARRETSON A few years later—'97 or something like that—I see she's playing in Oslo, so I call the promoter and explain I'm an old friend. We get back in touch, we have dinner together, and I explain to her I was moving to San Francisco because I was setting up my own music management company. Lydia asked if I would be her manager, so I professionally managed her from 1998 to 2004, but I continued even after I closed my company formally, and I continue to manager her business today.

A lot of my time with her in those first years was just about cleaning up really bad contracts, getting back her publishing, and also finding people who were pirating her music without her knowledge—a company in London was ripping off her masters and just putting them out. It was even happening visually, with her performances: there's a documentary about the Beat poets with people like Johnny Depp reading quotations from William S. Burroughs, and suddenly people were saying, 'Oh, we saw Lydia in this film,' and we knew nothing about it—we had to contact the people who made the film and make them pay Lydia. As well as that, I was getting things going for her professionally. I set up Widowspeak for her, as a publishing company; we tried to get her signed to Madonna's label but I think Madonna felt someone like Lydia was threatening to her. I do know the demo wound up on the coffee table at Madonna's home because a mutual friend saw it there.

LYDIA LUNCH I'm really excited when anybody wants to use my music, especially my spoken word. I want people to mix in my stuff; I want DJs to sample my stuff; I want people to download my stuff; I want my word to be out there.

CHRISTOF KURZMAN I was a music critic for Austrian radio, wrote for an alternative newspaper, and was a conscientious objector evading military service, so living illegally from my eighteenth to my thirtieth birthdays. Extended Versions was my first musical project. I'd co-founded a support group for conscientious objectors and met my musical partner, Helmut Heiland, and we started jamming in his flat's kitchen. Extended Versions would come to occupy a unique place in Austria's underground music scene—we even made the charts with our tribute album to Robert Wyatt.

For the track 'I Wish I Could Erase', I had *Adulterers Anonymous*, this book with some of Lydia's poems, and as our aim was to oppose enemies that included militarism, sexism, racism, capitalism. And as, to me, Lydia was one of the brightest figures in music—and still is—I used her words. Helmut and I would pick up various instruments—bass, guitar, a drum machine, cheap keyboards, a flute, anything from a Casio watch to an egg timer—then I would sing or read the text as we played. I never bothered her with the recording; I assumed wherever she went there were hundreds of songs being presented to her, or showing her influence.

WIKTOR SKOK I met Lydia in Warsaw in May 1998, on the *Matrikamantra* tour. Krzysztof Lach of Noise Annoys organised her Warsaw date in the Zamek Ujazdówski Centre For Contemporary Art. Lydia was very friendly. One of the first things I mentioned was that I used her voice on one of our songs, and she answered immediately, 'Use more! Do anything you want with it!' Just like that, it was magnificent. She had an amazing knowledge of contemporary Polish literature—she was familiar with masters like Stanislaw Ignacy Witkiewicz, Bruno Schulz, and Witold Gombrowicz.

Meeting her had zero dead moments. Her high energy made every moment unforgettable, an exchange of information, ideas, listening to her talk about issues, art, movies, literature, and life.

In the evening, with Joseph Budenholzer and Terry Edwards, she acted as master/mistress of ceremony. The art world elite of Warsaw, everyone, was present ... and she didn't make anything of it, didn't give a damn. There was this quite ascetic mastery of the music and musicians—she dominated and seduced the room with her voice and her words. Since then, I've included other samples of Lydia's spoken-word performances. My favourite is an opening passage of 'Dear Whores' from *The Uncensored Lydia Lunch*. It fits perfectly over my mix.

We did not ask Lydia for permission. We placed her voice on 'Times 1000' at the end of our first record, the first recording Jude ever made.* The sample goes over a loop, a raw wall of modulated noise, and this stunning voice: it sounded, to us, like the final ultimatum for the last days—the words 'Times 1000' were intended as an announcement of the last judgment, terminal justice, and a sombre ending. The voice fits perfectly—no mercy, no excuse.

BERNIE ROMANOWSKI I was listening to the album *The Joy Of Darkness*, a compilation of Jack Kerouac poems read by an eclectic group of artists. I was in college and would drive around listening to Kerouac's words, this pretentious bullshit. Lydia's reading of 'Bowery Blues', by contrast, is an immediate representation of her confrontational and contemplative style. We decided to use Lydia Lunch's reading to introduce our song 'Not Today I'm Not'.† The title is a quote from an uncooperative auto mechanic we encountered after our tour van broke down on a sweltering southern weekend in Berwick, Pennsylvania, as luck would have it within walking distance of an auto-repair shop. When our bass player and vocalist, Randy Larsen, asked the mechanic if his repair shop was open, the mechanic looked left, looked right, looked at the ground, looked at the sky, and said, 'Not today I'm not, but I can sell you a Coke.'

---

* Jude are a Polish extreme music band formed in 1993 and based in Łódź.
† A song by Romanowski's band Cable, a US underground rock band formed in 1994.

Cable was far from home and piss-broke, we needed help, and the mechanic knew we were fucked … and he didn't care. So the song starts, 'Not today I'm not, said that disgrace of a man. You're the biggest fucking loser in town. Cheapest fucking hooker in town. I can sell you a Coke, but you can't use my telephone.' Randy and I are sure the mechanic never heard it, but fuck that guy! I should admit that we never asked Lydia for permission to use the clip, so let me publicly apologise and thank Lydia for making this unknown contribution to our album. She gave us an iconic moment for which we will always be grateful.

DAVID KNIGHT On the first Arkkon record, the track 'Terminal Distraction', I took Lydia's voice straight from one of her records: 'Terminal Distraction' from Lydia's *Crimes Against Nature* box set. I might have done some subtle time stretching on it because my gear wasn't that advanced at the time. Being on tour, I'd realised how well Lydia's voice worked with these pieces I was coming up with. So I had this piece, and I thought she'd sound really good with this swampy feel, and when I put them together it sounded beautiful. Sometimes the stuff that works well, works straight away, you don't have to tweak it too much to force it to fit—you just know it.

NICOLAS JAAR When I was fifteen, sixteen, I downloaded *Conspiracy Of Women* as an audio file and it lingered on my mind. It's stayed on every computer that I've had since. One day, I was about to do a DJ set somewhere, and I just felt like all the music I had to play made no sense: *What am I going to play to people? What, we're just gonna dance and act like nothing is happening?* I just couldn't do it. I started finding noise records, drone records, set up a bed at the beginning of my set where there would be this dystopian psycho-ambience, and I would pick certain parts of *Conspiracy Of Women* on top of it. At some point, after doing that for about a year, I thought I should probably email this incredible person who did this. What influenced me, more than any one of Lydia's works, was the energy that she was putting out into the world—an energy of pure opposition, of resistance. Lydia is one of the first people who influenced me directly as an artist and as a human being. She is one of my only role models.

*

JOE BUDENHOLZER I met Lydia in the East Village in the early 90s at this place called King Tut's Wah Wah Hut, this seedy bar, junkies were always in the bathrooms, you could probably get crabs from the couch. We would hang out there and play pinball. At King Tut's there was this metal band she was friendly with, and they went out on tour. She ran into them in California, and it ended up in an orgy—she slept with the whole band. The band's girlfriends were in a band called Cycle Sluts From Hell, and word got back to New York, so, when Lydia returned, they wanted to kick her ass. There was a fight on the street, then the metal band were playing at the Cat Club, with Lydia opening. I was with her that night: she got up onstage, and her performance was a verbal history—the whole story—of the orgy. I had to smuggle her out of the club after that!

KEMBRA PFAHLER I was in my early twenties, discovering my sexuality. I always thought of Lydia as a 'sexpert'. I thought, *Will I ever get to this place where I can love sex and be fearless about sex?* She was such an adventurous paradigm. In the Lower East Side, when she was here in the 90s, the stories that we would all hear: an entire band, having sex with married people, people that were couples … she was never intentionally causing harm, but it was clear that there was irreverence for stereotypical behaviour, and that included heteronormative relationships. Her sexuality in daily life was completely parallel to what she was speaking of, and I thought that was very brave. I had a lot of trauma that I had to work through, and I just thought she was leagues ahead of her time. The people that she slept with would tell me stories about it too. I would just be listening with my mouth agape. She changed people's lives that she slept with, so it seems like the sexuality was such a benevolent education, as well as the art that she shared.

JOE BUDENHOLZER I was introduced to her through Richard Kern and Brian Moran, who was known as 'Blood Boy'. When I first moved to New York, in the mid-80s, I'd go to see Lydia perform spoken word, and Brian would be her opening act. He would always end up naked, covered in blood. I started doing the music for him, these industrial soundtracks, with Jim

Coleman from Cop Shoot Cop. Hanging out after the show was how I really connected with Lydia, and she was impressed, so she said, 'You should do some stuff for me.'

She came to me with this idea for an album—*Matrikamantra*—based on the works of E.M. Cioran.* She was heavily into *On The Heights Of Despair*. She started sending me tapes, then I'd put music on them and send them back to her. A lot of what I did with her was very like Angelo Badalamenti, sort of noir soundtracks. She would send me Mingus albums and things like that, and she'd ask me to work it into the mix—I'd disguise them so we didn't get any legal problems. It congealed for that album, but it really was a very big body of stuff we were working from, lots of different juxtapositions.

Before the album was done, I would meet her in Europe, and we would go on tour. My friend Ivan Lerner and I made a backing video of insect battles and giant sea creatures eating each other and stuff like that. I toured with her off and on for about two years—we'd go out for a week then come back.

TERRY EDWARDS There I was, Tuesday evening, post-dinner, slippers on, having a cup of tea, and waiting for *Eastenders* to come on. The phone rang, I pick up, and there's that voice: 'Hey, this is Lydia Lunch.' And I thought, *Well, of course it is, why wouldn't it be?* I had no idea someone had given her my number—Billy Chainsaw gave it to her, apparently.† She had just made the *Matrikamantra* album and she wanted a sax player based in Europe who did the kind of performance I did. Someone easy to get along with. She asked me, 'Do you drink at all?' Billy had sold me as being someone who wouldn't go into drunken rages!

We both sounded each other out: did we want to be in a bus with each other for five weeks? I spoke to Paul Smith from Blast First—I was aware of the Sonic Youth connection—and asked him if I should do it, and he

---

* A Romanian philosophical writer heavily associated with explorations of pessimism, misanthropy, and nihilism.
† Chainsaw is a UK-based artist, editor, writer, and publisher.

told me it'd be a good thing, that Lydia was fun to be around. I was more aware of her musically rather than the spoken-word stuff. *Matrikamantra* was almost a halfway house between the two—it was a pointer as to where she was going to go in the next decade.

I was bolted on to that first tour, given space to improvise, learning the structures of everything. The tour was almost completely programmed, by Joe—all the pieces were complete, so there wasn't much room for manoeuvre, but there was space I could work with, a lot of rope with which to hang myself, which I did on a nightly basis. The music Joe had created, this synthetic and manmade element, made it easy to play against. I was shouting or breathing through an instrument, so it fitted very much with it.

Joe, Lydia, and myself kept out of each other's way but were enough of a gang to keep up a united front playing live. There's a tendency at first to overplay when you don't know material very well, then you start to leave more space. On the second tour, Joe brought in a few more tunes—I think we did 'Knives In The Drain', and he programmed something for that, something slinky, so there was a real progression.

JOE BUDENHOLZER Lydia would tour with recordings too. She had a big amorphous mix of all the stuff that made up *Matrikamantra*, and she would use it while touring solo. The great thing is she would send me royalty checks for using the music I made. She was really good about that.

IAN WHITE I met Lydia on a plane on the way to the first gig with her, which was in Athens in 1999. That was entertaining. She just walked over and said, 'Hi. I'm Lydia Lunch.' I said, 'Oh, hi! I'm playing with you in a few hours.' I've played with her ever since. Everything changed every night—it was all very free and improvised but based around the structure of the songs on the *Matrikamantra* record. We were using some prerecorded ambient noises, and I'd pick up on it and then we'd direct one another.

I remember Jimmy Garrison and Elvin Jones, one of my favourite rhythm sections, they said if you don't have a love for someone you're onstage with, it doesn't work. Without sounding pretentious, it's true that when you enjoy being with them, so many things fall into place. Sometimes it doesn't work, we know that, but it's a journey and it's always a joy travelling with her. Even when Lydia does spoken word, she always had a rhythm, which meant I could pick out little bits, then she'd respond to the rhythm we were making behind her, and we could go places, take a risk. We always had a setlist and some ideas—you always set a few things in your head to guide yourself—but so long as you're listening to the people you're with, it will work. Lydia, even if she's in the middle of a torrent of words, she's always listening, and she'll let you get in there. She would never signal when she wanted to move on, but I got to know her body language. There was that understanding, without her having to say, 'Can you shut up now?'

TERRY EDWARDS Lydia gave me a copy of *Paradoxia* within a day of meeting her, so I was reading it while we were on tour. It was funny, thinking there was a woman in the hotel room next to me, and I was reading through her life story, going, *Oh that's very interesting*. What was an eye-opener for me on tour is that I think America needs Lydia more than Europe does. She really understands how America works and the intricacies and depths of that place. It's a great loss to America that she's not as accepted over there as she is in Europe. It was noticeable on tour that it was different. Maybe some of her observations on the American way of life, the way money works, are too close to the bone for them? The American mindset is very different, and she's very connected into the way America thinks, and maybe they don't like that she's so connected!

JOE BUDENHOLZER With Lydia, what influenced me was thinking that this was a person with a strong vision and a strong opinion about it, someone who could run for president—I've always thought talk radio would be a great medium for her. It made me realise that what I needed as an artist was to find my own voice, to not just be latching onto other people's sound. Seeing Lydia, how strong she was about her message, made me think, *Well, what's my message? What do I want to say?* It was inspiring to work with an artist who wasn't just there to earn a buck. Lydia was there with a message that was real. She would say it herself: '364 days of the year, these clubs can put on something crappy that will scrape them some money, but for one night they can afford to put on something that's actually special.' She would look for any excuse to cancel—if there was something that was wrong, if someone was a dick, she had the guts to just cancel. She'd as soon not do it if it wasn't going to be right.

KAMIL KRUTA I emigrated to the States in '92 and met Exene Cervenka. She really helped introduce me to people, told me how things work, because we were isolated in the Czech Republic, so I was in the early stages of learning how to get around. I met Lydia after a show in San Francisco. Her spoken word, it was very aggressive, and I wasn't used to the form—I'd never really seen spoken word anywhere. I was quite smitten.

Up to this point, I'd met people whose view of why you did your music, or your art—they all believed they had to get something together, get signed by a bigger label, to get the money to go on the road and support recording. There was a lot of competition, and it was really boring and inhospitable. Meeting Lydia, I saw somebody who was doing exactly what they wanted, without any cues from any other parties. She obviously had to survive, so she was making money in ten different ways, working all the time. But she was really independent and incorruptible. She gave me the strength and helped me to have the faith in myself. She was who she was, in all her art, and when you met her you found her to be just that—she's not some construct to shock you, she's just living her life and describing it. I really appreciate that honesty, because most of the cultural industries are lacking that—people doing honest things. She's a unique monolith.

JASMINE HIRST I've met quite a few famous people in my life, and they've all been awful—you get to be famous from pure narcissism, I think. Lydia doesn't have that. She sees people as they really are.

TOM GARRETSON It happens to the best of them, but, back then, a lot of people were caught up in their own myths, and the persona fabricated for the stage crosses out into their daily lives, and then they find out that it isn't a healthy thing to do. The ones who are not able to understand that the stage persona is completely different to how you should treat people—they tend not to last.

JOE BUDENHOLZER With Lydia, we'd be touring all around the world, and there'd always be these goth girls who would be her posse wherever we went. Lydia had written a lot about sexual abuse, she was very open about it, and it gave a voice to a lot of people who shared that experience and could see that they didn't need to be ashamed, because here was someone who spoke publicly and openly about it without any shame at all. They could see Lydia was empowered by her survival, that she was brave, and it was clear that's how a lot of women who came to see her felt.

KAMIL KRUTA In Prague, Lydia asked me to sit in with *Matrikamantra* at Palace Acropolis, and I organised the recording of the event. Lydia came about a week before the show with Joe, so we went to see a bunch of old castles, and we went to the 'bone house', Sedlec Ossuary, to see the bones in the church. In Prague, at this point, there were a lot of ex-patriots from the US, and, since the revolution, Prague had great shows almost every night, so there was a huge number of people who would go to shows and wanted to see Lydia.

I'd hired a friend of mine who was an amazing sound engineer, and the sound was so overwhelming there was almost complete silence between songs, because people were blown away—this wasn't one of the shows where people scream their opinions. It wasn't just spoken word, it was like watching a movie without pictures—there was a lot going on and the music was quite dark both in tone and in message.

Joe Budenholzer's way of sampling music and playing it back was amazing. He used a mixture of different esoteric sounds, world music, all kinds of things that you couldn't quite recognise because he would slow them down, run them through effects, recombine them so it became this paste you were familiar with but that came at you in completely new ways. His music flowed like a river—it was like being on a boat in a dangerous river, watching the landscape go by—described to you by Lydia, this catastrophic and bleak landscape.

There were cues where Lydia had told us, 'From here to here, play minimal' or 'This is where we're going to exit.' The lyrics were fixed, but the way she would enter or leave a song might only have been decided before the show. At first it wasn't easy to play with: I felt what Joe was trying to do, I was playing bass guitar, using a microphone through effects to create sounds; we had ideas, riffs, places where you could go crazy—and then you just try to keep it all flowing.

JOE BUDENHOLZER We were in Germany, and we got pulled over by the cops for having a taillight out. I'm worried she's going to say something, I'm wondering what's going to happen. Lydia got out and she totally charmed the cop until, pretty soon, he's handing her his nightstick and they're laughing and he totally let us go. She does have this strange relationship with authority. She's anti-patriarchy, she's anti-hierarchy, but she knows how to work the system. It's a yin-yang thing—she has a good amount of the thing she hates in herself, she's integrated it all in a very healthy way. It's her transcendent quality—she takes something oppressive and makes it liberating. I'm a sexual-abuse survivor myself, so that's something that means I resonate with Lydia and her work on that level. Her art is like alchemy, changing lead into gold—something that could poison and kill you, but she turns it into something of dark beauty. She's a real rebel, to the extreme, but there's a vulnerability, and she lets her guard down. I don't think she's ever gone to therapy—her healing process is what she does live. She shares, she performs, she changes it into this poetry that's brutal and beautiful and also very touching and very real.

CHAPTER NINETEEN

THE ANUBIAN LIGHTS

AFTER MOVING TO CALIFORNIA IN 2000, LYDIA COLLABORATES ACROSS 2001–03 WITH THE ANUBIAN LIGHTS, YIELDING AN ALBUM, AN EP, SEVERAL TOURS, AND THE ONGOING SMOKE IN THE SHADOWS PERFORMANCE SERIES.

NELS CLINE I had been aware of Lydia and her work since *Queen Of Siam*, which was an in-store favourite of one of the employees at Rhino Records, where I worked. Someone organised a meet-and-greet around that time, and Lydia showed up, refused to speak with anyone, and left with an armful of records she didn't pay for! This did not endear me to Lydia at all! After my initial irritation with her, I still found her fascinating and periodically powerful. That she was aligned with Sonic Youth certainly helped, but also she began a string of really interesting collaborations, particularly with Rowland S. Howard and Jim Thirlwell. It should also be said that Richard Kern's Lydia movie, *The Right Side Of My Brain*, and her book of poetry with Exene Cervenka, *Adulterers Anonymous*, were quite compelling. But I didn't cross paths with Lydia until she moved to Glendale, California, in 2000, and my then-partner, Carla Bozulich, introduced us. Carla assured me that Lydia was a wonderful friend and that her public persona was little like her private, one-on-one qualities, and that certainly turned out to be true. We hung out quite a bit then, and Carla and I persuaded Lydia to guest at a concert by our duo, Scarnella, in

San Pedro, at a coffee house called Sacred Grounds. We even got her to play slide guitar, which I don't think she had touched since Harry Crews! This is also where I got the quote from her—'The only thing worse than a guitar is a guitarist'—which was her perfectly contrarian way of introducing her—albeit brief—return to guitar.

CARLA BOZULICH I was on tour and Lydia had come to the gig, and she was very hot—you could feel the heat coming from between her legs. I slept at her house. There were these two super-naive redneck boys. They were brothers, and one of them I think was eighteen and the other one was another age, maybe, perhaps a little bit smaller than eighteen—he was so adorable and cute funny. Lydia's always had beautiful furniture, she just has a great eye for decoration and for collection, she'll just trash the whole thing everywhere she goes, and then she'll go to the next place and it's all different stuff but it's just as ornate. She'll have this whole new collection of curiosities.

She has a photographer friend called J.K. Potter, and he took us to the oldest cemetery in New Orleans—it's falling apart completely, and he just took tons and tons of photos of us.* I remember one of them in particular, because I'm always really resistant to what Lydia wants out of me, like she wants to just claw into me and get something out of me. So she was like, 'You just gotta be so sexy, and we're just gonna do this thing.' So I went there, and I was wearing a really short dress—you could see my panties, it was super-short—and I was like, *I'm just gonna lay here and read this Bataille book, so that's what I'm doing. I don't know what you're doing.*

She was, of course, amazing: holding on to this column and just wrapping around it like a snake, and these photos were very lovely. And that's the second time that I met Lydia Lunch. We hit it off, I just fell in love with Lydia and we're sisters. I just feel like we could just kill anyone without even touching them. I feel incredibly powerful, like, when I look around at the rest the world, it's abnormal, and I feel that Lydia has that

---

* Potter is a photographer and artist best known for the manipulation of imagery to create bizarre hybrids such as the picture found on the front of Lydia's 'Unearthly Delights' single, in which a human hand seamlessly replaces the lower half of Lydia's body.

same power, and we both understand that bottom-line fact that if we need it it's there. She's been through a lot, she's a fucking survivor, and she never bitches about it, ever.

LEN DEL RIO In 2001, the Anubian Lights were signed to Toni Schifer's label, Crippled Dick Hot Wax.* He had recently released *Matrikamantra* by Lydia, so we were labelmates. Tommy and I were well known for working with other established artists—at that point, we were Damo Suzuki's West Coast touring band whenever he came over; we were the touring band for Nik Turner from Hawkwind and worked with him on a number of records—so, when we went to Berlin, where Toni lived, he told us that Lydia was maybe interested in collaborating with somebody, and he told her he would speak to us. We went out to Lydia's house in Glendale, had a really good meeting—she'd heard our album *Naz Bar* and liked it because it reminded her of her record *Queen Of Siam*. We went out to eat, and she explained, 'Toni thinks you could write some songs for me to work with. Do you want to try something?'

We went back to our home studio in South Pasadena and began our normal process where one of us would come up with a riff, then I'd do a lot of the music-production end as the engineer; I would come up with the beats, Tommy would do the guitar and the bass, I would add the synths, then we'd try to find little samples and loops. We'd build these pieces. We had four or five tracks and we sent them to Lydia, who really liked them. That was the early demos of what became *Champagne, Cocaine, And Nicotine Stains*. She wrote the lyrics, then we invited her over to the studio to hang out—put her in front of the microphone. It was a lot of fun—Lydia would come over every weekend and record, sing a bit, do spoken-word poetry. It's among the more musical projects Lydia has done over the years.

The song 'Nothing But Trouble' was the first we did, and she more or less does spoken word, but she did a harmony on the chorus, and she liked how it sounded. So when we did the song, 'Champagne, Cocaine, And

---

* The Anubian Lights are the duo of Tommy Grenas and Len Del Rio, founded in the mid-90s.

Nicotine Stains', she's almost crooning it, and it really works. The next one was 'Potango Tango', and she takes it even further. She was maybe hesitant when she first came in; she didn't really know who we are or how it would work, but it worked out so well, it really broke the ice and built the trust.

We toured quite a bit together—something like twelve dates in Germany, Switzerland, and Austria. The big show was the Wave-Gotik-Treffen Festival—Gothic Wave—in Leipzig. Lydia headlined with us. We got on very well with Lydia. Her exterior onstage can be very gruff, but working with her creatively, she's really funny. Tommy has a great sense of humour, so we would joke around a lot, lots of self-deprecation, lots of talking about life, politics, the music industry. The booking agency rented a van and a tour driver, and we had a blast. It was interesting seeing the level of respect venue owners and tour promoters had for Lydia in Europe—touring in the US is very different, even if you're a big name, because they treat you as just another band, while in Europe it was at a different level. In the US, we played a few dates in Hollywood; we played Chicago and the Knitting Factory in New York. James Chance opened for us at the Knitting Factory, and he came up and played with us on a song, plus we got to hang out with the Bush Tetras, so we got to meet all these great people.

NELS CLINE There was actually a handful of shows in the US with Lydia and The Anubian Lights and yours truly as 'special guest'. They were not as peaceful or amicable as the Willing Victim run. Emotions tended to run high; Lydia yelling for someone to bring her a cognac, which she would chug down before smashing the snifter to bits on the stage; Tommy was very emotional; Len was sometimes awkward and got yelled at. I, for my part, was directed to be Lydia's onstage 'silent tormentor'. I found it fun and not difficult to affect a certain dark ennui or detachment, stoic, quietly and subtly snarling, never fully sneering. Sometimes, Lydia would look at me during a moment onstage, and I would acknowledge but never acquiesce, sort of turn away. It felt rather natural in that setting, at that moment. In this role, with my de rigueur suit and voluntarily added slave bracelet, I managed to—for the first and pretty much the only time in my career—attract unwanted attention from female audience members.

LEN DEL RIO It was a very productive time. Tommy and I would record instrumental music, then decide whether to get someone to come in and sing on it, or if we would sing it ourselves. It meant we usually had material ready, and we would see if things were a good fit for Lydia. She would also play us reference tracks: 'Can you guys do something like that?' Or she would tell us that she liked a certain aspect of a song, and ask whether we could make that an influence on something we did. We would often have something we'd done that we could rework or share with her.

Anubian Lights performed the music for around ten songs on the *Smoke In The Shadows* album, then there were two tracks that weren't released until Lydia put out the *Deviations On A Theme* compilation: a song called 'Baby Faced Killer' and one called 'One Body Too Many'. On *Smoke In The Shadows*, Lydia really took the lead in terms of wanting to do more singing. We were doing this slightly dark, electronic lounge-jazz, and we would coach her a little more about how she wanted to try it—we could overdub or double the vocals if there was something we needed to do about pitch—and Lydia brought in Adele Bertei and Carla Bozulich to help coach her on the vocals, and they were going to sing backing vocals.*

NELS CLINE Lydia had garnered some attention with this cool EP she did in collaboration with The Anubian Lights, which led to them attempting a full album, which became *Smoke In The Shadows*. The sessions were done at the house Tommy had then. He had this really cool basement setup, and one could record in the living room as well with tons of cool old gear if one desired. It was all a cool hang, with Carla and Adele around, Lydia smoking, everyone tossing out ideas. I still feel the record is wonderful …

---

* Bertei played organ in The Contortions and worked as assistant to Brian Eno at the time of the *No New York* compilation. She then started the all-female punk band The Bloods and continues to record and perform. She is also known as a writer and filmmaker, and acted in the works of Vivienne Dick and Beth and Scott B, as well as in Lizzie Borden's *Born In Flames* (1983).

and almost completely overlooked. Besides some killer tracks and grooves, it even has Carla Bozulich and Adele Bertei as backup singers on some tracks! Potent!

LEN DEL RIO Lydia moved to Barcelona—she was going to book some tours and we were going to try to work remotely. In the meantime, we were working more with Adele Bertei. We were supposed to go to Russia with Lydia, she had dates booked out there … but then we couldn't do it. We had signed a new record deal with a different label, and part of the deal was that we couldn't do any more side projects—it was in the contract. We felt bad, but that was just how it was. We sent the backing tracks to Lydia because, with all the drum loops and samples on that music, it would have been very hard to perform those songs otherwise.

IAN WHITE We used some of The Anubian Lights' prerecorded parts as backing when we performed in Europe. A lot of the stuff on that tour was more set because we were playing against grooves, songs, rather than ambient things with no start or end. It meant there were things we started to stick to, even if the songs continued to change. We always started these things individually, then we'd get together at the first gig, talk about it, but no one ever had to say, 'Do that, don't do that,' so it was fun to play and we'd change things altogether. The music has always been a living thing happening in the moment—every night is like the last thing you're ever going to do, so you go at it. There was never a stodginess.

DAVID KNIGHT We got all the way out to Moscow, me, Lydia, and Ian White—I was just there for just the one gig—but Lydia was staying longer, to do a solo spoken-word performance, and Ian would be playing with Gallon Drunk. Backstage, Lydia always has a bottle of cognac, and we each have one little glass, it's a ritual: swig, then off we go and hit the stage.

The soundman was there with us, he was hovering around the drinks, and Lydia asked, 'Would you like a drink?' She offered him the cognac. He said, 'Yes please!' and sat himself down with a pint glass and just filled it with cognac and necked it. Bit cheeky! Halfway through the set, I can hear the sound's getting a bit dubbed up, there's all this echo and stuff, and next minute apparently the sound guy fell forward, head down on the mixing desk, and slid to the floor. He collapsed, and suddenly the monitor guy jumps up and runs out to do the front-of-house sound instead! Lydia saw him the next day, and she let it be known she wasn't pleased.

LYDIA LUNCH I slapped him in the face loud enough to silence the room!

LEN DEL RIO It also meant that *Smoke In The Shadows* was never finished, even though the majority of the songs were done with us. Lydia probably wasn't thrilled about it, but after a period of time Lydia likes to move on anyway, so we figured it wasn't a problem. We suggested she just have those songs, make sure we were credited, then she could finish the album. She had a couple of songs with Nels Cline, a couple of songs with Terry Edwards, so she was able to finish the album. It came out on Atavistic, which was her label at the time.*

RON ATHEY When Lydia lived in Glendale, California, she lived with Gene Gregorits, who was an extreme self-mutilator.† This was a really personal time with Lydia—we were understanding his expression both on erotic channels and on 'concerned adult' channels. We were very present and honest about that: I had Gene play me in a video excerpt for a performance called *Joyce*, and Lydia writes a chapter about that experience in my book.‡ Instead of this being this thing that happened somewhere else, this bleeding person was somebody we shared an interaction with. I don't have a lot of articulate words about that, but that's a deep part of our bond that went into the physicality of that boy.

---

* Atavistic is a magnificent label founded by Kurt Kellison. It did more than any other in the 80s and 90s to recover and re-release the music of the no-wave scene, most of which had either never been commercially released or was released in limited editions and long out of print.
† Gregorits is a prolific writer of work focused on deviant sexuality, mental illness, and trauma. In a 2013 piece he cut off part of his own ear and ate it on camera. He is currently in prison for sexual battery.
‡ *Pleading In The Blood: The Art And Performances Of Ron Athey* (Intellect, 2013).

NELS CLINE Next, in 2003, Lydia put together a project called *Willing Victim: The Audience As Whipping Boy*. The 'seed gig' was a performance in Graz, Austria, as part of an international convention on sadomasochism in art. Lydia envisioned something with more poetry and visuals, new material, an ambitious idea. But with Algis Kizys, Norman Westberg, and Vinnie Signorelli being in New York, and Lydia and me being in Los Angeles, she decided to focus on more of a retrospective of her work, so we could just listen and learn the songs before hitting the road in Europe.

Norman has this special thing he does on the guitar, which really gave us a sound like no one else, while Algis and Vinnie had a signature overwhelming power. Lydia asked her future husband, a Spaniard named Marc Viaplana, to provide photographic projections for the shows. Marc was a real character: he taught photography in Barcelona, had written a respected book about billiards strategies, and was obsessed with the Anarchist movement and bombings of the 1920s. He and Lydia had met at some party, and I think that Lydia married him for dual citizenship—'You know, I'd never marry for love, Nels!'—though they lived together in Barcelona for years.

Lydia desired a longer run with this band and saw it as something to be presented in museums and other spaces, not on the rock club circuit, but getting something like that to happen was not easy, and such places usually schedule things years in advance. Lydia lives pretty much day-to-day, and, ultimately, she went back to the cheaper, easier, tried-and-true trio with saxophone and percussion, playing smaller but dependable shows.

CHAPTER TWENTY

UNIVERSAL INFILTRATOR

FROM THE MID-90S THROUGH THE 2000S, LYDIA HAS BEEN SOUGHT OUT FOR A WIDE RANGE OF GUEST APPEARANCES AND COLLABORATIONS THAT HAVE KEPT HER RECORDING OR ON THE ROAD MORE OR LESS CONTINUOUSLY.

VANESSA SKANTZE I was living in Washington, DC, and Lydia came down—this was '86—and did a couple of performances, and I was right there. I saw her do a show with Rollins at DC Space, and she literally sat down and put a beer in front of me—she picked me up! We corresponded, and I moved up to New York and worked for her and Widowspeak for a little while. I ran the gamut from writing press releases to being 'person Friday', which was delightful, because we would hang out and drink coffee, then I would go make copies and write these press releases that read like manifestos, but Lydia loved them. Then she made the decision to move down to New Orleans, so it sounded good to me as a place to go.

RON ATHEY When I first met Lydia in the late 80s, I remember us eating Thai food on Hollywood Boulevard, somewhere you always went before gigs. I was having an in-between period: I stopped performing, stopped taking drugs, was going through treatment. That's when I experienced, first hand, a huge part of Lydia's practice, which is, *I don't wanna fucking do this alone, get off your ass and make it fucking work! Stop daydreaming and do it!* The motivator, the drill sergeant, knowing that wiggly line where you can either do something, or you're not gonna do it, so do it. There's that point where you can't just be the artist, so what do you do? You either become a teacher or you mentor a couple people or the people you work with, and I'd never really understood that until that moment with her.

VANESSA SKANTZE I didn't perform until Lydia and I were down in New Orleans. She said, 'We're going to do some recording, why don't you read something?' I had a lot of crippling self-doubt—I'm the sort of person Lydia talks about supporting and bringing along. She was the first person in my life that believed in me as an artist—most of my life was geared toward feeling I had to prove myself every minute of every day.

I got to tour with her and Exene Cervenka on the *Rude Hieroglyphics* tour.* On the album that came out, when Exene says, 'It's not every day that three witches come to your town,' I was the third witch. My album *Pariah* was recorded after that, when Lydia was living in Pittsburgh. She had Joe Budenholzer do some sound illustration on one of the tracks, 'Rise'. Lydia really wanted those pieces recorded—she was the instigator, the ear listening to everything and working out how it should sound. There was hope that the record might be put out by someone we knew, so a bit of time went by, then I borrowed some money and ended up putting the album out using imagery from photos that she had done and photos that I had done. Lydia, from the beginning when I was writing these press releases, just encouraged and supported me to continue to write and to bring it out in spoken word. At a distance, looking back, I was declaring myself—in a punk way—and the word *pariah* had a sense of choosing to stand apart from this society and this way of being, embracing another way to be. I was never a personal confessional kind of writer—I never pulled on stories of my life, the writing was personal but more abstract, it wasn't depictionary.

JOE BUDENHOLZER It's noticeable that I wake up at 5am with every demon on my shoulders, while she wakes up—*Boom! Ready to go!*—and captures

---

* A six-date tour of Florida and Georgia that ran from March 18 to 24, 1995.

her demons on paper. Some people who go through the trauma she has go through years of therapy, while others, like Lydia, they're outsider artists, and they work, and that's just what they do to process it all.

BOB BERT I don't know what drives her, but it was always there and it never left. She just has this incredible drive I've never seen in any other person. She's always had a bunch of projects going on at the same time, and it's hard to keep track of her. She's always talking about getting a big paycheque someday so she could sit back and write another book, she always has a screenplay in the works, she's always pitching something to somebody.

MIRCO MAGNANI Minox was born in 1983. At the beginning, the line-up was me, Daniele Biagini, and Marco Monfardini, but a few months later, Enrico ('Fago') Faggioli and Raffaello ('Fello') Banci were added. Unexpectedly, a tragic event stopped us right when we released *Lazare*, a mini-LP. Enrico and Raffaello died in a car crash while driving to rehearsal. Shocked by the loss, we spent some time facing the abyss, then, after a few months, we recorded an album with guests—it's still unreleased.

At the end of the 90s we decided it was time to go back to Minox. After almost twenty years of listening to her, Lydia was obviously an icon for us, an important part of music history. I had deeply appreciated her album *Matrikamantra*, which was very inspiring to me—somehow it opened new horizons, and Lydia seemed to be peaking creatively. It directly affected our decision to involve her on our releases.

The first time I met Lydia was in Bologna, in November 1997, during her spoken-word act from *Paradoxia*. That performance in Bologna was a revelation! The idea of involving Lydia in the *U Turn* EP (1998) was getting more realistic—I was composing 'U Turn' and 'Subdevil', and we decided to offer a collaboration on those two tracks to her. We sent her the tracks and she was very clear. I remember she said, 'I love your music, it's very Argento.' That made us smile, despite the fact that I never liked Dario's movies much.*

---

* The film director Dario Argento is noted for his collaborations with the Italian progressive-rock band Goblin on several of his horror/chiller films' soundtracks.

She recorded her voice by herself, then she sent us tapes. We didn't give her any suggestions—we honestly felt like giving her free rein. We recorded 'Arp 2001' and 'Cobalt' after the December tour date, as, during the rehearsals, we had tried to give shape to those tracks to play live. We planned those tracks to be part of the next album, *Downworks*.

TOM GARRETSON Lydia has so many side projects going on at the same time, she collaborates all the time. I think that's how she's been able to make a living at this—so many people hold onto only one thing.

RON ATHEY I went to visit her in Barcelona and had real *home time* with her. Only Lydia would cook jambalaya in the heart of paella country! I joke that private time with Lydia, you get a spoken-word performance every four hours, like clockwork! I feel that's something you lose with other people, this idea of *life is a salon*. You can have some nibbles to eat, a drink, then share some writing, and then go back to the personal. It keeps a creative discussion going—you need to witness. You write in a bubble, and then you think, *Is that too negative? Am I jacking off in the corner?* It's always nice to deliver it, first, to people you trust, then you can get constructive feedback, or not, but it seems realer once that happens.

MARC HURTADO Aged fourteen, I started to work in music, cinema, staged performances with my brother. I couldn't work with other people, and I never expected to have a public who were interested. We named ourselves Étant Donnés as a tribute to Marcel Duchamp: it was the name of his last artwork, a piece for voyeurism—you look through a hole in a door and you see a naked woman with something alchemical in the setting. We were taking the same approach in music.

I saw one of Lydia's shows, before I knew her, and was surprised by how much power she had in her eyes, in her voice. I was scared when she looked direct into my eyes. She could make you afraid and make you fall in love all at once. When she moved to Barcelona, we started to exchange messages, because I knew Mark Cunningham. When we first met, the first thing she told us was that, at a show, she'd seen 'two guys watching me for the whole show without moving their eyes. I was wondering, *Who are these two psychopaths?*'

In 1998, I recorded Alan Vega and Genesis P-Orridge in New York, then invited Lydia to be part of the album—*Re-Up*.* She was the one artist I did not meet while making that record. She recorded in Pittsburgh and sent a DAT to us. Soon afterward, she moved to Barcelona. There was a place on Las Ramblas, a three-storey building with a big sign in red saying *Sexodrome*. It was a sex shop, a peepshow place. I decided immediately that the song Lydia did should be called 'Sexodrone'—it had a sexual power, and I felt you had to make the music mirror the person you have in mind.

For her, I wanted the music to be sexual, to be special, something very slow, almost static, but in a car going at two hundred miles per hour. For me, her voice was the stable element that I put at the centre of the track. I didn't think she could love it—maybe it was too much like industrial music?—but she loved it! She sounded comfortable and seemed at home. She's made so many different things, her music goes to many places, so we can't say she has one definitive style—the words are the one common point. They're the ultimate truth, and they have the power.

LYDIA LUNCH As somebody who considers themselves a writer, mobility is very important. I've moved so many different times for so many different reasons—economics, architecture, collaborators. I went from New York to New Orleans. I went from New Orleans to San Francisco, San Francisco to Pittsburgh, Pittsburgh to LA, then to Spain. Now, for me, it's not only a matter of collaborators but whatever I need at the time, whether it be the architecture, or just needing a cheap place to create because I'm not performing so much at the place I live, unless I decide to set up curatorial gigs, which I've done.

WAJID YASEEN I first met Lydia while I was producing music under the 2nd Gen

---

* Genesis Breyer P-Orridge was a co-founder of the COUM Transmissions art collective and the band Throbbing Gristle. He went on to form Psychic TV and the related occult group Thee Temple Ov Psychick Youth. He was an exponent of mail art, and from the 90s onward embarked on a process of surgical interventions with his partner Lady Jaye in order that they resemble one another as closely as possible, an expression of love they defined as 'pandrogyne'.

moniker. I was getting a name for myself, and, during this time, was invited to do a gig supporting Lydia at the Garage in London. There were three of us onstage: me, controlling all the electronics; Nadeem Shafi on voice; and Tiago Gambogi, a contemporary dancer. Both Tiago and Nad were topless, and one of the key memories I have is of Nad lashing Tiago on his bare back with a mic cable, clearly a painful and visceral experience for Tiago—he smashed a chair against the back wall onstage as a sort of cathartic response. I was in the crowd afterward when Lydia walked onstage making licentious comments about our topless smashing-shit-onstage performance. I liked how entirely comfortable she was with the frothing madness.

Uniform came about after arriving at a dead-end with 2nd Gen, I essentially locked myself away for a month producing the first Uniform album. Sleep deprivation, adrenaline, other shit helped piece it all together. The second album, *Protocol* (2006), was darker in sound and colour, but not too dissimilar from the first with regard to the compositional approach. This time, I decided to incorporate vocals. I felt an affinity with Lydia's anger after seeing her live. I remember standing at the side of the stage at one of the All Tomorrow's Parties events and giving her a hug as soon as she stepped off stage. The tenderness threw her a little, but I also knew she appreciated the honesty of the gesture.

We had mutual friends, James Johnston and Terry Edwards, so I called her after getting her contact details from James. I guess by the time I did approach her, she had sussed that I was an experienced producer and didn't have time or inclination to fuck about—having Alan Vega already on board helped too. There would have been no point asking Lydia to contribute if I was going to shape her content myself: what I wanted was her voice and her take on it. The track I'd made didn't need her voice to be tightly synched to tempo. All I was after was a sort of bitter spoken word. She used some sort of Dictaphone, and her delivery was exactly what I was looking for. Apparently she was walking down a street when she recorded it. Maybe her footsteps helped to convey precision. The recording was pretty short in length, but it worked. I placed it about three-quarters of the way in, and it allowed the track to build into its own form and have the voice arrive with some force. The 'Sex Is A Contract, History

Is A Trick' title was entirely mine: I have a file on my desktop with a collection of track titles that have come to mind, and it was simply one from the list. It felt perfectly suited. Brendon Labelle described the album as 'psychosexual', and that's about right.

BOB BERT Lydia's greatest work of art is herself. She created this being that's all encompassing, a presence in every medium. Lydia had this aggressiveness and power, like no other women or artists around at the time, and what's amazing is, here we are all these years later and she's pretty much exactly the same. It's nonstop. Sometimes, Lydia will call me up and I'm lucky to get three sentences, it's like, *I'm doing this, I'm doing that, I got this project going, I'm going to be in this movie*. It's great because every musical project she does is a completely different thing. She always said, in the early days, 'I just want to do it, execute it, document it, and move on.'

DALMAU BOADA Les Aus was formed with the intention of freeing the music and freeing ourselves through it. Our band at the time was called The Cheese, and, one day, we had the idea of playing a show in which all the music would be improvised and we would give instruments to the audiences, so we could all share in a common experience. That was the first Les Aus show. During the early years, we would play 'songs' that mixed structure and free music, but there was a moment—around the time we met Lydia— where we chose to only improvise what we played.

Lydia was living in Barcelona, and Arnau and I knew she and Mark Cunningham were playing music with our friend Adrian De Alfonso. One day, Lydia asked Arnau to play drums with her and, somehow, I ended up being part of the experiment. We met at a practice space in El Poblenou, and she had brought her electric guitar. She said it had been twenty years since she had last used it. I remember we turned the equipment on and got into a flow that just wouldn't end—a very fluid sensation connecting us to her. I was surprised by her way of looking at me, even talking to me, while the music was happening—I've never had that kind of intense eye contact from any other musician. Actually, thinking about it, the connection I had with her when we played did have its sensual moments. Our first performance was in Lausanne,

Switzerland, in 2007. We went there as Lydia's band—probably they wanted her, and Les Aus were the musicians who were experimenting with her at the time. I remember a moment where I was on the floor holding Lydia's leg and using her heel to play my guitar—no planning, it just happened.

PHILIPPE PETIT I guess my first meeting with Lydia was when I learnt English by reading her lyrics, and Siouxsie Sioux's, printed on the inner sleeve of vinyl records. I was a passionate music listener in the late 70s, totally into punk/post-punk—*Queen Of Siam* was an instant favourite when it came out. We met properly in the 90s when she came over to perform, and a decade later, when I started to make my own music, I asked her if she'd collaborate. I had agreed to release *Reciprocess*, a CD of collaborations to be given away with *The Wire* magazine, so I invited Lydia. She's a charm, so easy to work with. You can count on her, she's fast and so *pro*! I sent an instrumental, and the following day she sent me vocals. Intrigued, I asked if she'd do a second one, as I'd been invited to participate in a compilation for the Portuguese magazine and label This. She said why not, I sent over an instrumental, and the day after …

In just four days we had fifteen minutes of complete music, so we both agreed to keep on trying. It was July, it was warm; we needed to get something happening while everyone else was being lazy. Soon, we had an entire album, *Twist Of Fate* (2010), and were both very pleased with the result, so I suggested maybe we try to play live as a duet? A few weeks later, we were onstage in Norway—now that's how to influence fate!

MARC HURTADO I started to work on the *Sniper* album around 2009. I was working with Gabi Delgado of the German band Deutsch Amerikanische Freundschaft, but the album didn't appear. I had a lot of good songs, so I invited Alan [Vega] to make an entire record together. There's a song on the album called 'Sacrifice', and I proposed that Lydia sing a different version of the song at the end of the album—'Prison Sacrifice'—so it was like a duet between Alan and Lydia. I told her that we would keep the song 'Sacrifice', then she would go between the words of Alan, like a snake, to make it like a dream. She did a perfect job—there's distance to her voice which gives it magic. You hear the same music, but it's like a new song, because of how closely Lydia has connected her words to Alan's.

ZOHRA ATASH Flipping through posters in a mall in Virginia when I was fifteen years old, I saw that iconic shot by Ray Stevenson of Lydia with a tarantula on her chest and a framed picture of Jesus on a cross above her head. My mother hated that poster—she was really religious and convinced Lydia was one of the daughters of Satan, or Satan. The record she guested on with A Storm Of Light and me, it was an elegy to a post-fallout wasteland.* There are only a handful of artists who can make wine from the sour grapes that is the darkness of man, and Lydia Lunch is one of them. It's poetic nihilism that doesn't veer into maudlin dribbling or misanthropic smattering. She speaks the vernacular of violence that commingles chaos and hope through colourful prose without romanticising what's at the heart of darkness.

MERRILL ALDIGHIERI Lydia and I had no contact for the next ten years after *The Gun Is Loaded*. Making our next film together in 2007, *Road Rant*, was a series of disappointments we were trying to make lemonade out of. I was really disappointed I wasn't going to get a budget to make a real film of it with Canal+. That would have been a great breakthrough for me, even if I had to work as a ghost director with someone who had never made a film before. He was a cool guy, he had some interesting ideas, but I was a little jealous of him because though he had no experience he had a connection, while I'd spent my whole life making films and I couldn't get my foot in the door—so I thought I'd just keep my mouth shut and try to get in, but then that fell apart.

Meanwhile, there was a lot of positive energy coming from Lydia's publicist. They encouraged us to make the film happen. I hadn't seen her stuff, except for that one period working together but, starting with a number of performances in Paris, I was blown away. It was like it was the early 80s and I was seeing her for the first time, it was so powerful. I was struck that she had completely reinvented herself. Until I saw her on the tour, I hadn't

---

* Lydia collaborated with A Storm Of Light on two releases: an album in 2009 and an untitled record released in 2011.

realised that's what she's like every day: she's constantly reinventing, and, in each undertaking, she brings out new aspects of her performance talents, and with different collaborators it gives her work a lot of variety. It was an adventure driving around with Lydia all over France for the whole tour. My husband drove the van, and he was the translator. We went to five or six different places, drove all around the whole country in a week—it was exhausting. I recorded every set and then had to come up with reasons to choose certain bits from certain sets. And I did a lot of things with effects to embellish the stages with phantom ghosts of what she's talking about—she was talking about a lot of intense stuff. I ran around to clubs, I got friends to do funny stuff. A friend of mine was running lesbian parties in Paris, and I went to a club to film a girl who was doing a performance, twirling flaming batons while naked with some guy in chains. Stuff like that.

Some of her songs touched on the theme of war—in the same way *The Gun Is Loaded* did. She talks of 'manmade disasters', and it connected with my own childhood—the first times I heard about war, about nuclear weapons, the 'duck and cover' era of school drills in case of bomb attacks. I had a sense of awe: *How could we let this happen?* I wish art could combat or change it, like with a magic wand, and there's a little child in me hoping that this work is going to be the magic wand which will give us this utopia where we're finally free of it.

*

LYDIA LUNCH I may have found more sophisticated ways to express, but the themes remain the same, the themes have always been the same. They've always been about the abuse of power, they've always been about the need for the individual to struggle to survive everything that is dealt against them, whether it's economically, religiously, their gender, their obsessions. It's always been the same themes, and it's like most writers: you write the same book over and over. You just have to find new ways of expressing it. It's why I had to release an anthology called *Will Work For Drugs*, which showcases the variety of types of writing.

RON ATHEY The last thing I looked at was Lydia's book *Will Work For*

Drugs. Lydia has the best dark humour and knows to layer some of it on when things get too gnarly—she can lighten it that way. One of the most amazing performances I saw was at London Fashion Week 2011. This is a fashion crowd, some of them don't have any idea who she is, and it was amazing to see her, in that audience, top everybody. She topped everyone! She was funny, then harsh, then charming again, then harsh again. I could see the cycle, and, by the end, everyone was submissive and in fan mode and hearing it. She didn't even refer to fashion. I love that—why go to the lowest common denominator and take the piss out of fashion when you're already in the odd position of performing at a Fashion Week event? That's activism: to go in where the audience aren't necessarily in the Church Of Lydia, but they all were afterward.

ELISE PASSAVANT I had no idea who Lydia really was until I met her in 2010. Life brought us together: an Icelandic volcano spews dust into the European sky, strikes everywhere, unbelievable tension in crowded trains and cars. That's the day I come to Bourges, to document an event organised by the French writer Virginie Despentes. Lydia and Virginie were reading, in French and English, a piece from Lydia's book *Will Work For Drugs*, called 'Death Defied By A Thousand Cuts'. I was filming and something happened, something visceral. I started shaking; I felt something deep in my solar plexus, an inner sensation. I had to put the camera down on the floor at my side. I kept recording but I had to see and hear this for myself, not through a camera lens.

A little later, I felt compelled to go toward this woman, but … what was I gonna say? Am I gonna sound stupid? Am I gonna get punched in the face? My gut said, *Just go*. Ten minutes feeling like a full forty minutes of mental, psychic, physical back-and-forth. I walked toward her, I thanked her, told her how moved I was by the reading. Lydia's blue eyes on mine, her pale skin, red lips. She took my hand, gently kissed it, thanked me, and gave me a hug, though of course I am French, so I don't do hugs. I was stiff as a metal pole—I truly didn't see it coming. The following day I sat by her on a blanket, a sunny picnic, as she told stories. It was pleasant to just shut up and listen.

Time passed, I was impacted by a number of personal, familial, tragedies. It was Christmas and I wanted out: out of my apartment, out of Paris, out of habits and routines. I sent Lydia a eight-word email: 'Name one desert you'd like to go to?' She replied, 'Desert or dessert? Mojave or chocolate avocado mousse?' Me: 'Desert like *deserted.*' Lydia writes back, 'A deep escape from the rat race to oblivion? A very interesting proposal and a wonderfully generous one, o sister witch! Let's discuss.' A few more emails and a trip was planned: a two-week road trip through the Zaragoza Desert and its abandoned villages. Our main stop: Belchite, one of Lydia's favourite spots on the planet. I understood why the minute I saw the ruins through the windshield of the car. Here we were, two witches, though mortal flesh and blood, on Christmas night, drowning their sorrows with the ghosts in the ruins of a city destroyed by humanity's ignorance and stupidity. Belchite, its walls scarred with bullet holes from summary executions, open skies above and bombed-out cathedrals. There was such beauty in all that decay. It was the perfect playground for me and my camera.

A few weeks later, I was moving in with Lydia and her deadly cat, Buster. When you're near Lydia, you're caught up in the middle of a gigantic mass of unstoppable energy. You can't be close to such a force, such inspiration, without winding up pretty creative yourself—even if you have a lethargic nature, like I do. Every other day, she would come up with an idea, a song, a piece of spoken word, a collaborative female-led workshop concept, even. And every other day, I would invite her to my room to show the imagery I wanted to use for each piece she gave me. I remember not a single moment of discord. She was encouraging, cheerful, enthusiastic. Everything flowed at speed, a very organic process. We would watch movies, TV shows; I was the lone (and delighted) spectator of countless readings. And she would feed people: she hosted countless suppers for the intriguing people who would visit her.

LYDIA LUNCH The reason the cookbook came about was that when you're poor, you gotta cook anyway.* I like the idea of touching things that are going in other people's mouths. It's a form of witchcraft; it's a very intimate thing,

---

* *The Need To Feed: Recipes For Developing A Healthy Obsession For Deeply Satisfying Foods* (Universe, 2012).

feeding people. I like knowing some of my cells are going down their throat and living inside them. It's a form of impregnation. Everybody loves you when you cook for them, so I started cooking for people just out of poverty and hypnotism.

In *True Blood*, the vampire series set in Louisiana, Michelle Forbes plays this witch who would have these food orgies and drug people. She said she based the character on Ken Russell and me. I'm like, *I gotta try to cash in on this vampire shit*. It's a hedonist's guide to good food, sexy food, musical selections; the history of food, especially spicy food. You can be tortured with habaneros and jalapeños—the Mayans and the Aztecs used to torture children by making bonfires of hot peppers. I like facts like that.

The last chapter has the 'hazard' sign because I've lived in so many toxic zones: there's this site very close to the house where I was born; then I lived in New York, above a plastics factory; then New Orleans, which is the anus of America, cancer alley. Pittsburgh, San Francisco, Richmond with its 350 chemical plants, Los Angeles, London. I have made a pentagram of cancerous locations to live in: like a weekend detox is really gonna cure you from all that crap, right? Food is important, but the problem is so much of it is contaminated in America.

ZOE HANSEN Lydia has no time—she's constantly thinking, her mind is constantly going. If she's not recording something, she's writing, she's publishing, she's performing, she's taking photographs, she's got the cookbook—she's endless. One of the girls from L7 said to Lydia once, 'You know, we're show folk!' And they are: they're like old-style carnies, gypsy fortune-teller types, something going back centuries, always on the road, selling your wares, bringing along whoever wants to be part of it, and everyone is pretty much welcome.

TOM GARRETSON Lydia's changed a lot over the years—my god, it'd be pathetic if she was just the same person she was when she was seventeen and starting Teenage Jesus. To me, it's only a positive thing that when a person grows older, it doesn't mean that someone like Lydia ever sold out or conformed to any other standard, but she's developed herself in her own direction—

age gives us nuance and depth we didn't have when we were younger. She's a Gemini, multifaceted—and, coincidentally, born on the same day as the Marquis de Sade—so it's part of her nature to explore other areas of creativity, without limits imposed on her by others. I call Lydia the hardest-working woman in showbiz.

*

GIANNA GRECO I'd been into music since I was ten years old, mainly self-taught, first punk, then everything from stoner to Balkan music to jazz. Since then I've run a club, founded an indie record label, worked as a sideman for several bands while studying and working as a bartender. At the end of my studies, I decided to give music a real shot. I stopped playing as a sideman, gave myself a two-year deadline ... and, six months later, I received a proposition: to join Lydia Lunch's Putan Club. As you can imagine, I said yes. I'd been listening to her music since I was fifteen, I'd read her books, I knew a lot about her work. Putan Club has existed for more than a decade—it was François's idea, a test bed for all his various projects.

FRANÇOIS-RÉGIS CAMBUZAT I started with punk back in 1978, in London, then I later fell into jazz and contemporary classical music. In 2012, during a tour in Mongolia, a musician friend—the son of a Kazakh bard—told me about shamanism. He explained that, in Xinjiang, it remained pure because it was strictly forbidden by the Chinese authorities. Back in Europe, those words were still ringing in my ears. I was left wondering what made me live within music, why—ever since my first concerts, when I was roughly twelve years old—performing onstage took me elsewhere, why it would make depression or toothache disappear. I am an atheist; I am not a neo/proto-son-of-Woodstock, either, and I hate the populist image of shamanism. I come from punk, from a tradition of savagery and experimentation—that's what I see as shamanism. Gianna and I stayed for many months in Xinjiang, learning, recording, and filming.

GIANNA GRECO François explained to me this idea he had, using lyrics as a means of elevation, with the help of music and images, and asking Lydia to act as the shaman. I was intrigued. You might ask why ... well, as musicians, every time we're onstage, we get high, we go somewhere else—and why Lydia? We love her writing. We expressly asked her not to sing. We wanted it to be spoken word, so she could slowly lull people's minds into entering this creepy and violent world—the real world. The first—and, as far as we knew, last performance of Lydia Lunch's Putan Club—took place at the Theatre Garonne, Toulouse, in March 2012.

FRANÇOIS-RÉGIS CAMBUZAT Lydia is the 'Dea Ex Machina'. We follow behind her like faithful dogs. Technically speaking, the hard part is simply to control the computer. Everything else that happens is catharsis. The idea has never changed: we want to leave Lydia completely free, to be the shaman, to be the person who carries people to some faraway place. Gianna and I are just the vectors that help that journey. Think of the way that the guitar is the slave of the dancer, or of the singer, in flamenco music—just a foundation on which they stand to try to touch the *duende*.* Everything was ready by the time Lydia joined us, forty-eight hours before the ceremony. I knew that Lydia wanted—artistically, not just physically—to kick ass so hard it might move this whole planet forward. It needed sufficient budget, of course: 'Your Love Don't Pay My Rent' is a very true and honest statement.

GIANNA GRECO It wasn't a *concert* because Lydia isn't really singing; but it's not a reading, either, because she's neither seated, nor reading from a pulpit. We decided to play out in the audience—something François and I were doing regularly as a duo—so, with Lydia, it meant she was around them, whispering these gloomy, violent, indecent, powerful, cynical, revolutionary texts. And we're there, sweating with them, and on them, a kind of orgiastic ritual that leaves us all broken. It's not entertainment. Art isn't placed on this Earth to entertain, it's there to awaken minds, provoke, shock. That's what we were trying to do together.

---

* A Spanish term related to a state of heightened ecstatic emotion and energy, the rapture desired by flamenco dancers, but likely also familiar to musicians and performers (and audiences) caught up in the creative force of an artistically expressive moment.

FRANÇOIS-RÉGIS CAMBUZAT Lydia is always shining! A whole tour with her is something special. No frenzy, no stupid behaviour, no jerking around. I really think she's an intellectual—she's curious and cynical about this world. The sweetest moments I remember were when she was sleeping in the back of the van, and she'd wake up, ask for a stop for coffee and a cigarette. To know Lydia automatically becomes to truly respect her.

*

DAVID LACKNER Family In Mourning is its own world, and the album, *Eulogy* (2017), is like a relic from that world.* It originated in Lydia's imagination— she had wanted to do it for a long time. When she met Dominic [Cipolla] and saw him in an undertaker's jacket, that connected the dots. Family In Mourning is this bigger concept of a funeral service Lydia had: people could hire her as an officiant, Jasmine Hirst as a videographer, and we would be the band. Jasmine has the ability to interact with spirits, so she's a huge part of the extended family, even though she isn't musically involved; she took the cover photo, and she was a sweet person to have there during the process. Lydia saw herself as the widow, Ben [Lord] as the gravedigger, Dom as the Edgar Allan Poe undertaker; I was a mix of altar boy and priest. We were characters in that world, and she was the centre of it. It's a big crew, a group of like-minded people, but we wouldn't be Family In Mourning without Lydia.

During a tour, Lydia and Dom were rapping about this concept, then, when we got home, we felt it was time to write the album. We wanted to move fast so Lydia didn't change her mind—luckily she liked most of it! We did demos, listened to the tracks together, and made plans how to develop them, then it was a long process of recording. The initial tracking took a couple of months, then adding things here and there was another few months.

Once the recordings were in a good place, we sent them to Lydia. She's very much the big-picture person: *Is this song worthy of being on the*

---

* Family In Mourning featured a varied cast of musicians and collaborators, including Dominic Cipolla, David Lackner, Ben Lord, Adrian Knight, Aaron Dugan, Christian Lee Buss, Gabrielle Muller, Genevieve Kammel-Morris, Derek Vockins, and William Robinson.

record? Stuff like that. I'm someone who will obsess over the bass and kick level, while, if she hears something she doesn't like, she'll say something, but she doesn't want to be picking apart the little things, so we had a certain amount of freedom, so long as people liked it! Seeing her perform a lot, seeing her style, she really brings everything to the stage, and she doesn't leave anything for tomorrow. That translates in her recording as well—she brings everything to everything she does, or she just doesn't do it. I noticed she's always thinking about words and phrases, or she's got a story or a feeling in her head, and she's working out how to express it.

MATT KORVETTE I feel like there is an inherent reckoning of the male species within Pissed Jeans' work, and who better to be involved in that interrogation than Lydia Lunch?* She's the optimal judge, jury, and executioner, as far as I'm concerned. We've always wanted to make records that reflect us in that moment—not just creatively but where we are in our lives and relationships and whatnot. We were up for something new, maybe a little risky, and we thought we could use some Sub Pop money to force someone cool to hang out with us. *What would happen if Lydia Lunch produced a Pissed Jeans record?* seemed like a great question to answer. I wanted to feel excitement, nervousness, and to get to meet this person who seemed almost more than human.

We got her on board by spring 2016, then into the studio in August 2016. It was more about her presence, learning from her attitude and approach, rather than asking her if we should change the melody to a chorus or whatever. The best rock music is all about feel and style, not technical prowess. We had a rock-solid engineer on board, so Lydia was there to go over lyrics, tell us stories, show us her fucked-up videos, go out with at night, flick a cigarette down Sean's shirt—an accident, allegedly—just let us bathe in her presence, whip us around a bit. She gave Brad [Fry] perhaps the most painful back massage of his life; I took her to a goth night and felt like I was the coolest

---

* Pissed Jeans are an American punk-rock band active since 2004 and currently consisting of Bradley Fry, Randy Huth, Matt Korvette, and Sean McGuinness. They have released five albums, of which four are on Sub Pop, including *Why Love Now* (2017), produced by Lydia.

dude on Earth, bringing the person who created the damn aesthetic; asking her about anyone from Ministry to The Ramones to The Geto Boys to Guns N' Roses and getting some great story or anecdote out of her.

It probably wasn't a traditional producer/band relationship, but that's not what we were looking for anyway. She was also a fantastic encourager—her feedback was hugely helpful in having us feel confident. I'm not sure I've met anyone else whose presence utterly fills up a room, even if we're just sitting around eating Indian takeout. She was involved and sharp and had a great entourage of witches around her. With a lot of these punk legends, they can kind of be idiots, or vegetables, or stuck in the past, or clueless, but she was the opposite of all that. Which was a relief! I was even prepared for her to only be looking to cash our cheque, but that wasn't the case at all. Really, best-case scenario here.

THOMAS SAYER ELLIS It's hard to be a poet, specifically a black poet, and not have the traditions within the community clash and mix and remix at some point in one's life. You're always hearing and participating in some form of poetry, especially if you grew up in the church and were drawn to the poetic dictions of the Spirituals. I co-founded a writers' group in Boston called the Dark Room Collective, and during one of our seasons we paid tribute to Bob Kaufman, which sent me digging into aspects of his life and work, and I carried around in my body many of his poems, especially 'Would You Wear My Eyes'. At the Jack Kerouac School Of Disembodied Poetics in Naropa, it seemed the right thing to do, given that the Kaufman legacy carries with it the sticky shadow of him having been overlooked quite a bit by Beat lovers, Beat students, Beat teachers, and Beat fame.*

---

* Kaufman was an American poet, surrealist and jazz performer. Kaufman rarely wrote down his poems, focusing instead on memorising them and presenting them live. He died in 1986 of emphysema and cirrhosis, aged sixty. The Jack Kerouac School Of Disembodied Poetics is a part of Naropa University in Boulder, Colorado, founded by Allen Ginsberg and Anne Waldman. Each year the school invites a wide range of guest faculty to take part in the summer writing programme of workshops, lectures, reading, and performance. The intention is to expand the creative potential of the learning environment for students and to spark writing and creativity.

Going in, we simply planned to make one song, but real life, real passion, heartache, and all of that stepped in. There's a tradition at Naropa of asking visiting poets to record a poem, so I recorded 'Vernacular Owl', my anti-elegy for Amiri Baraka the previous year. When I was invited back, I knew what to expect, and I planned a tiny bit. The idea was to see how many members of Heroes Are Gang Leaders we could get there for the week, to take advantage of the opportunity to record.* Margaret Morris, James Brandon Lewis, Luke Stewart, and myself, but we did add Devin Brahja Waldman on drums for a few tracks; then Heru Shabaka-ra on trumpet and Randall Horton on vocals, once we got back to New York. Those contributions, along with Thurston Moore and Lydia, provided an extra layer of texture. It actually sounded like we knew what we were doing, when, in fact, it was all improvised, talked on the spot, and done, one take per song.

While passing Lydia on the hotel balcony, her door open or her sitting on a chair, chatting with her in the parking lot, unique quick responses in the key of 'rasp', at the dinner table at the Hotel Boulderado, nearly the Venus Fly Trap of attention: all of these moments hipped me to the way Lydia performed and unperformed. In the studio she listened to me, while not listening to me, then poured her version of 'Mother Everything' onto the song. I hoped for a burst, even for anger, but had no idea what we'd get. I sat with Lydia, briefed her on the content of 'Would You Wear My Eyes', she had a drink or two, then owned it. The song took its own direction in the studio, becoming something of a matrimony of the Kaufman text and the difficult times Margaret and I were experiencing as a couple. I just thought I was losing my girlfriend, why not lay it all on the line? I told Margaret the same: just put life, the truth, on the record.

LYDIA LUNCH Umar Bin Hassan, The Last Poets. I had a concept called No Wave Out, so I'm going to meet him, and what the hell am I supposed to say to a sixty five-year-old black man living out in Baltimore, about who

---

* Heroes Are Gang Leaders are a socially active avant-garde art collective combining jazz, poetry, spoken word, and hip-hop to celebrate black culture.

and what I am? God knows what he vetted, because there's nothing in my career that would appeal to him on the level I need to appeal to him, whereas everything he's done has appealed to me. Somebody who came out of a ghetto uprising? OK! As somebody that spoken word was very important to, that rebellion and protest were important to, what is he going to see? How is he going to relate to this? The only way was, having dinner, and through humour, I got him to see who I was. Where we truly relate is experiential human survivalist protest and mandatory expulsion of the evils we see into some kind of poetry. My *career*, quote-unquote, has led up to No Wave Out, because it combines all of it: the word, which is first and foremost most important; the sense of protest; that true humour; the musical collaboration with improvisational musicians; out music—this is where this has all been leading up to, and, through my humanity, that's where we came together. Highlight of my life.*

DAVID LACKNER Having such a freedom, taking her trauma and turning it back on the world, there's a freedom she exuberates. She's a spokesperson for these feelings, and her music resonated with me at a specific point in my life—they're universal feelings that will never become un-relevant. She's a bit of a martyr for staying there and keeping that energy going—it's impressive she can maintain it and keep creating from this place that is helpful for a lot of people.

EXENE CERVENKA Lydia has worked really hard, and I admire her a lot. She's like me—she just came up saying, *Sure, I'm a kid, and I have this much talent and this much nerve.* For me, it was driven by fear, but she was always more confident: and I'm just going to do this, and I'm going to make it happen for me the way I want it to be. What was driving me at the time is that all of this was really fun: it was fun to go to New York, it was fun for people to come to California, doing different projects, doing spoken

---

* No Wave Out is a collaboration between Lydia Lunch, Weasel Walter, Tim Dahl, and Umar Bin Hassan of The Last Poets. They recorded together in mid-2015, and have performed live several times in recent years.

word—then, eventually, you realise you're in so deep you better make the most of it, because this is your life and you're not getting out of it. People don't realise how self-motivated you need to be; they don't know how much work you have to do. Lydia showed up in New York with just her body and her brain—that's all she had—and she made a career out of it. Her skill was, *This is who I am—I'm going to sell me.*

RICHARD METZGER Look at somebody like Lydia or Kembra Pfahler: nobody has come up out of the next generation or the one after that, to knock them off their throne—it hasn't happened. You'd figure that this generation would have another Lydia, but today's young people are medicated on Prozac, so they're not self-medicating with acid or coke. Think about the kinds of people who were hanging out at CBGB's and places like that— that's why that generation was so extreme. If you're taking drugs that are exacerbating your insanity then you might end up forming a band like The Cramps. Today, a budding Lux Interior or baby Nick Cave, they're so heavily medicated on psych drugs by the time they're teenagers that they aren't capable of creating anything interesting, original, or extreme. Had Prozac been marketed in the 70s, would punk have happened?

TOM GARRETSON In this business, it's dependent on the age groups. My generation is busy sitting at home in front of the TV, drinking beer every night—that's the sad reality of the punk generation, that, for the most part, they turned out to be their parents. The original punk generation is just as pathetic as the hippie generation became. But Lydia was never punk. From the start, her work went way beyond that. What Lydia has done is to welcome each successive new generation to discover her work. Teenage Jesus, when she did the revival shows, a brand-new audience of eighteen, nineteen, twenty-year-olds started appearing at those shows, and they sold out every gig. For the most part, you didn't find fifty-year-olds there—the people who liked early Lydia Lunch. They're at home with the kids and a spouse they hate, paying off the mortgage, drinking away their woes and voting Republican.

ABOVE Medusa's Bed: Lydia Lunch, Mia Zabelka, Zahra Mani (photo by David Visnjic).
LEFT Outlasting the boys: Weasel Walter, Lydia, and Tim Dahl on tour (photo by Bob Bert, Retrovirus drummer extraordinaire).

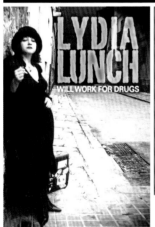

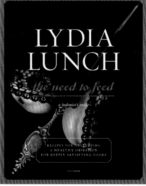

OPPOSITE PAGE Lydia manifesting inside the audiovisual artwork of Elise Passavant (all photos by Elise Passavant).

ABOVE Lydia and François R. Cambuzat at the Putan Club (photo by Daniel Margreth). **LEFT** Lydia's books *Will Work For Drugs* (Akashic Books, 2009) and *The Need To Feed: A Hedonist's Guide* (Universe Publishing, 2012).

ABOVE Retrovirus killing it (photo by Kathleen Fox); Cypress Grove and Lydia (photo by Beatrice Ciuca). **RIGHT** Lydia in the spotlight (photo by Tom Garretson).

OPPOSITE PAGE, FROM TOP Ian White, James Johnston, Lydia Lunch: Big Sexy Noise (photo by Tom Garretson); *A Fistful Of Desert Blues* (RustBlade, 2014); Lydia with Pissed Jeans' Matt Korvette (photo by Matt Korvette); 'Hand Alley' (photo by Jasmine Hirst).

OPPOSITE PAGE, FROM TOP *My Lover The Killer* at Deutsche Oper, Berlin, February 2018 (photo by Eike Walkenhorst); Medusa's Bed making live magic (photo by Udo Siegfriedt); testifying at PopKultur Berlin, 2018 (photo by Udo Siegfriedt); playing Suicide songs with Marc Hurtado, 2019 (photo by Sébastien Greppo); in cheery defiance with Gianna Greco (photo by Gianna Greco).

ABOVE Another view of *My Lover The Killer* in Berlin (photo by Udo Siegfriedt).
LEFT Family In Mourning (photo by Jasmine Hirst).

RIGHT The poster for Beth B's film *Lydia Lunch: The War Is Never Over* (photo by Annie Sprinkle); Lydia's *So Real It Hurts* (Seven Stories Press, 2019).
BELOW Beth B and Lydia Lunch (photo by Curt Hoppe).

CHAPTER TWENTY-ONE

BIG SEXY NOISE

BARRING A BRIEF 2003 TOUR UNDER THE NAME THE WILLING VICTIM, BIG SEXY NOISE IS LYDIA'S FIRST ROCK BAND SINCE SHOTGUN WEDDING—AND HER LONGEST-ENDURING BAND PROJECT TO DATE.

LYDIA LUNCH Some of my records have to be recorded live because that fervour only happens in a live situation. The Big Sexy Noise record, I wanted to title it *Courtney Love, Four Years, Two Million Dollars—Lydia Lunch, Two Days, Four Hundred Pounds—You Judge.*

JAMES JOHNSTON I'd released a record, *Dora Suarez*, of the crime writer Derek Raymond. Terry Edwards and I did the music. Terry wound up doing a million different things with Lydia, so I ended up joining up with her as well. Sitting in vans together, getting to know one another, it was all pretty natural that we would become friends, and, as we enjoyed it, we kept touring. In 2007, we did an instrumental for the Gallon Drunk album *The Rotten Mile*, and we asked Lydia to add lyrics and vocal for a B-side version of a track for a single. That was the first real thing together. Then the four of us went into a small studio and did an EP, super-stripped down and raw, really fun to play, fun to do. It was really rejuvenating for all of us. It had been a lot of fun touring together, so it seemed like a great idea to record together. Pretty soon after that, we had the whole of the first album done too, and we were touring a lot—it was really fast.

TERRY EDWARDS Big Sexy Noise was completely Ian's idea. He just suggested to her she should have a proper rock band—enough of the backing tracks stuff and improvising, she should just do it. James started playing more with effects pedals and making these octave-based noises, rather than having a bass player in the band. It was always a four-piece band, very much guitar-and-drums-led. Four people against the world, as a band should be.

IAN WHITE Big Sexy Noise came about because we were hanging out with each other, and I asked Lydia, 'Don't you feel like doing a heavy rock band?' And she said, 'Why not? Let's go!' I'd fancied stripping everything back, so with James being such a fantastic guitarist I thought we should go for it. It was a throwaway idea but she went for it.

TERRY EDWARDS We just rehearsed some ideas, and we decided just to move straight up into the recording studio the next day, because it sounded so good and we wanted to record them in that state. That EP catches the spirit of the band: a few ideas from James and Lydia, then Lydia's song 'Gospel Singer' from Harry Crews, and 'Kill Your Sons', the Lou Reed cover. It had a *reliving your teenage band* feel to it, and Lydia was clearly enjoying having a band around her.

JAMES JOHNSTON We went into rehearsal almost immediately and started trying ideas out. Guitar going through a bass amp and a guitar amp sounded great. We demoed a load of things—me and Ian—then sent them to her. She recorded over them; it was so straightforward, and everything she did sounded really good. It was a chance for her to do something different lyrically; it gave us a chance to get out on the road and to do a different type of music, something much simpler; it seemed like such a good idea. As soon as we tried it out, it worked. A lot of the lyrics are really funny and so spirited.

IAN WHITE James started turning out all these fantastic riffs that would provoke her to create all these amazing lyrics. They're poignant, they're well observed; sometimes Lydia is like a stand-up comedian and other times she's a philosopher.

LYDIA LUNCH My recent performance on Martin Luther King Day, people were actually laughing. I'm like, *Exactly! I never said you couldn't laugh!* Just because I don't wait for the punch line, because every line has a punch line, I never said you couldn't laugh. I'm constantly laughing. I'm the funniest person I know—funny as fuck, matter of fact. The only reason I'm not a comedian is the timing is very different. I study comedians—I mean, most of them suck, but I do have a few favourites: Dennis Leary, Chris Rock, Bill Hicks, George Carlin, Lenny Bruce. The timing is very different, and they have to allow a release of laughter. When I do spoken word, there is no relief. If I just changed my timing, I'd be very fucking funny.

TIM DAHL I love Lydia's vivacious, loud, aggressive side. It doesn't bother me that a woman is like this at all. In fact, I wish more women were like that. For me, it's witnessing other people's reactions to it, because I can't believe that other people are still blindsided by such a character. One of my best friends is from the Deep South—they're funny together, and he was kind of religious growing up. But anyhow, there was one night where they're hanging out, and she said, 'Dave, if you put your fingers in my vagina, you'd swear I was a virgin.' And he said, 'Well, that's not very ladylike, Lydia.' And that collision, for me, was hilarious. I love them both.

CARLO MCCORMICK She has the same, really assertive, cruel kind of tools as a comedian who's been working the stand-up circuit forever. She's got ways of slaying you that belong more to stand-up comedy than they do to rock'n'roll stage banter or art performances.

TIM DAHL Lydia is a maximalist. Even with the extreme intensity, the expression, the insight, the intellect, there's always an overtone of humour in it as well. Sometimes it's direct—only humour—but humour is in a lot of it. Her humour, it's fast. It's witty. Almost Don Rickles's one-liners. Just sharp, clever, funny, and mean. I've talked to Lydia about this all the time: the best humour is mean-spirited humour, because mean-spirited humour isn't really mean. It's addressing subjects and making observations about the things that people feel very uncomfortable about, and let's put a spotlight on it. And you know what? It's OK. We can laugh. Why not laugh? We all know the horrors, let's also laugh at it. That's a great, very healthy way of filtering this planet. When I was a kid, I remember my dad got a phone call from a teacher: 'Always laughing too much.' And my Dad pauses, he goes, 'What's wrong with laughing?' It's very important. And she does.

IAN WHITE She seemed alive again, being in a rock band for the first time in so many years. You really saw the love of life, the comedy, all of it came out of her. We knew this place called Fortress Studios, a real shithole, but it was brilliant, and everyone there was one hundred percent into music. Lydia would come over and sleep on somebody's floor; we'd get into the studio, work through the songs, and more or less write them as they were being recorded. It was so quick, and we were all howling with laughter—it was a joy!

JAMES JOHNSTON A couple of years later, we had the second album, which we maybe spent too long on, if I'm being honest. After that, there was a version with a fantastic live record, recorded in Italy as the three-piece. That came out because the original label went bust and disappeared along with a chunk of our money—that was typical of our luck.

IAN WHITE An unfortunate experience. This guy in France vanished with all the money—and the masters—so we never saw a penny. The live record, a tiny venue, a brilliant night; the guy running it had a reel-to-reel downstairs and gave us a copy, and he'd gotten the balance just right. We never had any record company money—it was all paid for by us. We got that record pressed up ourselves, and we were selling loads on tour. It emphasised that we were fed up of tinpot record labels, and no one was going to pay us to do it, so we just focused on having a record pressed to go on tour, and we would just try to tour endlessly.

ELISE PASSAVANT There was this really catchy tune by Big Sexy Noise. It's a grey, dull, Parisian afternoon with my friend So Noel. We decided, totally out of the blue, to shoot a video for the song we both loved: 'Your Love

Don't Pay My Rent'. Half a day of shooting, a couple of days editing—done! Then we emailed Mademoiselle Lunch. Twenty minutes later, So and I were going out, there's a phone call from a weird number. I remember joking, 'It's gotta be Lydia Lunch calling to thank us.' Ha! Well, it was Lydia calling to thank us, that's how fast the woman is. I barely caught more than a few words: 'Fucking ... awesome ... great ... fucking genius.'

I suggested we would do another one with her in the near future, and she was back in Paris a few weeks later, so I ended up in her hotel room. Lydia had the idea of a 'book trailer' for *Will Work For Drugs*. Visually, everything was inspiring that day. The wallpaper, the young 'bunny boy' she invited for the occasion, the music playing in the background. We shot for an hour or so. I had no idea what I was going to do with the footage. A couple days later, Lydia sent me a soundtrack and a voiceover. It all clicked. The book trailer was ready in less than a day. Again, a few weeks later, I was invited to join Lydia, the excuse being to make another video for Big Sexy Noise's song 'Ballin' The Jack'.

Of course, when it comes to Lydia, work often rhymes with leisure. I still have this vision of her welcoming me at the door: a combination of sexiness, nonchalance, grace, and genuine sweetness. All sorts of delicacies on the table. Stories. Nectars. Laughter and, again, something organic, simple, easy. It's a witchcraft thing, I'd say. I remember leaving after those few days, me in the taxi and her a few feet back on the curb, yelling at me with her warrior-rasp of a voice, 'I fucking love you!' Where I come from, we don't say those words so easily. I was touched.

JAMES JOHNSTON I loved all of it. The total abandon and freedom, everything second nature, getting lost in this incredibly brilliant noise and hilarious interjections from Lydia between all the songs. Then we kick off again into this glorious sound, everything locked in and so simple. Almost all of it was rhythm guitar, then some sections of free guitar noise, which I love.

IAN WHITE When it was the four of us, with Terry, there was a certain dynamic creeping in that none of us were comfortable with. There were backing vocals, more instrumentation—it was straying away from what we were thinking. So Terry went, then we worked just as a trio—that was a major change.

TERRY EDWARDS I was astonished, though, that they did a show in New York without telling me—it felt a bit like they were frightened to tell me they just wanted to do it as a three-piece. I'm still surprised by it, but they're shy people offstage.

IAN WHITE We'd be sitting in bars, talking to truckers, whalers from Iceland, she'd be laughing, it just became even more of a party, and we really looked out for each other. For a lot of people, the conditions might not be comfortable because it wasn't glamorous, but Lydia and I never cared if we were sleeping in a cupboard under the sink in someone's kitchen. You'd think she might be a diva, but she's not; we've shared shit rooms before, and she's having a great laugh. We were feeding off each other, and, as we got more relaxed, we'd start trying stuff; we'd signal to each other that we wanted to go off something, or Lydia would start saying something we hadn't heard before within the structure of an existing song. It really progressed; we felt we could do anything, and we weren't bound by anything.

JAMES JOHNSTON Lydia is nonstop; her mindset and attitude are unique. It's exhilarating being around that. She's so fucking good at what she does, and we all knew each other so well by then, and liked being around each other, that we knew from the start we wanted to make it a proper band together. If you get on with people and you don't have to compromise how you are or how you play—everyone has freedom, space, so they can express themselves—it makes it a very creative environment. That's the only point of something like Big Sexy Noise.

IAN WHITE Lydia is so active. She never stops; she's sort of my hero on that score. I've never met anyone more committed to the cause than her. I was terrified of her for a while, but she always put me under her wing—I was quieter than her, so maybe that's why it worked. We never accept what is given, neither of us, and performing music is the total reason for existing—that's how we both feel. We shared so many passions, and we both have spent so long going away from mainstream society that we could talk about anything.

Certainly I—and Lydia too—didn't want Big Sexy Noise to end. But James was very honest that he was losing the desire to be on tour, and Lydia and I respected that.* I still hope it might come back. James does things I've never seen, things I've never heard, when he performs! It was a little heartbreaking when he explained we needed to stop. Even just on a prosaic level, we split all the fees three-ways, and it was still her name they were coming to see, but the ethos of the band was very specific—we even did all the interviews together. Dealing with promoters, dealing with fans, it was always the three of us together, and she did a good job of letting people know that it was her, me, and James. I really respected her for doing that.

---

* Big Sexy Noise played their final show on June 22, 2019, in Norway.

CHAPTER TWENTY-TWO

NEMESISTERS: MEDUSA'S BED AND SISTER ASSASSIN

AFTER AN INITIAL COLLABORATION WITH MIA ZABELKA IN 2009–13, LYDIA FORMS MEDUSA'S BED WITH ZABELKA AND ZAHRA MANI. AROUND THE SAME TIME, SHE PERFORMS IN SISTER ASSASSIN WITH JESSIE EVANS AND BEATRICE ANTOLINI.

CATHI UNSWORTH As I got to know Lydia better, she taught me something of the world, because she's been to places that I'm lucky enough not to have. She's always been very self-aware and very good at putting things across in ways that can make you understand very big concepts—she can put them into a nutshell. Things I've learnt from being in her company, from her music and her writing, some of the ideas come over in my novels. She's definitely had an impact on how I write and how I present female characters: the woman who gets to places she shouldn't go and pokes her nose in and sees things she shouldn't see, and gets there through her own wit and ingenuity—that's the power of Lydia. Lydia feels like my brilliant older sister.

EXENE CERVENKA Lydia is very encouraging of people. I've met a few people she met when they were really young—people with really dark history—and it's amazing how many people credit her with keeping them alive and keeping them going. I didn't really have anyone, except my sister, that I looked up to, and I don't think Lydia did, either, but I guess part of what she is and what I am is someone for young people to discover and relate to. It's about surviving a crappy childhood, and she's a real light in her darkness to a lot of people in their darkness—it's a big part of her ongoing legacy and life story. She's there for people: strangers and friends alike.

LYDIA LUNCH There's a massive hole left out through history, from the female point of view. Women, we used to be warriors. How have we devolved from Medusa to Madonna? From Kali to Courtney Love? From Durga to Uma Thurman? I don't get it. We need to get back to the goddess.

ZAHRA MANI In 2009, in Vienna, Lydia was performing at a festival called Phonofemme. I curated a Balkan evening there with a film by Marina Abramović, all sorts of artists; Pauline Oliveros curated an American evening; and Lydia was actually in the Austrian evening.* She did a piece that was basically solo spoken word, but she also played with Mia Zabelka and Christina Nemec.† That's where we each heard each other live for the first time—and the pleasure was mutual. Lydia and I are very different musically, and generationally too—I was born in '78—but there's a basic kind of engagement with sound. We share a sense of humour—that helps— we got on immediately. Another thing that definitely connects me with Lydia is improvisation as a principle, in music, in life, in a way of doing things. I find that when we're together, whether it's onstage or talking about what to eat or what to do next, most of what we say is, 'Why not?'

MIA ZABELKA Zahra and I have been working together for a very long time, so we had already developed a musical language together. When we

---

* Abramović is a major figure in extreme performance art active since the early 70s. Her work includes the *Rhythm* series that took place across 1973–74, in which she exploded aspects of pain, audience complicity, and her own human limitations. Oliveros was a contemporary composer best known for the concepts of 'deep listening' and 'sonic awareness'.
† Nemec collaborated with Lydia and Mia Zabelka on the performances *The Gun Is Still Loaded* (2009) and *Battle Scars* (2010). She runs the queer and feminist-focused music label comfortzone and was the 2019 winner of the City Of Vienna Prize For Music.

invited Lydia Lunch for Phonofemme, she entered as Zahra and I were soundchecking. Lydia came into the space and said, 'Ohhh … I like that sound.' It was kind of a noisy, dark, ambient-industrial sound. And this was the start of a wonderful collaboration and friendship.

ZAHRA MANI The idea of Medusa's Bed came about quite organically. The idea was to basically do this experimental spoken-word thing with three women in a way that hadn't been done before—something new—with Mia's crazy violin, with Lydia's dark vocals, and with my sounds. So what happened is that we started exchanging music and vocals and lyrics, and kind of sending them back and forth.

LYDIA LUNCH I refuse to play guitar in America, for the most part—I just don't endorse the playing of my guitar in America. It's something that—especially if it's a three-piece female improv, which is a very unusual setup—it's best kept to Eastern Europe. They have always understood weird jazz, though this isn't jazz—it isn't even definable by a genre, because Mia's classically trained, and Zahra has incredible musical knowledge as well.

MIA ZABELKA Medusa's Bed is a kind of radio play, a live radio play, with words, ambient sounds, free improvisation, and the great thing about Medusa's Bed is it's really created in the moment—it can't be repeated, no performance can be repeated, it's always different. It's always a challenge, of course, because the situation is always different, the space is different, the venue is different; we are in different moods, and also the audience is different, the technical environment is different—it all influences our playing and our performance, so we can create something very unique at each performance.

ZAHRA MANI We improvise. The three of us meet before we go onstage: sometimes it's the same day, sometimes it's the day before; we don't plan anything we do. We have this basic stock of sound and text, but that always changes, and Lydia sometimes uses new lyrics; a couple of times, we've covered pieces like Suicide's 'Harlem' or Tom Petty's 'Breakdown', which is more a reference to the original than a cover, because it's a kind of tribute that we do something so completely different with. We all work very differently in our approach to music and instruments: Mia improvises on her electric violin, uses a lot of analogue effects, and also plays free improvisation on the classical acoustic violin; I work in layers of complex sound and tiny short fragments that I build up, I make crazy sounds with field recordings, with the sounds of nature, and I deconstruct the bass guitar; and Lydia does what she does, something that I don't know anyone else is doing with spoken word and performance, in terms of her power and in her idiomatic way of being onstage.

LYDIA LUNCH It's really like three different ships battling it out to find the same dock, kind of a tag team, not a battle. It's just based on instinct about what's going to build. Also, we're the ones that are always laughing, which is an outrage for improvisational music, because usually it's a bunch of straight white guys, or, as I call it, 'the crack dick syndrome of music' that just sounds like masturbatory frustration played usually by white guys. This is the antithesis of that.

ZAHRA MANI We played this crazy gig in a thunderstorm at Maria's Kleines Haus in Austria. It was sunny and hot, and then this huge bank of clouds rolled in, and the lightning was getting closer and closer—and we just found it hysterically funny. We were sitting there onstage, listening to the thunder joining our music, and we started laughing with each other onstage, and that was a magical moment, and that's something that we've kept. One of the main things in our communication onstage is the shared pleasure, or humour, or irony, in our exchange with each other. Maybe it's a female thing, in the sense of being together and not everyone just doing their thing, and at the same time it makes the whole process alive and dynamic.

MIA ZABELKA It's very important to interact with each other so we look at each other. We also have fun onstage—this is a very important factor, that we really enjoy improvising with each other, playing with each other, communicating with each other. Improvisation is communication onstage with each other, but also with the audience. So, we also involve the audience, and this is also really fascinating in Lydia Lunch's art world—how she communicates with the audience. The audience is always part of the whole thing.

*

JESSIE EVANS I was nineteen, I moved to San Francisco, and put an ad in the paper saying I was a saxophonist who loved X-Ray Spex and was looking for people to play music with. I started playing bass and sax in some different projects, like Leper Sex Killer On The Loose and The Knives and Subtonix, and later formed The Vanishing. Around that time, I was introduced to 8 Eyed Spy and Teenage Jesus, as well as *Queen Of Siam*. At the time, I wasn't a singer yet, but it wasn't long before I pushed the singer of my group off the stage during a coffee-shop gig on college campus, where I got drunk and peed in the garden—that was the beginning of my music career ...

Later, I was living in Berlin, touring Europe with my solo project. The first time I met Lydia was in May 2008, when we shared the stage at Ladyfest in Madrid, at the Nasti Club. I'll never forget it: she sat next to the sound guy during our soundcheck, just grilling him over how he could improve our sound—it was so sweet and supportive. She was very nice to me, like a big sister—we hit it off immediately.

BEATRICE ANTOLINI By the time I was about eighteen, nineteen years old, I felt I'd met Lydia through her various works, her records, and her many lives. She is a truly historic figure in music. She passes through Italy quite often, and I had the opportunity to admire her at a concert at the Locomotiv Club in Bologna around 2008. I was in the very front row of the audience, and she was onstage and staring at me so intensely. To my surprise, she then reached out and took the cigarette I was smoking from my hands and smoked it onstage while she sang. I was amazed. What a bomb! I was delighted both with the concert and with the gesture.

CARLA BOZULICH When I watch Lydia, I get right in the front, as close as I can— sometimes a foot away. She just focuses on the people that she can see, and it could be love, it could be power, but we're in it, and she's taking the power from the room, seizing it like, *This is mine!* The fact that she can lock onto something and be like, *You are a part of this, and I'm going to fuck with you or I'm going to fuck you*—whatever it is, that's one of the huge reasons I love Lydia. If you're going to try and experience Lydia Lunch, the best thing you can do is to get your body as close to hers as possible: that's no. 1. Secondly, her stuff is pushing things to the boundary, and it cuts a swath in the audience. If you're willing to take it in and take that fucking knife and cut yourself open and see what's in there, she's perfect for you. And if you're scared of that, or you need to be way cooler than that, or whatever your problem is, then get the fuck out.

BEATRICE ANTOLINI After that show, I made Lydia's acquaintance in rather a bizarre way. I was told that there was no percussionist for a gig Lydia would be performing in Cagliari. Her people were in contact with my booking agency, who promptly called me and asked if I could go. It was such a powerful moment, strong emotions within me, but I'm adventurous, I'm curious, so I said yes! Lydia Lunch was going to perform with me? I was going to perform with Lydia Lunch? I was concerned that, maybe, it wouldn't work, that I'd be an ugly figure onstage …

I found myself in a rehearsal room on the beachfront of Cagliari, there were pink flamingos outside, and this magical atmosphere that day—then Lydia arrived, and, to me, was just so surreally beautiful. My first impression of her was that she was so unlike the people I was used to in music. She was so focused, this air of natural brilliance, so awake and alive—it's an impression I now know to be absolutely true. For the show, I only had to play in three or four pieces, but after a first test she declared, in a firm voice, 'You're going to play the whole concert.'

JESSIE EVANS Sister Assassin came about because Lydia had those shows booked and invited me to join her on sax. I believe the promoter from one of the gigs presented Beatrice to her, so when we got there we met her and just went into a rehearsal together and worked it out. I don't think Lydia really had any idea she was going to play with Beatrice, but it was actually a pleasant surprise, as she's not only a very talented multi-instrumentalist but she's drop-dead gorgeous and a very nice girl.

BEATRICE ANTOLINI One thing to point out is that we didn't improvise—we had genuine structures we learned and worked to, and each song was treated very seriously in that regard. I was playing acoustic instruments, like timpani and other percussion, over an electronic part. I remember feeling, when I heard the initial songs, that we could do so much to make them interesting in a live setting, which is, I feel, the task of any musician—to be interesting.

JESSIE EVANS As we didn't have much rehearsal, and I had come directly from another tour with little time to learn the material, I'd have to say it was probably almost one hundred percent improvised. It was really fun to share the stage with those girls. Just being in a girl group was incredibly refreshing, and it somehow always seems unexpected for the audience.

BEATRICE ANTOLINI The name, Sister Assassin, came about after the show in Cagliari. The promoters asked about playing other dates, so Lydia decided we needed a name for the project—she chose it. We performed five times together as a trio, and each one was extremely powerful. I played the drums standing up—Lydia wanted me to—and I was so focused I got blisters on my hands but didn't give a damn, barely noticed. I sang the choir parts with Lydia—a true honour—and I remember I had a djembe and various other percussion equipment to hand. Jessie Evans played the tenor sax, and she was great. She's a musician I respect a lot because, like me, she creates and produces her own records. She's a real artist, not just some session musician—true creativity as it should be.

Part of the setlist was cover songs that Lydia interpreted as if they were her own. She weaved an atmosphere that, if it was a colour, I'd say it was crimson red. The audiences were in ecstasy every night because each concert became this magical and theatrical act, all this energy pouring through Lydia's clear, powerful, and beautiful eyes. People left our concerts, and, instead of feeling like they'd been at a regular theatre, they felt catharsis, a purification—as if they'd been attending and participating in a spiritual ritual.

JESSIE EVANS What inspires me most about Lydia is that she continues to explore and make new music with a vast array of musicians, always pushing new styles and working on new projects. She said that she never wanted fame, and I find that inspiring, too, as it goes so against what we're trained to want in life. Attention is one thing, and it's interesting to hear someone say that it doesn't appeal to them. It's a very antisocial thing to say, but it's sincere in her case. She understands the importance of speaking to the few people who get it. And that she's literally never gonna stop what she does.

*

BETH B Nowadays, women being confrontationists, it's become part of our culture. When Lydia was doing that in in the late 70s, early 80s, that was forbidden. Especially for women. And to talk about things that she was talking about—especially for her, and the things she was talking about—she was going into material that good girls didn't do. But she was the bad girl.

THURSTON MOORE What was so amazing about that community of Teenage Jesus and The Contortions, the no-wave scene, was that there was this eradication of the hierarchy of gender. It wasn't female power; it wasn't male power. It was just like that dialogue between men and women had equal power, and it was a given.

RON ATHEY Lydia is pretty traditional. She's a fem top—you know she's not gender nonconforming. I don't think she's that complicated. She's an aggressive female. And she's an icon. I mean, I remember this period well. OK everyone has a stupid orange Mohawk and these clothes; now that we're getting in our thirties, how do you look? There were some people that were role models and she was one of them. She always went to the next thing: being kind of gothy, to being kind of like white-trash housedress with messier hair, being kind of lounge lizard. She went through a lot of slick looks at different times when I don't think anyone else was making the move to evolve.

CHRISTINA BIRRER The sexuality and feminism, for me it was interesting because the themes were quite extraordinary, and I understood there was this other basis underneath it. She's always been talking about violence, pain, and sexuality in her texts. As you see the story continuing to unfold now, thirty years on, you start to understand why it was there: this undercurrent and inherent flawedness in the patriarchal hegemony that she was able to put into words.

THURSTON MOORE I never got the sense of Lydia's work being explicitly about female experience. And she transcended it so early on—she had such an idea of what the power of sex was at such an early age, and she took it upon herself to explore it in the most explicit and charged way. And that was apparent to everybody who crossed paths with her, whether you were friends or enemies with her. That was something you knew she so *owned*. A lot of people, be it male or female, who sort of have that as part of their personality, you realise that it's informed by something that is precipitous, that is: it could be dangerous. For Lydia, it never really felt like that. I felt like she had eradicated and transcended any danger, and she became what she wanted with it, and so there was nothing more dangerous than Lydia Lunch at that point.

LYDIA LUNCH I have a cock-rock band, I have a hard-rock band, I have a blues-rock band—that pretty much means I work with men in those vehicles. It just doesn't matter to me. I see people as individuals—I don't care what's between their legs unless I want to get there.

RICHARD KERN If there was something Lydia didn't like, she would get right in the face of that person and just lay into them. People can use that as a reason to dismiss her, but her doing it all these years, you do it here—one person's affected. You do it here—one person's affected. All those people add up over time, and a lot of those people go on to do their version of the same thing. Her male fans, they all just like worship her—*Oh, master!*—that kind of shit. But the women fans look at her for what she's done, for standing up to people and saying what she thinks all the time. That's very different! And people who aren't heterosexual, they've also championed her for a long time, because she doesn't give a fuck about any gender stuff either. She could care less, you know? The crazier the better, for her. Lydia was doing this stuff way before anybody was thinking this stuff. Back then, I would be in a room, and they were addressing me, and Lydia's like, 'What're you talking to him for? Talk to me! I'm in charge here.' And she was. Me and all the guys that work with her, you ask any of them, we're just following her around.

PAUL ZONE It's underrated, to this day, how much of the no-wave scene was gay or bisexual. Lydia had a gay following from the beginning. When you're a woman in the music scene you're always going to attract a gay audience, whether you're Patti Smith or Debbie Harry, who couldn't be more different. Lydia had that toughness that everyone liked—she could kick a guy's ass if she wanted to.

LINK WRECKAGE Lydia's lyrics on *Shotgun Wedding* contain themes that are a long-time presence in her work. If you dig into them, you can see those ongoing concerns, and, of course, Lydia was very much a feminist at a time when people weren't really bandying that word around—she had that power and that strength.

WIKTOR SKOK Lydia expresses everything the average feminist can only dream of. She represents a strong femininity—a person and a persona all her own. She gets by without sloganeering, without trivia—an explosive force. I don't believe she can be seen as a 'feminist artist' because her art, her expression, has a sincerity that is above any tag as limiting as 'female art' or 'male art'. The quality erases these simplifications.

THURSTON MOORE I felt like, in a way, it went beyond any gender politics and her recognition of people's work. It had nothing to do with gender. It was just like the work needs to stand alone, and regardless of who you are, if you're male/female, black/white, she was like, *Your work needs to be what it is*. In that sense, what she was doing in the 70s was creating an environment for artists to come into where you didn't feel an imbalance of gender in the community. When people talk about rock'n'roll as being either a boys' world or a 'boys dressed up as girls' world, that's not what we experienced. We saw change; the rules were changing when we went to New York because the most powerful players were Patti Smith and Debbie Harry. And Lydia, and Lucy Hamilton, and Adele Bertei, and Anya Phillips, and everybody who was on that scene—it wasn't that it was female-centric for any sake of presenting, like, a new power-leader female, it was like a complete eradication of hierarchy in gender there.

KEMBRA PFAHLER Do we ever ask an artist like Henri Matisse or Pablo Picasso, 'Why are you so controlling with how you're doing your work? The hours that you're putting in to the day, the amount of lovers that you're having come into your art studio, the amount of people that you're painting every day?' Lydia Lunch is a great American artist! It's disrespectful to even try to analyse her masculine and her feminine parts: she is showing us, through her work, how to integrate both of those genders. She's an artist, and it takes a lot of time and concentration to do the amount of work that she does. She's always on tour, writing books, making records. Whether or not that's masculine or feminine, I can't answer that succinctly. I wouldn't be so bold as to try to analyse a great artist completely.

MERRILL ALDIGHIERI When we were in Paris, they had a get-together at one of the stores that was featuring her book. One of the people who came was the book translator of *Paradoxia*. I wish I'd filmed this, but I was speaking with him and he was telling me how he was having a hard time deciding whether to use the crudest words in his vocabulary or to make something softer and more poetic for the French audience. That struck me as an interesting dilemma that I would have liked to explore with Lydia and him together.

KEMBRA PFAHLER For female artists, we're so much more inclined to want to dissect their behaviours, their words, who they're sleeping with, if they're acting controlling because they're women—we don't treat men the same way. For me, her work is so much about that, and so rooted in that stuff. And it's always trying to erase old paradigms and old behaviours, and to also hold those people accountable for their behaviours too, like they need to be taken down and out. Her use of clear, strong language around the abuse, around the violators, around the disease—she's relentlessly pointing us in this direction of seeing where the harm is coming from and eradicating it. *We've got to get rid of it, take it down.* That's where violence comes in. That's where a gun comes in. That's where extreme behaviours come in. It has to be taken down, by any means necessary. Obviously. We've seen that the way men have done things isn't working. It takes a complicit individual to show us the way, and someone that's able to embody both male and female principles.

CHAPTER TWENTY-THREE

RETROVIRUS

WITH A BACK CATALOGUE OF SONGS THAT HAVE BARELY BEEN PERFORMED, LYDIA IS PERSUADED TO CREATE THE WILLING VICTIM RETROSPECTIVE, THEN TO REFORM TEENAGE JESUS & THE JERKS. RETROVIRUS IS THE NEXT LOGICAL STEP.

JAMES JOHNSTON There was a fuck-up with visas. Big Sexy Noise was meant to go to the US, then we couldn't, so Lydia put together Retrovirus and toured with them instead while we did Gallon Drunk at the same time and I was on tour with PJ Harvey for most of two years. Lydia wanted to tour as much as possible, so she always had a band that was ready to go.

TOM GARRETSON Years ago, we had a conversation, and I told her she really should go back on the road with some of her old material. Finally, after a couple of years, she put Retrovirus together and started exploring her back catalogue, revisiting the older Lydia songs. I did smugly say, 'I told you!' And it's been very successful in introducing a new generation to her work.

WEASEL WALTER In the 80s, when I was a teenager, I was looking at the 70s New York scene from the outside, through books and records and stuff like that. I became obsessed with the mystic ferment of 70s New York—it seemed idyllic in some regards. Creatively, because New York was such a blank slate at that point, because it was so devastated financially, it seemed to have no rules. And that appealed to me. Also, at the time, there was more press for this stuff. There were people who were championing the movements in the arts scene in New York, and it was all pretty well documented, considering how non-commercial it was.

BOB BERT Even to this day, when Lydia introduces me to people, she always says, 'Bob has seen me perform live more than any other human.' It's probably true, because I saw her very first spoken words—anything she did, I was there. Even though Lydia moved out of town, anytime she came to town I was there. Around 2011, she contacted me and was trying to get me involved in some project that she had in her mind. I couldn't do it at the time because I was taking care of my wife [Linda Wolfe], who was on her deathbed. After Linda died, I contacted Lydia and said, 'Count me in.' Not long after that, in 2012, she contacted me and proposed this idea for Retrovirus. She had Algis Kizys from Swans on board, but we couldn't find the guitar player. We contacted Paul Leary of the Butthole Surfers and all these other great musicians, and no one came through. Finally, Weasel Walter got wind of it, and he's like a no-wave historian. He contacted Lydia.

WEASEL WALTER A lot of Lydia's work is very focused on articulating dark tendencies in the psyche, and there's a certain amount of therapy that's generated from that for the person who does it, as well as possibly the audience who relates to it. And that darkness resonates with a lot of people, it resonated with me as a teenager, it resonates with me now. There are constructive ways of dealing with rage and anger and violence and all these things, and I think it's more constructive to put it into artwork.

LYDIA LUNCH Weasel was into my music at fourteen, when he was still in Rockford, Illinois. He saw a picture of me, found out about Teenage Jesus, and got into no wave. I was having a difficult time trying to conceive of a guitar player who could cover my guitar, Robert Quine's guitar, Rowland S. Howard's guitar, and Weasel was the man for the job—he understood the music and how to bring this new intensity to it.

WEASEL WALTER I had a reputation as an expert on no-wave stuff. In 2012, a friend of mine got a hold of me: 'Hey, Weasel! Lydia Lunch needs a guitar player,' and I said, 'Thanks, I'm on this.' So I wrote her, and I said, 'Hey Lydia, I heard you need a guitar player. I'm the guy.' And she wrote me back, 'Well, there's these other guys I'm thinking about,' and I said, 'Well, check out this video clip,' and I sent her a clip of me playing guitar with my band Cellular Chaos, which is me going absolutely bat-shit nuts on the guitar. And she took a look at it, and she said, 'Yeah, I can work with you. You got the job.'

LYDIA LUNCH I had written an introduction for this book called *Ripped: T-Shirts From The Underground* by Caesar Padilla. That was displayed at an exhibition at the FIDM Fashion Institute of Design And Merchandising in LA. Caesar suggested that I bring a band there, and I thought it was a good time to do something like Retrovirus. After doing so much music for so long, and because of the way that I conceive/collaborate/record/document/go on, a lot of the music had never been done live, or it was done for ten shows in Europe, or for ten, fifteen people. It was time to bring it to a new audience, with a new intensity, because I felt there were not enough women doing brutal, ugly, intense music at that time. Also, many of the musicians I played with are dead, so I wanted to recognise their contributions: George Scott from 8 Eyed Spy; Rowland S. Howard from *Shotgun Wedding*; Robert Quine, who played on *Queen Of Siam*; Gordon Stevenson and Bradly Field from Teenage Jesus …

TIM DAHL I came to New York in '98. I wanted to play music, I knew the musicians I loved, but no one cared. It was kind of like, *Here I am!* But no one's waiting. I had bands, music that I was writing, people I was playing with that I liked, but I couldn't make a living doing it. I met Lydia because Weasel was in the band with her, and he would come over to my house— in fact, he brought her over. It was a hot summer evening, I was grilling, Weasel comes by to eat a cheeseburger, Lydia comes along; I served her drinks and gave her grilled meat and we laughed. A few of my friends were around—it was just sparring all night, all daggers, but all with love. I really think the audition was, *Do I like this person?* We got along famously, so I get a call from Weasel saying, 'Algis Kizys is out. If you'd like this gig, I recommended you, you might get a call from Lydia.' That same day, I got a call: 'Are you free?'

TIM DAHL Retrovirus is playing basically her quote-unquote greatest hits. Pierre Boulez has a great book about music called *Orientations: Collected Writings*—he always says you can never synthesise the past, but if you are going to reference the past, you have to have, at least, a contemporary perspective on it. So we're playing her older songs, but it's a completely contemporary interpretation that's still true to what those songs are. That's why, when you go to a theme park and someone's like, *Here's Dixieland!* ... but New Orleans, 1915—I mean, come on, there's a band playing Dixieland, but that's not a brothel and there are no guns. If someone already took the risk of being an innovator and coming up with an artistic creation, it's easy to play if there's twenty-thirty-forty years of distance and society can kind of recognise what that is. It's easy to play with all the permutations and refine that. With Retrovirus, there was no intention of trying to synthesise the past—there had to be a danger, otherwise it wouldn't have worked.

LYDIA LUNCH The only groups I've ever done more than one recording with are Big Sexy Noise and Retrovirus—and Retrovirus is a revisiting of the various musical schizophrenias I have in an attempt to expose people to these songs they've probably never heard.

WEASEL WALTER My style is a synthesis of all the masters and mistresses that came before me. I mean, in the Retrovirus set, the ghosts of all these great guitar players are sort of whizzing around my head—Bob Quine and those kinds of people. It's my job to amalgamate their voices a little bit and make it my own and do it in a modern way. We don't want to be like a stodgy old county-fair band, we're trying to bring modern energy and a modern perspective. But Bob Quine, for example, he's a legendary guitar player, and it's an honour to hold his chair, in a weird way. I want to do it justice by letting these people speak through me, because a lot of them are dead. Maybe I'm next!

TIM DAHL Lydia gave me a lot of freedom, and still gives me a lot of freedom. I still have to play those songs for Retrovirus; the interpretation has to realise the songs, but, within that margin, Lydia lets me get away with murder. What can you sneak in? Going back to me quitting all those background jazz gigs, going into where I am now and planting the seeds. I wanted to come back and make my own music, but if someone was going to hire me, they were going to hire *me*, not just a bass player playing the song. It had to be on my own terms otherwise I would have gotten out of music altogether. I had to be an artist, as opposed to just a hired gun. Lydia totally allows me to be an artist within her designs. I couldn't ask for something more, in terms of a gig like that.

BOB BERT Lydia's kind of interjecting with little stories, like we do that song '3X3' from *13.13*, and she's like, 'This song is about fucking a guy in a parking lot, and then his wife finds out, and then she fucks with you as she's better than he is.' Every song has a great introduction! When we play 'Mechanical Flattery', from the *Queen Of Siam* album, she's like, 'This is the invention of goth blues: it's not the Nick Cave remake, this if the first goth blues song.'

WEASEL WALTER Lydia Lunch is just such a raving egomaniac that she challenges the rest of Retrovirus to meet her at her high level of insanity. And we have our own insanity, and I think that we are up to the challenge. But there's no overshadowing anything, because Retrovirus are all maniacs, and the whole point is to take things as far as it can go. And we live like we act onstage: we're totally insane. And that's the point, to be real rock'n'roll, where you're kicking ass and taking names, not staring at your feet trying not to get in the way of the bass player. Lydia allows me to do whatever I want. Nominally it's inside her vision, but, basically, I have free rein. I can come out onstage just swinging my balls as hard and mighty as I want, and she's totally like, *Bring it on!* Her ego is so massive that there is no way you can upstage Lydia Lunch. So, it basically takes the whole platform and raises it—the standard is higher, which is why Retrovirus is one of the greatest rock'n'roll bands on Earth, because there's no competition. It's just an onslaught of narcissism and mania and insanity. And that's what we stand for.

Being on tour with Retrovirus, it's like being part of a gang where, mostly, our every whims are taken care of. And you're allowed to have extremely lavish temper tantrums every night in front of hundreds of people at very high volume, and I can't think of anything more Dionysian than that.

It's very *libertine*. We are a gang, and we're threatening. And we enjoy this kind of sadistic activity, and its good fun. It's good work if you can get it.

BOB BERT She's the only spoken-word performer I've seen, like, a million times and it's constantly enlightening, entertaining, truthful. I've never met anyone as together with her every aspect—the way she deals with people, her creativity, the way she's dealt with the trauma of her childhood. We've all met people who've been through abusive childhoods, and everyone's dealt with them in a different way. Some people go through a half as much as Lydia might've gone through and spend their whole life going to therapy, never get over it. Lydia came to New York at the young age that she did and she says she's never going to give up her power to anyone. She never looked back. She refers to every day as her birthday, and she's the one dealing with everyone else's problems, she's like a psychiatrist.

LYDIA LUNCH One story: I was at a Retrovirus rehearsal, and I was very, very, tired, which I rarely am. There was a pole; I go up to the pole. It's not something I did a lot of—I did it very seldom, I was the laziest go-go dancer or stripper you've ever seen, I was so lazy! I would just sit there, spread my legs, get the money. I did it maybe five times in my life, until somebody walked in who knew me from New Jersey, so I'm like, *I'm never doing that again*. So, somehow, Dominika—the wife of Tim Dahl—heard this story and said, 'I love exercise videos! Really ridiculous ones!' And I'm like, 'I don't know how we went from the stripper pole supporting myself in rehearsal because I'm so exhausted, to the story about my floor show, to doing this exercise video, the *Lazy Girl Exercise* video!'* I do not exercise. I like to box—I'm strong and pretty fit. Exercise is boring, unless you have somebody do it for you. That's how that video came about.

---

* Available now on Vimeo, Lydia's four-minute workout routine. The author would like to recommend it wholeheartedly.

CHAPTER TWENTY-FOUR

CYPRESS GROVE

FROM 2009 ONWARD, WORKING WITH GUITARIST CYPRESS GROVE, LYDIA HAS EXPLORED HER LOVE OF THE BLUES— FIRST SEEN IN THE DAYS OF DEVIL DOGS— AND HER APPRECIATION FOR KICKASS COVER VERSIONS.

CYPRESS GROVE The Jeffrey Lee Pierce sessions came about when I discovered an old cassette of Jeffrey and myself rehearsing potential songs for the album we made together—*Ramblin' Jeffrey Lee & Cypress Grove With Willie Love.** It was originally going to be a country album but sort of morphed into a blues album. None of the songs on the cassette made it to the album, and they were mostly unfinished. I was struck by how great they sounded. The recording quality was, of course, terrible, given that they were recorded on a boom box in my bedroom. But I thought if I could get them recorded properly and have friends, colleagues, and admirers of Jeffrey guest on the tracks, then people might be interested to hear them.

'Walkin' Down The Street (Doin' My Thing)', the original track was a weird jam thing, but there was a song there—it sped up, it slowed down, it changed key. It was the end of a session, they were all drunk, Jeffrey was making the lyrics up as he went along. I tamed it, sent Lydia the original and my version, and suggested to her, 'I'm not sure if you can make anything of it, if there's any way you can turn this into a song?' She

---

* Pierce was a singer-songwriter, guitarist, and founder of the band The Gun Club. He died in March 1996, at age thirty-seven, of a brain haemorrhage influenced by drug and alcohol abuse.

tried a few things, then settled on a spoken word over part of it, then made up this rock vocal chorus, and that was it—she really glued it together. Brilliant how she does that—you can give her anything and she can see how to make a song out of it.

LYDIA LUNCH To do the blues correctly, I ended up working with Cypress Grove—that's a continuum from *Shotgun Wedding*. He invited me to be part of a tribute to Jeffrey Lee Pierce, so I recorded two songs and told him, 'This is great, we have to work together.'

CYPRESS GROVE 'St Mark's Place' is just an acoustic guitar and a bass, and I'd noticed Lydia has this wonderfully fragile quality to her voice sometimes, this broken, sensitive, and vulnerable quality that I felt was exactly what that song required. I asked and Lydia just went ahead and did it. When we first started working together, I thought maybe it'd be taking her outside of her comfort zone, but the truth is Lydia has so many voices—her rock voice, that spitting voice she does, then she has a really tender voice with a lovely vibrato. She says she's not a singer, but she is. She'll never win *The X Factor* but she has beautiful qualities to her voice and really knows how and when to use them. It sends shivers up my spine sometimes.

JOE BUDENHOLZER I really like her singing. I was sad she didn't sing more at the time we toured together, but she straight up told me she didn't want to sing anymore at that time. She's an amazing singer—she uses these microtones and atonal elements—but I know she gets criticism, which is so unfair.

WIKTOR SKOK It was always, from the beginning, Lydia's voice that struck me. In the first years of high school, I didn't even understand English. I was touched by her voice, the directness, the purity, Lydia's venomous timbre. I became a follower very early, waited for every sign of activity. When you hear something with the words 'Featuring Lydia Lunch', the result is always the same: it winds up as 'Lydia Lunch And', because her voice is so in-your-face, she's at the front of every appearance.

CYPRESS GROVE I sent her my ideas and the next day she sent back the finished song! I thought, *Wow, I've never heard her sing like that before.* That's when I realised we had to do more stuff like that. I just gathered my courage in both hands and asked her if she would like to do some songs with me. She wanted to hear any ideas that I may have had, so I sent her a few skeletal ideas. It got the ball rolling, so, gradually, we started sending stuff back and forth.

LYDIA LUNCH I was in Barcelona, he was in London, so I would send him on a wild goose chase: *Go listen to a Hazel Dickens song, bluegrass, then write me something that doesn't sound like it!* Or, *Go listen to Buckwheat Zydeco's version of 'When The Levee Breaks' and write me something that doesn't sound like it.* He kept coming up with all these amazing songs, and we started recording between Barcelona and London—I hadn't even met him yet.

CYPRESS GROVE That opportunity arose about three months after I suggested the idea. She was staying in Whitechapel. I suggested meeting up at the Blind Beggar pub—where Ronnie Kray shot George Cornell in the head! This would be our first face-to-face meeting, and I was pretty nervous. As it turned out, she was, of course, delightful, and she immediately became the sister I never had. We spoke about a lot of stuff that night, and I found myself really opening up to her. As she was leaving, she gave me a copy of her book *Amnesia.** I asked her to sign it. She wrote, 'Learn to forget.' Best damn advice I have ever been given!

The first album was about three years in the making. We would bat ideas backward and forward—it even got to the point that I thought it would probably never come out. She said to me, 'I don't want people to think of this as Lydia-lite,' so it felt a little like a guilty pleasure, with no prospect of being released. There was no deadline, so it just took what it took.

LYDIA LUNCH *A Fistful Of Desert Blues* with Cypress Grove, almost all those

---

* A 2009 volume published in Spain and accompanied by an audiovisual CD performance.

songs were about one person who now sits in prison: my last extremely tragic love affair. It cured me, in essence, because at that age I knew what I was getting into—I knew it was horrendous and ridiculous, almost a teenage trauma lust-bond. That person was a brilliant artist, writer—and writing matters to me—who couldn't control himself. You can't save anyone from themselves, you know this, we know this always, you have to save yourself. But I would not give up on that last traumatic experience, because it was a kind of final—we hope—nail in the coffin of my obsession with mania, with somebody who is as uncomfortable with a certain part of their life, somebody as driven, as obsessive, as lusty, who just pushes beyond the edge then pushes a little further.

For me to be attracted to people, they have to go there. They have to either be extreme genius or extremely damaged—that's just where the attraction lies, because it calms something within myself, as well as allowing that playing field for the little demons in me to come running, whether it's the puppet master or the perfect victim. I'm not a victim, but I will be a chalkboard for someone else to write out their fantasies if they need. I feel like I do live in service of the therapy of other people who have no room to play certain roles, or games, or conditions. They're not safe to do that anywhere, but they are safe with me. But are we really safe from each other? Not necessarily.

CYPRESS GROVE Stefano Rossello of Rustblade Records was putting out some of Lydia's old stuff, and he asked if we had anything new. We just had to decide, of the tracks we had, what to put out—I left the selection and running order to Lydia. I was still surprised it was going to be released—I thought it'd probably be one of those things that comes out after everyone on it is dead! So, after *A Fistful Of Desert Blues*, there was the *Twin Horses* split release with five songs, and we did 'Hotel California' specifically for the record—Stefano wanted each band, us and Spiritual Front, to do a cover. Lydia had been threatening to do that song for a while—I thought she was joking! During our intense periods of recording, we would try out all sorts of covers, mostly for fun, but as our collection grew, we thought we should put out a covers album.

LYDIA LUNCH Most of the songs on *Under The Covers* with Cypress Grove, people have heard these songs hundreds of times, but they've never heard the lyrics. Is it my voice hypnotising them into hearing them? Whether I hated the music or the way they were performed, the lyrics on all the cover songs I do are amazing. They're all dying, though—I must've killed like five rock stars by covering their songs!

GLYN STYLER We were riding in a van to Memphis for the *Shotgun Wedding* recording session and she played Led Zeppelin's *Physical Graffiti* and Alice Cooper records all the way. When I commented on her choices, she said, 'There's nothing embarrassing about it. We all love it, don't we? Admit it!'

LYDIA LUNCH I love classic rock but I rebelled against it, obviously, most of my musical career, most of my life. Then I realised that classic rock— we're talking mid-60s to mid-70s—was far more perverse than what came afterward, because you were able to get away with so much more. So much of it is about drugs, war, sex, and done in such a bizarre way. There was no genre of music owning the Top 40, so you could have The Temptations doing 'Ball Of Confusion' and The Doors doing 'The End' two years apart, and both being Top 40 hits. There's no way, now, that something so perverse, or the juxtaposition of 'Ball Of Confusion'—a political song— and 'Riders On The Storm'—about serial killers, basically—could both be hits. Politics mattered, and it was a more individual time than has been recognised, because now everything has to be a specific genre—you have to fit into a box. There's no point to modern popular music, but luckily there are still people doing underground music that matters. Music about being a true individual, and about something beyond the production.

KEMBRA PFAHLER If you think about what ugly music actually is, compared to listener-friendly or beautiful music, I think about artists even from the 60s, like Janis Joplin—who really was able to let her hair down and sing with such gusto, without a speck of makeup—and Nina Simone really went there with a lot of her songs. When you're striving toward getting close to feelings and being extremely honest, there's room for glamour, but it's not entirely necessary. And when you're pushing boundaries with music, you have to be unafraid to be ugly. I just think that most of Lydia Lunch's artwork has been so ahead of her time, the rest of the world is kind of catching up to her.

LYDIA LUNCH I feel that some of my writing is very unglamorous. It's brutally fat-free; it's masculine, and I deliver it in a very masculine way, but from a feminine view. That voice did not exist—though Wanda Coleman had it, Angela Davis had it—but there weren't many women in music that allowed themselves to be that brutal or ugly.* I always tell women, 'Don't be afraid to be ugly.' I'm not gonna be the one smiling pretty to please anybody.

CYPRESS GROVE She really is ferocious onstage. The way she chews up hecklers, that really is her—it's not an act, it's what she does. But when you get to know her, she has a gentle side, but she doesn't suffer fools, and you mess with her at your peril. I remember a gig in Torino, when we were doing the *Under The Covers* record—quite a small club—and she started going on about how beautiful Italian women were, and how Italian men look very nice, but why do they all have to wear these fucking beards? She pointed to some heavy-looking guy in the audience: 'Why have you got that beard?' And he basically told her to fuck off.

Here we go, I thought. *This isn't going to end well.* I was nervous because he was really tough-looking, and he really didn't want to go, but she took him on: 'OK, get him out. I'm not playing any more until he's out.' Of course, he wouldn't move for ages, and with it being such a small club, I'm not sure what we could have done if he'd decided to batter hell out of her. Mercifully, he left of his own accord. She stared him down with that electric stare of hers, not sure he got his money back. It's not worth getting into a conflict with Lydia—you'll always end up on the losing side.

---

* Davis is an enduringly radical political figure who has tackled the challenges of racial, social, and economic inequality in the US. Coleman is the author of a substantial output of dexterous and powerful poetic works, and potentially the most prolific African-American poet of all time, who focused strongly on racism and the intertwined challenges of life in the USA.

CARLO MCCORMICK Pity the poor person who heckles her at a concert, because she will tear them down and make them realise that whatever compelled them to hit the screen with whatever they did, she's going to find where that came from and make them really own it.

JESSIE EVANS Lydia is a very seasoned performer. She's in charge and doesn't take shit. I remember seeing her at the Bataclan in Paris once, where she called out some guy in the front of the show who was misbehaving. She told him to go to the back of the room, and he did. A friend said she saw her pee onstage once too. Cut from true punk thread, an inspiration on how to rule the stage!

CYPRESS GROVE Lydia's audience, they're malleable, they're a broad church, they like to hear what she's doing, because whatever she's doing, she's never done anything shit. When we played together, it was always billed as Lydia Lunch With Cypress Grove, so they knew it wasn't going to be Teenage Jesus stuff or anything else; they knew what they were coming for, and—as far as I could tell—they were appreciative. Touring with Lydia is tiring, she's full on from first thing in the morning until last thing at night, while I'm not a morning person—you just adjust. A few weeks at a time was very good fun. I remember all the gigs we did together with great fondness, and I still don't know how she manages it—she's on the road all the time. I sleep for weeks after a tour, while she's off to Australia the very next day—I'm stunned by the stamina. She's made of iron, and she presumably sleeps very well at night!

CHAPTER TWENTY-FIVE

COVENS AND CATASTROPHES

*COLLABORATION AND CREATIVE CONNECTION
BECOME THE FORMATION OF SUPPORTIVE
COMMUNITIES FOR THOSE ENDURING DIFFICULT
TIMES, MEMORIES OF PAIN, AND EMBEDDED
TRAUMA, LYDIA'S IMPACT EXPANDING FAR
BEYOND THE LITERARY AND THE MUSICAL.*

JASMINE HIRST I'm an artist in the fields of photography, film, and painting. Art, for me, has always been a way to heal. I made art about the sexual abuse of women and children because—from my own background, the abuse I experienced, and that of every woman I knew, and men too—it was endemic. So, when I started, my work was very confrontational. I got death threats—they'd be left on my work in galleries—some men tried to sue me saying I was discriminatory against men, when I was only talking about rapists and perpetrators—it was heavy. I also had my art on T-shirts and women wearing them were being threatened in the street. This was what Australia was like. It was really violent, especially in the suburbs.

BETH B I couldn't live the rest of my life hand-to-mouth, so I started making documentary films. I decided to make a film about juvenile sex offenders, and I didn't realise at the time how it related to the sexual abuse I suffered when I was a child, but I felt compelled to make the film.* How are these

---

* *Voices Unheard*, released in 2003.

children, who are abusing children being rehabilitated—how are they being helped? How do you have empathy for your abuser? If you cannot find empathy then there is no healing, no way to enlighten yourself or to make a better choice. It was looking at these children, stuck in the cycle where they were abused, so they abuse; their abuser was likely abused; and it just goes on and on. There was a boy, he was sixteen, and he said, 'I'm just like a drug addict: my addiction is sexual abuse, and if I do not take care and talk about it and think about it every day, then I will abuse again.' It's incredible for a boy of that age to realise that about themselves, and to have that be so much a part of who they are, knowing they have to be so vigilant. It was a very hard film. You saw that in most institutions these boys were not getting any help that would make a difference. There was just one place where they were talking about it in such frank terms, and you could see the boys were feeling remorse and empathy for their victims—and that's what it needs to be about.

JASMINE HIRST When I discovered Lydia, it saved my life, because I thought, *Oh my god, there are other artists out there*. Lydia was making work about the darkest parts of our psyche, the shadowlands of society, and—at the time—there was always no one else doing that. The first time I saw a photograph of her, I was in my late teens. I was in this arts collective in Sydney, and we got a government grant to make work about girls and unemployment—it was going to be shown to girls in schools. We were making a calendar, and I looked at the girl next to me's work, and there was this picture of Lydia, who I knew nothing about and had never heard of. I was struck by it: *Who's that woman?* And the girl told me, 'Oh, it's Lydia Lunch.' That was the first time I heard of her.

It was her writing and her interviews that got me interested. Something profound happened to my soul when I read Lydia's words about the abuse inflicted upon her—I thought, *Oh my god I'm not alone*, and also, *I can make art about it*. A lot of women go into self-destruct mode, while Lydia was someone who rose up. When I read her words, I took it as a sign that I could heal my wounds, that I could rise up.

ZOE HANSEN You don't have to have travelled the same road in order to get it.

One of my favourite books is *Paradoxia*—that's when I became a real fan of her literature. When I'm around Lydia, it feels like teacher and student; Lydia can school me anytime, and I'll always listen. Lydia appreciates the life that I've led, and there was a wink-wink, *I know where you're coming from*. I'd been writing my whole life, but I decided I really wanted to get serious. I sent something into an anthology, and it was accepted. The book was called *Hos, Hookers, Call Girls, And Rent Boys* by David Sterry—he was mentoring me. I knew everyone in downtown Manhattan, so I was able to put on a show at the Bowery Poetry Club and incorporate women, mainly ex-sex workers, to read. So I had started, then I met Lydia and I became more confident.

DONITA SPARKS Lydia has a lust for life—she gives it all, no matter what she's doing, whether she's onstage, chatting up a stranger, chatting up a friend. She's always got shit to report. She's always doing something, hustling; she's a connector with people. She's always offering: 'Hey, have you ever done spoken word? You've got to do it!' She wants to reel you in, but she's so encouraging. 'Write something! Perform something! Do it! Do it!' She's a renaissance woman, and she encourages others to get out of their box and try. It's a very generous, non-coveting way for an artist to be with another artist. I really cherish that about her—she always wants to bring her friends in, and they don't even have to be well known. I've seen her bring in young women who are just total newbies. She's almost a mentor.

LYDIA LUNCH I'm writing real stories from two things, either my world perspective—which could be considered psychopathic—or my personal experience. I don't write fiction, so *Paradoxia* or *Will Work for Drugs*, these are all real-life experiences: how can they be shocking? You're reading it for two hours, I lived it my whole life, but it's shocking to you on the page? I don't know what you're talking about. I'm just trying to tell the truth, knowing that other people have experienced similar things and it's not for everybody. Telling the truth is controversial now, because we are so full of bullshit and lies. Orwell was right: the truth is a lie, the lies are truth, so telling the truth according to the way I tell it will always be controversial.

God, trigger warning? Safe space? Safe for my voice? You shitting me? Unbelievable. I'm not too controversial, everyone else is just too fucking straight and scared.

JASMINE HIRST Synchronicity often happens in my life. I heard she was coming to Australia to do a spoken-word performance—this was 1997—and the day of the show I thought I really needed to give her some of my art as a gift. Just by chance, I was walking in Darlinghurst, the inner city of Sydney, and I bumped straight into her. I said, 'Oh my god, Lydia, I have a gift for you!' That was my first meeting. I saw the show and I just wanted to cry, because it was the first time I'd seen a reflection of my own life and my experience in Australia. At the time, I had filmed Aileen Wuornos, the female serial killer, on Death Row. I asked Lydia if I could interview her for my film *You Can Execute Her But You Can't Kill Her*. Lydia said, 'Absolutely, come up to my hotel room.' It took a minute! I grabbed a cameraperson, and I believe we did it the next day. People like Lydia—and others, like the performance artist Penny Arcade—they've had a very similar life to Aileen, but they ended up onstage while Aileen finished up on Death Row.

ZOE HANSEN The first time I encountered Lydia was 1984. I was seventeen, and I'd run away from London to New York and was working at MTV as a stylist. I had a very close friend—who passed away from AIDS—who adored Lydia, and he took me to see Lydia perform. But we lived very different lives. Our paths didn't cross until *The Heroin Chronicles*. I met Lydia through Jerry Stahl, who edited the volume that Lydia and I were both in. So when we had an opportunity to do a reading in New York— Jerry, Lydia, me, Nathan Larson, Eric Bogosian all read—we all became really tight.[*]

Lydia and I were instantly attached. She's an artist through-and-through and has gathered this incredible circle of writers, musicians, performers— everyone that is excited to produce and to do things. Wherever she's lived, she'd have dinner parties, cook magnificent meals, and people would come

---

[*] St. Mark's Bookshop in the East Village, January 24, 2013.

around after her shows. I met Jasmine at one of these gatherings at Lydia's and we became inseparable—we hung out every day. Jasmine is a medium, a psychic—I don't know how she describes herself, I've never asked her, but I know what she is.

We bonded a lot on witchcraft, the three of us did—Lydia, Jasmine, and I. It's a really natural thing with some women. It's as natural as Mother Nature, an old hippie-ish thing of being at one with nature. That's what witchcraft means. There are spells and things, but they're really part of meditation, and the dark stuff, I love doing that, but I haven't done it recently, because it does come back to bite you in the ass, and I don't feel like paying for anything right now! I felt there was something broken in me that couldn't be fixed unless I found something truly pure, and what Wicca gave me was a purity of understanding—it allowed me to draw good, put away bad. I saw things that I really couldn't explain. It's very powerful, and that's why I'm still with it all these years later. I've been practising it for forty years, and Lydia has always had an interest in witchcraft. I have experience of spell casting, rune reading; different methods that Wiccans have used traditionally.

JASMINE HIRST Lydia is the strongest healer I've ever met in her life. I'm a psychic, a medium, and a healer. I communicate with the dead—a gift from my mother and grandmother—and Lydia is the strongest psychic I've ever met in my life. I've watched her, over the years, bring the outcasts of society—the most wounded men and women—into her fold, and she heals them. She does it in many different ways. She's a big collaborator, that's the first thing. She collects artists and musicians and writers. The people who are rejected from our society, she invites them into her home, she feeds them, she heals them. Particularly women who have suffered sexual assault and abuse, there's an amazing transformation I see when they're with her.

ZOE HANSEN I've seen women cry in her arms many a time. I'm not talking one-offs, it's all the time—she holds her arms out to people in the front row and they hug her all the time.

ELISE PASSAVANT Lydia had toured with our performance *Dust And Shadows* through Europe and the US. By using live visuals and body-mapping techniques, I would make her disappear and reappear in a patchwork of moving images from Belchite: an abandoned asylum, burnt forests, cosmic black holes. On the road, I saw huge Hells Angel–looking guys crying and begging me to translate to Lydia that she was their hero. I saw victims of abuse and trauma breathing again and feeling reinforced while sucking up some of her monstrous energy—she's like an enormous universal charger. And she's also the sharpest warrior nature ever created.

ZOHRA ATASH I wanted her on my music, and I want to put a new generation of fans onto her. It's got nothing to do with 'para-social interaction' bullshit, where people project Herculean notions onto any dummy with a 'verified' status on social media. Lydia is that fucking badass, rad as shit, high priestess you see in those images. I've told her this, and I would tell anyone, she's my rock'n'roll mama. She's head of the coven, mother, like Mother Nature. She's the life-giving, nurturing aspects, but she's also the gale-force winds that'll fan the flames of a cleansing wildfire. It really just depends on how she vibes you.

One of the most striking memories I have of her is when I confided in her something deeply personal and she put her hand on my shoulder as we spoke—it was, and I say this without hyperbole, what I reckon a mother's touch would feel like to an infant child. It was deeply healing. I was taken aback but how much so, honestly. I'd hugged her many times, but in that vulnerability, in that time of need, she was a soothing balm.

CATHI UNSWORTH I had a very funny experience with Lydia in the Tongues Club in Brighton. I actually passed out while she was speaking—the only time I've ever fainted in my life. Lydia and I have joked ever since that this was her opening my third eye! It was a small crowded room in the upstairs of a pub on the long road that goes from the station down to the seafront. She started talking, and my vision started going from colour, into black-and-white, then it went into total widescreen, so all I could see was a black background with a white line down the middle, then it contracted to a small dot like you would see on an analogue television, then I fainted. Luckily, I fainted onto Billy Chainsaw, as he was sturdy enough to accommodate my fall. It was part of Lydia's magic spell, and my writing and perceptions became a little better after that!

CHRISTOF KURZMANN I was looking forward to seeing Lydia perform in Vienna, then, the night before, I had a weird dream. I was backstage at a festival with her—a big grass space with individuals tents in it. The organiser of the Vienna Jazz Festival looks into our tent and says something unfriendly, so Lydia and I leave and drive to Linz together—end of dream. The next day, I mention it to my friend as we head to the concert. Then, somewhere after the third or fourth song, Lydia starts talking to the audience and suddenly—out of nowhere—states, 'I have this feeling tonight that someone in the audience has a big fetish for me and they're standing somewhere there!' And she points her finger directly toward where I am standing. All I can say is, I was never attracted erotically to Lydia, though I admired her work and performance.

JASMINE HIRST Lydia and I started doing psychic readings together, which are fucking amazing! We complement each other—we see different stuff. Sometimes we're in different places and I'll speak to her in my head, say things to her, and there'll be a phone call or a text immediately— sometimes she answers the question I had, other times she just says, 'You called?' She's so much more than just writer, artist, performer—she's an amazing psychic too.

ZOE HANSEN People who know Lydia know she is a very generous person. She'll give of herself until she makes herself sick. She's done so much for me I probably made her sick last year. I was going through trauma, sleeping on her couch, and she literally nursed me back to health.

JASMINE HIRST Another time, I was with Lydia in New York and I was doing a reading for Weasel Walter, then I looked at Lydia and suddenly our surroundings started to disappear, and I was in the woods somewhere. I looked at Lydia, into her eyes, and I went back hundreds of years, and I said to her, 'Oh my God.' Lydia replied, 'Yes, you're right. We're back there.' I was witnessing her being executed. I don't know if it was France or England, but I could smell peat, a mouldy forest-y smell, and we could both see it. I would describe what I was seeing, she would describe what she was seeing, I was literally watching her die—she was being hung, drawn, and quartered. I saw the life go out of her eyes. She was saying things that I hadn't said to her, but it was exactly what I was seeing too. Lydia told me that two other psychics had brought up that experience with her. I was the third to confirm it.

Our first reading together, Lydia and I were up in the Hudson Valley, visiting friends, and Bibbe Hansen lives up there. She came over and I did a reading for her. Bibbe had so many dead people around her, from the Andy Warhol era, so many. Lydia was sitting next to me, and she could feel them moving—so she started talking too. It was organic. We'd fill each other's gaps. Whenever she felt someone needed a reading, we would do it together. Lydia and I don't advertise—it's just for friends of hers. If people are particularly tormented then Lydia will suggest they come and we'll do a reading for them. Lydia will take the notes and I'll do the reading— she'll interject with things. I remember once, we were in the West Village and she brought a friend, we started doing the reading, and I said to the girl, 'Who's Riley?' and the girl's face went white. She said, 'Riley is the man who raped me.' Because Lydia and I both know and have lived how sadistic and cruel and horrific this world can be, people who have been tortured are drawn to us, because we can feel those dark wounds. I know it doesn't sound very healing, but, by the end of it, the energy from Lydia is pure love. We understand these wounds, and the person always leaves with that different energy, compared to what they carried in with them. There's something about communicating and being heard—it helps us live with our wounds when we can speak to people who truly understand our experience and our injuries.

LYDIA LUNCH At the end of my dark tunnel is light forever. A lot of people like to paint their own fear on my face—too regressive, too passionate, too aggressive. There's nothing to compare it to because it's so brutal, unglamorous, and romantic, but in the darkest way. I'm throwing a temper tantrum in order just to get to the other side of it. I find it very beautiful when people have that awareness of what I do, because most can't see beyond the surface. Obviously, there are people who love it and they want it and need it, because I'm speaking to the darkest parts of individuals who have been traumatised.

*

ZOE HANSEN The three of us started talking: Jasmine could take care of the psychic side, I would do some readings, we would put on a 'coven night'. We would call ourselves The Coven when we were at her place in Brooklyn because there was this particular circle of women who were always showing up, and she was always bringing in different people. We did a couple of places including Soho House, New York.

JASMINE HIRST For The Coven, Zoe did a reading about witches, Lydia did a spoken word about the history of witches, then she read something I had written about 'What Is A Witch?', then I did a group psychic reading. Penny Arcade was in the audience on the last night. She was the first reading I did, because her dead people were the loudest. The audience were members of the club, friends of Lydia's, friends of mine, friends of Zoe's, people who had read about it—a mix of people, maybe a hundred people. It was exhausting for me—I don't normally do groups, and I was very nervous. I'm an introvert and I didn't want to be onstage. It was a lot of readings in a very short space of time, but I'll do anything for Lydia!

ZOE HANSEN Jasmine is very graceful, very talented, so she'd bring an elegance to the night. Lydia and I would work off each other: she's the draw, the superstar, I had some real stories—insane life stories that just happen to be about the actual life I've led. I was a madam, a brothel owner, worked in the sex industry for many years, a massive drug history, a little humour and insanity thrown into the stories. Then Lydia would tell her stories, spoken word accompanied by music, then Jasmine would quieten the room and do a psychic reading, pulling whatever she could from the feeling of the audience. The nights were pretty packed.

JASMINE HIRST Lydia has an enormous amount of positive energy; I'm more of a sponge to negative energy. Some readings, because there's a healing going on, I get that healing energy as well, but sometimes I am drained and I have to go to bed for a day. I have to spend most of my time alone. I can't bear to be around other people too often because I'm a sponge, I can't protect myself—and I have tried—so I'm constantly picking up energies.

ZOE HANSEN Generally what happens is, the audience, often they want to see the real shit, they want to see Lydia enraged. At her spoken-word shows, she does these very strong, very emotional pieces that really move the audience. We would draw in a great crowd for them—it worked to their advantage. We would draw a crowd of women who were roughly our age, in that range and everywhere in between, people who wanted that different storytelling experience. We did the Roxy for three months—not an easy room to fill, but it was great! Lydia is one of these people who has made it out alive. Others either gave it up, or didn't make it. She did, and she still has, so good on her—that should be celebrated. People around the East Village really appreciate Lydia because she was a huge part of the scene around CBGB's and other venues, so people are thrilled to see her when she's in town. People get excited when they see her on the street here because she represents a time that is only available through books, film, and through her.

VANESSA SKANTZE I was living in New Orleans and I came across Butō, initially through being exposed to Sankai Juku, one of the most known groups that travel and tour.* When I found it, I felt I was always on the way to this, and that became the main creative river of my life to this day. I was fortunate enough to train with Atsushi Takenouchi, a truly amazing

---

* Butō was founded by Tatsumi Hijikata in Japan in 1959. According to Skantze, 'Butō was very much a radical and transgressive art form in keeping with a lot of the art forms going on at that time. There's a very Japanese theme coming through with the violence that had happened in the culture following the destruction caused by the bombing of Japan, also the prevalence and influence of the Shinto religion and the sense of animism, ghosts, ancestors, a different perspective on the dead compared to western culture. Coupled with this was a great inspiration from Jean Genet, the Marquis De Sade, Antonin Artaud, and Yukio Mishima.'

teacher, a wonderful dancer, and a transmitter of the truly deep inspirational movements of the dance. Believe it or not, as avant-garde a form as Butō is, they have their feelings about what a woman should or should not be like onstage, and how forceful or intense, or not, you can be. I've come across that judgment in different places and in different ways, Atsushi never had that—he was always supportive of me. It's often not in so many words, but people will tell you things like, 'You could be softer.' There's nothing wrong with developing range, but I've been practising this form for seventeen years. I would come across this idea of what I was meant to be.

The Post-Catastrophe Collaborative Workshop*—the one that I had the good fortune to be a part of, in Ojai, California—it was about creating space for women to find expression, different ways of expression, find liberation—a retreat with different people focusing on different aspects of creativity. It was a lovely place; I led some Butō workshops in an avocado grove, which was wonderful. It was interesting in the breadth of age, of people who were going through chemo, coming through divorces, going through intense life things; Lydia was such a source of inspiration, and being able to cut through imposed external barriers so people could explore their own voice. There was the woman who hosted us, then Adele Bertei came up, a musician from the area, a writer, a yoga teacher—an interesting mix—and everyone stayed there at this little retreat. I led a few different movement practices with basic patterns and ways to feel energy and transformation in the body, a little life-and-death passage exercise, some partner work with people to create unknown movement and form—it was a way people could experience their bodies as vessels of transformation, to not think of dance as movements they were executing but rather as life erupting inside. Lydia did a little of that, then led spoken word and reading, people brought texts, and she did a workshop in performance and strategies and possibilities. Everyone did something at the performance event on the last night.

---

* The Post-Catastrophe Women's Workshop concept was created by Lydia as a retreat and creative space for sharing in which guests are taught artistic modes of expression, and given the opportunity to present their work and feelings. They have been staged in Europe and America.

SADIE MAE I was also enrolled by Lydia in the Post-Catastrophe Collaborative Workshop in Rennes, France, in 2012. It was epic. Lydia and most of the women did not understand one another but still, the electricity was in the air, under their skins—a different type of undressing, I guess. It was all about what Lydia is naturally great at: reinforcing strength, confidence, fierceness in women who have experienced or are enduring trauma. Every morning, this confrontational beast was camped on her two legs right at the entrance door and took it upon herself to give hugs to each and every one of the women involved in the workshop, charging them up as if they were soldiers preparing their internal weapons for war. The performances from the women were grand.

LYDIA LUNCH Workshops are important to me because I think a lot of women write, or they should write. They need to document their experiences. The best part is, it inspires women, gives them a place to be free, to experiment and find their voice, whether they're going to use it in a public format or not. Usually, after the workshops, I make a public performance, so at least they can get that under their belt. We don't have war, we don't have sports; you gotta have a coven. In a sense, the workshops are just an extension of what I consider a coven. It's just creating in a group of women—if we had a clubhouse, we'd call it that, but we don't. It's important that women have collectives. And every workshop I've done so far, it's really inspired them to take matters into their own hands and do other things. It's great.

CHAPTER TWENTY-SIX

MY LOVER THE KILLER

AN ALBUM-LENGTH COLLABORATION WITH MARC HURTADO, INITIATED IN 2012, CRASHES HEADLONG INTO A LONG-AGO MEMORY OF THE LATE 70S: LYDIA'S EX, JOHNNY O'KANE …

LYDIA LUNCH Johnny O'Kane? So you're talking about a lover I had when I was seventeen? All right, let's go back in time …*

IAN WHITE The funny thing with Lydia is, she loves to talk … but she never talks about the past unless you ask her to. She lives in the present and in the future. Bit by bit, night and day with one another, she'd tell me things. I don't think for one second she's ever tried to make things grander or better or worse than they were, she never embellishes things. As I got to know her, I realised it was always one hundred percent what she said it was.

JASMINE HIRST When Lydia and I reconnected in New York, she invited me out for coffee in the Lower East Side in this coffee shop that's been there since the 70s, and she hadn't been there in over twenty years—but the owner knew what her order was. We sat in the back and her dead lover,

---

* O'Kane appeared in Eric Mitchell's *Red Italy* (1979), alongside Lydia in Beth B and Scott B's *The Offenders* (1980) and in Gordon Stevenson's *Ecstatic Stigmatic* (1980). He also briefly performed in Teenage Jesus & The Jerks.

Johnny, appeared behind her. I started doing a reading about him and told her that he was pushing his hand into her solar plexus—she said, 'Oh my god! I've been feeling that all morning.' Unbeknown to me, she'd had an awful pain there.

BETH B I knew Johnny when Lydia was with him, and that was a very violent relationship. I remember going to the hospital with her. She called me: 'Oh, Johnny OD'd. He took a bunch of sleeping pills because I was threatening to leave him.' Lydia was at the hospital, I went there, and I'm confronted by Lydia in a nurse's uniform, wheeling Johnny in a wheelchair—horror replaced by humour.

LYDIA LUNCH Johnny O'Kane had created this perfect, stylised representation of the male idol. We're talking James Dean, Robert Michum, Marlon Brando—every movement was so stylised. They don't make men like that anymore. You have somebody who comes from a very drunken, damaging, poor Irish background. He's trying his best to break out of that by running away and creating this matinee ideal of male perfection. But underneath that is the battery that a child has withstood from the age of three. How do you get over that?

MARC HURTADO I was thinking of making an entire record with Lydia. She said OK and told me to send her music. I sent her loops, some of natural noise, some of electronic, some industrial sounds, some of drum-bass-guitar like industrial noir jazz. She was looking at songs she had, music she had made, and she started by sending me one track—'I'm Sorry But I'm Not'—with her voice and the loops I sent, then other music from elsewhere. We worked like painting, building up layers. By herself, she built things from her work, with my loops and her vocals. You could understand that she was speaking to a man and apologising for things like stealing his guitar, but not being sorry, because it was clear he did so much wrong to her too.

LYDIA LUNCH You take it out on each at first. I never considered any relationship I was in domestic violence. It's more psychological violence, psychic violence, or just being a bit psychotic, because it was beautiful and fun, and we had to play somewhere, so we played with each other, because most other people didn't want to play with us, because it was too much. So, when you're too much, you find somebody else who is too much, because if you don't, you're forever unsatisfied. And that's not going to be 'the boy next door'. That's going to be the boy who spends all his time in the garage, sniffing gasoline, getting high on paint fumes, drinking whiskey out of a milk carton. You know, all that cute shit.

MARC HURTADO She had been in love with him—she told me she'd never been in love like she had been with him. He was quite violent, a junkie, he put her in danger many times. He always said, 'I want to save you'—from what? It was from him. He killed her animals and painted with their blood on the wall. She had to escape in the end—she went to Los Angeles with Marty Nation. Johnny came looking for her and found her, knocked on her door at five in the morning.

LYDIA LUNCH I was looking for somebody that understood what it feels like to have your blood boiling inside you, and that's not every man. I tried my best with all of them, because I saw their potential in the worst, and in the best, way possible.

TIM DAHL Lydia Lunch gets away with murder onstage—but there's a subtext. People feel blindsided, particularly men. I mean, there's often a castration per set with Retrovirus, and I'm wondering why do these guys do this to themselves? They set themselves up: they'll say something, and she'll just stop the music and publicly humiliate them. I've thought about this, and I still haven't figured it out, but there is a level that's sexual. They want to be dominated. And, in her performance, there is a bit of that domination/ submission that's being explored, and some of these guys, or ladies, show up to be dominated. Fine, she'll dominate them.

NELS CLINE The chemistry between Lydia and certain male members of her audience is that these certain men showed up to be tongue-lashed and insulted by Lydia, and she was more than happy to oblige them! She would call out someone who had shouted something and ask them to step up to the front of the stage, and then unleash myriad cutting insults—some of them rather creative—after which the humiliated offender would drift away, smiling beatifically ...

LYDIA LUNCH If you've both been traumatised, then you see this wounded person, but you also see the person before they were battered. You want to see that beautiful child, and your beautiful child—which is hard for you to recognise because they're hiding in the closet—wants to connect with that person. But then the maniacs come out, because, well, the children aren't always in the same playground at the same time, but the monsters are often circling.

BETH B It isn't that we *find ourselves* in these strange power relationships, it's that we choose to enter into them and then we choose to stay. The addiction to that emotional connection can be so strong that we can't extricate ourselves from the great highs, the ecstasy, and the great lows of devastation and misery—it replicates the family dynamic. I was in that precise situation for five years, the individual was both extremely rage-filled and also very depressed, which was the exact combination of my mother and father. How could I leave? I was home.

MARC HURTADO She told me we needed to find a name for our project. She sent me ten titles, and *My Lover The Killer* was such a powerful name, the yin-yang, the story of Lydia Lunch. Three days after, she was going to the US to rehearse with Retrovirus for a tour. She phoned me some days after: 'God, something incredible happened.' She had arrived in New York and met up with Bob Bert, who was a big friend of Johnny, and through Bob they got in touch and he explained he was a steelworker now, he had two children, a girlfriend. Lydia felt that he had changed, that maybe they could get a drink together and have a chat. So, she was staying at Marty Nation's sister's house in Los Angeles, Lydia and Johnny were going to meet ... and Johnny didn't show up.

LYDIA LUNCH He straightened out for a long time, he got over his initial behaviours to become the union labour leader for construction, making a lot of money, going to the job, and doing fine … until he snapped. Why did he snap? Because he was going to come to see me again, and what did that bring up in him? Lost love, the insanity that resides within him that he's kept at bay for so long that he knows he can't really keep it at bay any longer because it's going to rise up, and it's going to do something? I have no idea. Sometimes, if it's too much, somebody might have to take themselves out, but as to why they have to take somebody else out? I don't understand that. You can't stand it? Take yourself out. But Johnny had stabilised for a long time.

MARC HURTADO Johnny chased his girlfriend into the street and shot her in the head, two bullets. He then went back to the house, called the police, and told them that he shot his girlfriend. Then he shot himself and died the next day in the hospital.*

BETH B Johnny O'Kane, his story is exactly what we're talking about here. The trauma resides inside of us, it never goes away; it gets triggered in a multitude of ways, and you never know when. You have to be vigilant. Johnny erupted in this explosion of violence that ended his life and another's. I don't know what precipitated that but, from what *is* known, it was historical. He wanted to obliterate himself and everything around him. You don't get out of the cycle by being silent. You need witnesses, you need to talk about it, you need to get it out.

MARC HURTADO Our project passed from fiction into blood-red reality. When we started, we were working from a story, 'Ghost Town', that talks of her experience with Johnny. With the name *My Lover The Killer*, she predicted what became real. Lydia can't escape it—the themes of her life, the actions, it all comes back to her. We laugh about it, but, yes, she does have a power, a magic. Some people think she's a witch. Some days later,

---

* On November 2 and November 3, 2012, respectively.

she told me she wanted to continue—she wanted to write about Johnny. For Lydia, it was a more universal story, about many men in the world, not just this one.

VANESSA SKANTZE One of the positive aspects of this time has been seeing the notion of gender opening up to liberating non-binary visions. I'd like to see the notion of 'male gender' dissolve and mutate as the world goes forward. Something like the #MeToo movement has been important for allowing people to realise that they are not responsible for what has been inflicted on them. There are strong feelings—particularly in the wretched, fundamentalist, puritanical aspects of the United States—that are so beyond the pale, in terms of blaming victims and making them responsible not only for their own suffering but how they're dealing with it. Opening that notion up and saying, *This has happened to me and it never should have—you should be punished for feeling you get to do this because of who you are.*

LYDIA LUNCH I don't blame the victim. I blame the parents of the victim. I blame them for not teaching girls from the age of five that if somebody touches you and you don't like it, you punch them in the nuts, you scream in their face, and you run away. I blame them for not teaching little boys how to act with respect. But who were our parents, and who taught them? Nobody. And what's Hollywood? If you want to be an actress, go off-Broadway, do independent films, otherwise you are willingly going into a corrupt corporation, run by mogul pimps, who are looking for the next well-paid call girl who is going to dress up sleek, portray this ideal that nobody can live up to, personify the mouthpiece, and sales-rep selling the corporate product.

What I don't understand is how twenty, fifty, one hundred women took twenty years? It's not like they're twelve, they're not three, or five—they could have just walked in and said, 'Get naked now, we're getting a little revenge on you.' They could have cracked a dick. #MeToo was a movement started by women of colour to articulate a situation which is rampant in all areas of feminine existence, which I've been screaming about for forty years now. Women in low-paying jobs don't have any choice! Their voices have always been loud, but nobody's been listening to them!

Wearing black as a protest? Honey, what have I been doing for forty-five years? It's not enough to wear black—I'm wearing black to mourn the death of intelligence. Why don't they scream about the minimum wage? Why don't they talk about the rape of the planet? If somebody would pay me a hundred grand to not talk about fucking them—oh, please, sign me up! You know why I've never been able to sell out, or sell up, is because they're not going to convince me to play puppet to corporate whoredom.

BETH B I saw Lydia give a performance in the club Berlin in New York, where she's raging against the starlets. People were aghast. I was behind the camera and so was I. *Lydia! What the fuck are you saying?!* I was so upset, but that's the beautiful gift. When you see art, or you hear a performance, that makes you so upset or uncomfortable, where suddenly you're in a panic or in an argument, that's real art. I had to laugh at myself as those feelings came up inside me, because that's exactly what we want to do as artists. It's been great that people have come up to me saying, 'I was really upset by what Lydia was saying about the Hollywood starlets having to get a grip, crack a dick!' She's saying something outrageous, in a way, but the subject matter is so complex, and the media has made it so black-and-white, and it cannot be black-and-white. We have to look at grey zones, because that's where the work is. You cannot apply every theory or remedy to every situation. Lydia qualifies that atrocity she spouted by saying, 'I don't blame the victims, I blame the mothers and the fathers, that boys are not taught the right lessons.' She expands it out into a bigger conversation: *What is the culture we are growing up in?* That needs to be addressed and we are all responsible. The individuals will always continue to be the individuals, but it's the culture that is propagating this kind of abuse, and we need to talk about it and look at it.

LYDIA LUNCH If it wasn't an *extreme*, I couldn't feel it at some point, because I had basically flatlined as a protection against trauma. There comes incredible anger and violence, and then there comes flatlining, where you're dead, you don't feel anything, unless it's extreme. Hence why there is, as the French well understand, the need for sex and death to relate very closely, because if sex was only that 'mini-death', well, it's too mini for me.

The reason I was pushing beyond normal experience was because I had to be brought to the brink of something explosive, because, otherwise, I didn't feel it. I had to go beyond what normal people would tolerate, or what they wanted, or what excited them. And there's a victimology, a magnetism, with people about this kind of extreme relationship, because you're not going to settle for somebody that doesn't understand the dynamics. I knew from a very early age that I was on a cycle that I wanted to get off of, that I didn't want to perpetuate a cycle of abuse. I didn't want to be just reactionary because of what was done to me, or what I saw in life, or the political dimension I was already fully aware of. I had such a stubborn insistence on resistance and survival.

THE WAR IS NEVER OVER

BETH B Making a film about my mother, Ida Applebroog—that was a love letter to her, one allowing me to appreciate her while acknowledging the profound differences between us.* She gave me so much inspiration regarding the possibilities open to women to break away from the roles expected of them, to resist the suppression of their creativity. It was also a coming to terms with myself and my relationship to her, acknowledging some of the things she gave me were fraught with the disturbance she suffered and continues to suffer.

Until my mid-forties, I believed I would never have a child, because I felt that meant I could not have a career, I could go mad, I might end up in a psychiatric ward—that was the message I told myself, based on what happened to my mother. In my mid-forties, I decided I wanted to do this, to make a life with another human being, and to give them the care and nurturing that I felt I'd missed in part of my childhood. I wanted to create a different kind of family. I couldn't have one biologically, it was too late, so me and my partner in life, Jim [Coleman], we adopted our daughter, Lola.

Call Her Applebroog led naturally into wanting to make a film about Lydia because Lydia, to me, represented a revolutionary vision of *woman*. When I met her in the late 70s, there simply were not women like Lydia Lunch.

This film was so much about myself, my concerns throughout my career—they're all focused in *Lydia Lunch: The War Is Never Over*. All of the themes that I've been unravelling these forty years are manifest in this film: abuse, the cycle of violence in our culture, sexuality, giving voice

---

* *Call Her Applebroog*, released in 2016.

to the unheard, knocking down the patriarchy, dominance, submission, trauma, recovery … it's all here. As much as Lydia is this iconic figure, her struggle, that continues on to this very day, gives each of us permission to be imperfect, to look at our flaws, and to continue to struggle ourselves.

*

LYDIA LUNCH Big Lou, I don't want to use a term like schizophrenic, because I'm functional. Big Lou is just when I get too aggressive and violent. I don't break shit, I've never thrown a plate in anger, I don't punch walls. It's this frantic, physical feeling and there's no reason, necessarily, that leads to it. You can't predict, *OK, this leads to that, and here comes Big Lou*. He's always lurking but doesn't always come out. I do have to be tapped out by my friends in my own fucking house if I start becoming too aggressive.

WEASEL WALTER Big Lou is the violent male killer side of Lydia's psyche embodied. Big Lou is a friendly way of personifying her worst, most heinous, psychological elements, so that we can joke about it instead of having it come alive. The thing about Big Lou is that I'm so glad we can laugh at it, because Big Lou is the embodiment of the absolute homicidal, raging murderer that Lydia could be, if she was left to her devices in a way that didn't work out so well. Lydia has the gene that could be a killer, that could be a murderer, and she's dealt with it. The joke is, when Big Lou comes to town, everyone starts crying, because they know their blood is going to be smeared all over the wall. It's Grand Guignol, it's horror movie, or whatever. There's a side to Lydia that's that extreme, and it's not for everybody. We have these joke scenarios about Big Lou coming to town, and what Big Lou does to people, and it's not pretty.

LYDIA LUNCH I never feel as if I'm doing damage, I never want to do damage to anyone I know—I'm paid to be damaging. It took me a long time to realise just how ruthless I can be, because I don't feel the effects of that kind of behaviour. I've never felt insulted—oh there have been insults aimed at me, there are volumes written about how people hate me or what they think I am—their fear painted on my face—but I've never felt insulted. I've never felt demeaned. I've never felt any of that crap. Because I don't feel it, it makes it hard for me if I'm rat-a-tat-tatting. I might be actually wounding somebody or just going on too long, so Big Lou needs to be tapped out sometimes.

BETH B Mental illness doesn't just go away, it isn't cured. People think that someone goes for treatment, they're hospitalised, they get antidepressants, they go through therapy, and they're cured. I've had a hard reckoning with that because I've been in denial about the impact that mental illness has on a person, and upon all the people around them. When you're in a relationship, or a household, with that person, it becomes a shared dysfunction. There is no way out of it except to find a sense of community where we can really talk about it and tell our truths without shaming, without guilt. Getting it out of the body is what is therapeutic, having witnesses. We are witnesses to Lydia's traumas, and, by virtue of embracing that, we can witness our own and bring those into the light. As long as they stay in that dark, dank, fetid place, there's no way to heal.

TIM DAHL A friend of mine, a musician in Scotland, just let himself get destroyed by Lydia. He's sucking on her stiletto heel after she's walked through the puke-soaked Friday night streets of Glasgow. I'm just like, *Why are you doing this?* He loved her, and she was loving to him. It got so extreme. She has a whole line of folks wanting to be dominated by her in Manchester, and this guy cock-blocked them. He showed up there, and they both went in for round two. I was backstage, the party had moved somewhere else, and I was getting something and I saw them. Brits, they'll have, like, a candy-bar diet, and he had all these fucked-up teeth. I hadn't seen him for years, and he had this whole set of brand-new teeth, and Lydia knocked one of his teeth out! *Oh my god*, I thought, *he must have spent a lot on that!* He kind of looked around, he put it in his pocket, but then I went to get something and I saw them, and this was after all his black eyes and all that stuff, and then I saw them whispering … it's a friend of mine, and he's been through a lot. And after this two-day humiliation, mutilation, I got a glimpse after all this. They didn't know I was there, and he said to her, 'You don't know how much I've suffered.' And she hugged him. I know it doesn't sound like anything but,

but I saw something so dramatic over forty-eight hours, and then it finished in one of the most compassionate ways. I don't even know why that got me emotional, but it did. There's a performance, and then there's the personable really one-on-one focus that, when Lydia is in your life, she'll give you if she cares about you, and Lydia will give you that attention. She didn't know this guy, but somehow they bonded over forty-eight hours.

BETH B In all my interviews, I would ask, 'What is the most disturbing thing you've ever witnessed with Lydia?' I could not get anyone to really talk about it until Tim Dahl. I'm very grateful to Tim because I had the material I wanted from Lydia, talking about the monster in her, but I needed somebody to be the witness. Tim witnessed it, and he brought it into the light, and there's something very powerful about this outside party who loves Lydia and admires her, but who also sees the monster that is still within and has great empathy for what she struggles with.

That, for me, is the journey I'm so grateful for being able to take with Lydia, and that she trusted me to tell her story. I want to show the grandness of this woman, but I also had to—out of respect to her art and her work—go into what she continues to struggle with. I was a little scared at what her reaction would be, but, when I showed her the film and the Tim Dahl bit came up, she didn't skip a beat. She just put her thumbs up. *Yes!*

Tim understood her, and he wasn't afraid to speak it, and that's about having compassion for ourselves and for others who are suffering. That's a huge part of Lydia's work—to find compassion and forgiveness for the people suffering, because the people who harm us are suffering.

LYDIA LUNCH I don't feel I'm projecting an armour, but I'm a warrior. I'm never against the individual—I'm against systems that suppress and oppress individuals. The realest people see that, and that's why they come to my show and work with me. I want to laugh and have a good time, party, rebel with pleasure—I want to laugh because otherwise *they* have won. I deal with very negative things in a very aggressive way because I use the language of the enemy—but underneath that is sweetness and light. I'm defending the shy boys against the bullies.

TIM DAHL Lydia and I agree on how, as an artist, you filter this planet, and there's a lot of trauma and there's a lot of suffering out there. Everyone filters this planet in their own way. There's not one way to do it. I look at Richard Pryor: how do you deal with trauma? Some people cry, some people get politically active, some people become catatonic. Some people can't handle it, some people laugh, some people express it through words, through music—there's not one way to do it. The fact that Lydia can artistically filter this planet's suffering and trauma is a gift. The ability to do that is tremendous—it's a gift to society. There's so much pain, and it's very important to give back if you have those gifts. The amount of blood and suffering and trauma that we are all standing on is tremendous, and you better give back. And to sit back and just take a nap and justify taking a nap is actually offensive. You have to give back, and so Lydia's giving.

BETH B So many people talk about politics, social issues, but when it comes down to being honest about themselves, they're full of shit. Lydia says she's still struggling—that's the takeaway. I'm not trying to find a solution in my work, because there is no answer. There are momentary revelations, self-knowledge, owning our part in the scenarios of our lives, but our disturbances remain with us, and we have to be vigilant, ever aware, not to repeat the cycle of violence, the cycle of dysfunction, the cycle of denial.

Lydia Lunch: The War Is Never Over is about the cycle of abuse that many of us have encountered and dealt with for our entire lives. And there is no solution, but by telling our stories, it gives a way to identify with others and to bring it out of those dark clandestine places, and to work toward not continuing that cycle. I love the title because it's the war that manifests in every aspect of our lives. It's not just the war raged worldwide by the US, it's the war within ourselves. Lydia's film is transformative in that there's a great celebration of her and her work, but it's a much more complex message that the film has: it's about each and every one of us.

CONTRIBUTORS

BARRY ADAMSON has been creating all of his life. Perhaps his greatest creation is himself as a multi-disciplined artist. The self-taught musician rose to prominence as the bass player in post-punk legends Magazine. His establishment as a solo artist came after a three-year stint with Nick Cave & The Bad Seeds and heralded the release of his seminal first solo album, *Moss Side Story*. Having released nine studio albums, including the 1992 Mercury Music Prize–nominated *Soul Murder*, Adamson has continued to tour globally and recently released a brand new anthology, *Memento Mori*.

MERRILL ALDIGHIERI is a multimedia artist who invented the job of video jockey in nightclubs in 1980, introducing MTV to the concept before it began. Recordings of a year's worth of legendary live shows form the basis of her current rockumentary series, and she has won Emmys for computer animation on *Sesame Street* and for her PBS documentaries. She only meets her heroes when they are swearing sobriety, so has drunk apple juice with Lou Reed, Jim Carrol, Lydia Lunch, among other atypical teetotallers. Five years after moving to France, she could speak French like Daffy Duck on Quaaludes … she's better now, and talks like Bugs Bunny.

BEATRICE ANTOLINI is a songwriter, producer, and multi-instrumentalist who lives in Bologna, Italy. She has written and produced her own records and collaborated with Italian and foreign artists.

ZOHRA ATASH is a singer, songwriter, and producer. Her current project (with Josh Strawn) is the goth-industrial-experimental-pop group Azar Swan. She has lent her singing to recordings from a variety of diverse acts, from Ancient Methods to Del Judas to Publicist UK, and been a touring performer with Storm Of Light. She is the fourth daughter of a family of Afghan refugees, a proud voice for the diaspora, and, with her family, has worked in and helped build their auto shops, hair salons, restaurants, international business operations, and Afghan charities. She grew up all over and currently resides exactly there.

RON ATHEY is an American performance artist associated with body art and extreme performance art, with many of his works incorporating elements of S&M to confront preconceived ideas about the body in relation to masculinity and religious iconography. His earliest collaborations were with Rozz Williams in the early 80s, moving on to make his 'Torture Trilogy', consisting of the ensemble pieces *Martyrs & Saints* (1992), *4 Scenes In A Harsh Life* (1993–96), and *Deliverance* (1995).

DON BAJEMA was adopted by a World War II hero and a nurse in the psych ward at Camarillo Hospital. He lived in trailer parks throughout the USA, eventually settling in San Diego, where he lived with the Fawks family. He was an athlete of some promise and was selected by the US Olympic programme to compete in the decathlon, but spent his time in the 70s importing weed and hanging around the beach. Acting and writing changed his life. He is eternally grateful to Sam Shepard, Jim Carroll, Henry Rollins, and Lydia Lunch. He lives in New York City with his wife and children.

BOB BERT has drummed in Sonic Youth, Pussy Galore, Chrome Cranks, Knoxville Girls, and more; then fronted his own band, Bewitched, laying down swampy, tribal grooves on over thirty albums. He also put out the critically acclaimed magazine *BB Gun*. As an artist he has been in gallery shows since 1979, and as a fine art silkscreen printer he printed Andy Warhol's editions and paintings until his death. Currently, Bob is drumming for Lydia Lunch's Retrovirus and Wolfmanhattan Project. In 2018, his book of photos, text, and *BB Gun* interviews entitled *I'm Just The Drummer* was released to great acclaim.

BETH B is an award-winning director of independent feature-length documentary and narrative films as well as network television documentaries. B's career has been characterized by work that challenges society's conventions and that focuses on recasting and redefining concepts relating to the mind, the body, and women's issues. Her films have been shown at museums and cinemas worldwide as well as film festivals, including the New York Film Festival, Sundance Film Festival, Berlin Film Festival, Toronto Film Festival, Nuremberg Int'l Human Rights Film Festival, Locarno Film Festival, and others.

CHRISTINA BIRRER is a research-based artist working on *Anomalies Of Geography*, an interdisciplinary conversation regarding climate change based in the Mojave Desert, using GIS, cartography, and community-based social engagement. 'Sister, sister, hear my heart. It's time to bring the family back. Together we must remember Earth. We must remember what life is all about.' (J.Trudell.) In previous lives she has explored feminist and post-punk iconographies, gathered millions of acorns to secure the genetic bank of Ireland's indigenous ancient forests, and been involved in life-long learning and the development of organic community gardens. 'Healing is created one mind-net at a time.'

BOB BLANK has worked with artists as varied as Sting and Kid Creole And The Coconuts. His credits in production include Lydia Lunch's *Queen Of Siam*, Fonda Rae's *Over Like A Fat Rat*, Lola's *Wax The Van*, and Class Action's *Weekend*. Bob is cited hundreds of times in Discogs and Allmusic for engineering and production, dating back from the days of his famed New York studio Blank Tapes. Transitioning to a career as a competitive dancer, Bob and his partner Martha Estevez won the Latin World Championships for SR3 in 2014. Bob lives in Connecticut, USA.

DALMAU BOADA started playing with a hardcore band at eleven years old and, since then, has lived a life in music with numerous collaborators and friends. Music defines Dalmau in the best ways. He has worked as a producer, a sound engineer, and as a solo and group performer.

DOUGIE BOWNE has played with a who's who of vital artists ranging from John Cale to Iggy Pop, Marianne Faithful to Jack Bruce, as well as carving out an impressive musical vocabulary during ten-plus years with Lounge Lizards. Across the years he has performed on and produced a wide spectrum of critically acclaimed and award-winning music. In 2014, Dougie wrote the soundtrack for the film *Watchers Of The Sky*, and more recently he has finished four pieces for the Quadrilatere project, as well as collaborating with Amanda K. Miller on a short ballet premiering in late 2019 in San Francisco.

CARLA BOZULICH is an American musician based in Los Angeles, best known for her works with The Geraldine Fibbers, Evangelista, and under her own name. She has also written numerous articles, pieces of short fiction, poetry, and criticism while also being involved in performance art in various forms.

JOSEPH BUDENHOLZER moved to the East Village in the 1980s to participate in the underground theatre and music scene. He studied theatre and music at New York University, Nikitsky Gates Theater in Moscow, and Sofia Art Institute in Bulgaria. His band Backworld has released seven albums. Collaborators include: Lydia Lunch, Beth B, Richard Kern, David Tibet, Jarboe, Isobel Campbell, Little Annie, Antony Hegarty, and Neil LaBute. His operatic works are *The Hound Of Heaven*, *The Women Of Berlin*, *The Divine Invasion*, and a new adaptation of Frank Wedekind's play *Earth Spirit* with Obie award-winning director Bob McGrath at Ridge Theater, NYC.

JESSAMY CALKIN is a journalist and features editor of the *Telegraph Magazine*.

FRANÇOIS R. CAMBUZAT is a sonic activist triggering detonations with Putan Club, Trans-Aeolian Transmission, L'Ifriqiyya Electrique, Low House, Machine Rouge, Alevilik Aşkına and other urgencies. The resistance is organised with the archaic and immediate ways of our century: voices, electrical rumours, military tanks, and counted words. From fresco painting to the most daring conceptualism, from avant-rock to modern contemporary music to the most brutal techno, from a kiss on the mouth to a kick in the ass: 'Macht man Kunst, um Geld zu verdienen und die netten Bürger zu streicheln?' (Tristan Tzara, 1918)

EXENE CERVENKA is well known for being singer/songwriter in the seminal Los Angeles punk band X. She is also a member of The Knitters, a bluegrass, folk, and country outfit that features members of X and guitarist/song-writing legend, Dave Alvin. She has been a published poet and writer since 1975. Exene has performed on spoken-word stages with Wanda Coleman, Henry Rollins, Jello Biafra, Lydia Lunch, and many others. Exene is also proud to be on the list of singers, musicians, and bands who have

not been inducted into the Rock And Roll Hall Of Fame.

NELS CLINE has spent more than three decades, performing across over two hundred recordings, as a guitarist and composer in the arenas of jazz, improvised music, and rock. He has collaborated with artists including Thurston Moore, Zeena Parkins, Ben Goldberg, Carla Bozulich, Bobby Previte, Mike Watt, and Elliott Sharp. Nels's group The Nels Cline Singers has been performing for eighteen years, he has made over twenty solo records, and he has recently performed with The Nels Cline 4 and CUP, a duo with his wife, Yuka C Honda. He's best known for his work with Wilco. Nels and his wife reside in Brooklyn.

TIM DAHL is a bassist and vocalist best known for his work with the noise-rock band Child Abuse and Lydia Lunch Retrovirus. He also writes and performs for the jazz ensembles Pulverize The Sound and GRID. Dahl has also performed and/or recorded with many notable musicians, including Yusef Lateef, Archie Shepp, Eugene Chadbourne, Tatsuya Yoshida, Mary Halvorson, Rhys Chatham, The Flying Luttenbachers, Tyshawn Sorey, Jandek, Kool Keith, and Von Lmo. Tim lives in Brooklyn, New York, where he is an active member of the music scene.

LEN DEL RIO (aka Len Haynes) is a recording engineer, songwriter, and electronic musician. Len and his long-time songwriting partner, Tommy Grenas, with their band Anubian Lights have collaborated with an eclectic variety of artists, including Nik Turner (Hawkwind), Lydia Lunch, Damo Suzuki (CAN), Simon House (Hawkwind, High Tide), and Joel Vandroogenbroeck (Brainticket), among others. Anubian Lights' songs have been featured in various television shows and films, including the blockbuster *Ocean's 8*. Len is an Adjunct Professor and Lecturer at San Francisco State University and Santa Rosa

Junior College, where he teaches courses in audio production, video production, and mass communication.

VIVIENNE DICK's early work is associated with the no-wave music and film movement of late 70s New York City. Currently, she is making a film about revisiting friends from this period and seeing how their lives are in New York today. Her work is distributed by LUX UK.

CHRISTOPH DREHER has played in bands since the late 60s, notably Die Haut (1980–2000), collaborating with singers like Lydia Lunch, Alan Vega, Kim Gordon, Jeffrey Lee Pierce, Kid Congo Powers, Debbie Harry, and Nick Cave. As a filmmaker he has made numerous documentaries, including the TV series *Lost In Music*, *Pop Odyssee*, and *Fantastic Voyages*, as well as music videos and experimental films. He has been a professor of film for twenty years and editor of two books on auteur TV series (*The Wire*, *The Sopranos*, *Deadwood*, etc.), as well as co-author of a volume on *Breaking Bad* (with Christine Lang).

RICHARD EDSON was a founding member of the Workspace art collective in Albany, New York. In San Francisco he was a founding member of the art/punk band The Altarboys. He was also a founding member of the club/performance space Club Foot. In New York, he was the original drummer of the seminal punk/noise band Sonic Youth, and a founding member and drummer in the white boy funk/punk band Konk. As an actor, Richard Edson has been in over eighty films and TV shows, including *Do The Right Thing*, *Good Morning Vietnam*, *Platoon*, and *Stranger Than Paradise*. He has just completed *The Pit*, his first novel.

TERRY EDWARDS has, over four decades, charted a career from punk-funk pioneer with The Higsons to leading world-class musicians at the Barbican (London), NCH (Dublin), and Town

Hall (Adelaide). He is at home playing sideman to PJ Harvey; Bowie collaborators Woody Woodmansey, Tony Visconti, and Mike Garson; Bertolt Brecht specialists Ute Lemper and Blixa Bargeld; plus an exhaustive roster of rockers and rollers. Terry keeps his eye on the sky by working with emerging artists such as Nadine Shah, Hardwicke Circus, and Plastik. He fronts instrumental trio The Near Jazz Experience and maintains a busy solo career.

THOMAS SAYERS ELLIS is a poet, photographer, and bandleader. In 1986, he purchased a stolen camera and began taking photographs. In 1989, after attending James Baldwin's funeral, he co-founded the Dark Room Collective, a literary gathering for emerging black writers. Ellis is the author of *The Maverick Room*, *Skin, Inc: Identity Repair Poems*, and *The Corny Toys*. He is the recipient of a Whiting Writer's Award and a Guggenheim Fellowship. In 2014, he co-founded—with saxophonist James Brandon Lewis—the literary free-jazz band Heroes Are Gang Leaders as a tribute to poet and activist Amiri Baraka.

JESSIE EVANS is a Californian singer, saxophonist, producer, and visual artist currently living in Brazil. For the past twenty years she's shimmied her way from San Francisco to Berlin to South America with her bands The Vanishing and Subtonix and solo collaborations with artists Bettina Koester (Malaria!), Toby Dammit (Iggy & The Stooges), Budgie (Siouxsie & The Banshees), Warrior Queen (Jamaica), and Pepe Mogt (Nortec Collective), among many others. Armed with her sax like a machine gun, her performance mixes burlesque and punk energy with world beats to create a lush mix of intergalactic vamp and cosmic wave.

KATHLEEN FOX is a Peabody Award–winning producer on the drama *Queerskins: A Love Story*. With over a decade of experience producing, directing, writing, and creating video and print content for global campaigns, her specialty in virtual reality extends to short-form documentaries and editorial features for social, web, and television. Fox is co-producer on the feature documentary *Lydia Lunch: The War Is Never Over*, a film by Beth B. From 2007 to 2017, Kathleen acted as Senior Director Of Photo & Video Production at NYC & Company. Kathleen wrote, directed, and produced multiple web series and brand campaigns.

TOM GARRETSON is a multidisciplinary Native American/Norwegian artist working in the fields of photography, sound, writing, theatre, and performance art. He has worked extensively in the music industry as a live producer and producer of recordings, as an artist manager, and as an industry professional with PolyGram, Sony Music, and Universal Music. He has managed Lydia Lunch's career since 1998.

GIANNA GRECO left everything behind her. A heroine of the Italian electric musical scene, she lives today between Pamir, France, and Tunceli, and follows only what makes her tremble. With François R. Cambuzat, Gianna is the co-founder of Putan Club, a hyperactive unit of musical militancy. She is also the co-founder of Trans-Aeolian Transmission, the research cell at the base of L'Ifriqiyya Electrique and many other risky and impossible journeys.

CYPRESS GROVE is a London-based guitarist, singer, songwriter, composer, and producer of The Jeffrey Lee Pierce Sessions Project. He has worked with Nick Cave, Mark Lanegan, Thurston Moore, Mark Stewart, and Debbie Harry, among many others. His collaboration with Lydia Lunch has produced three albums: *A Fistful Of Desert Blues*, *Twin Horses*, and *Under The Covers*. In 2018, he composed and recorded material for the award-winning Italian film *Lucania*. Present projects include a new solo album and further film work.

ROBIN HALL was a co-founder of Jack Ruby in 1973. Along with friend and guitarist Chris Gray, the duo relocated to New York City, where they were joined by Randy Cohen and Boris Policeband. The band had changed line-ups by 1975, with Robin and Chris joined by George Scott III and Steve Barth, until the group's demise after Hall left the band and New York City in mid-'77.

LUCY HAMILTON goes by many names and pseudonyms. She is probably best known as one of the members of the no-wave band Mars, under the name Connie Burg (or China Burg).

ZOE HANSEN came from London to New York at seventeen years old in the early 80s, living at the Chelsea Hotel and in Hell's Kitchen before settling in the East Village. Hansen has worked as a stylist, clothing-store owner, streetwalker, speedball addict, escort, massage-parlour owner, writer, and brothel madam. She has been writing and telling tales of her life for many years.

MICK HARVEY is renowned as a musician, record producer, and composer who has been active for forty-plus years and is perhaps best known as a member of The Birthday Party and The Bad Seeds, and for his long-term collaborative work with PJ Harvey and Nick Cave. Aside from scoring more than a dozen feature films and documentaries, Harvey has also released eight solo albums, four of them being a series of translations of the songs of Serge Gainsbourg. Harvey resides in Melbourne, Australia, but spends a few months each year travelling and working in Europe on his various musical projects.

JASMINE HIRST is a photographer, filmmaker, painter, and psychic medium who divides her time between making art and speaking with the dead. Jasmine's films are in the collection of the New York Filmmakers Co-op of the

New American Cinema Group and have been screened at Lincoln Center, the LA Museum of Contemporary Art, and the Sydney Underground Film Festival. Jasmine currently collaborates with Lydia Lunch on photographic and film projects, and her photographic art has been exhibited at the Casa Del Pane (Milan), Sprengel Museum (Hanover), Illuminated Metropolis Gallery (New York), and Lethal Amounts Gallery (Los Angeles).

KRISTIAN HOFFMAN had his first brush with notoriety on PBS's noted reality show *An American Family* before he started the band Mumps. He has toured with The Contortions, played on James White & The Blacks' *Off White*, started his own loungeabilly band The Swinging Madisons and a folk parody band called Bleaker Street Incident, and wrote music for Klaus Nomi. He has since released four acclaimed solo CDs, toured and performed with numerous musicians, and is now the musical director of the Brookledge Follies; he collaborates with Prince Poppycock, plays in a 30s-style harmony band called The Roswell Sisters, and performs with Timur Bekbosunov.

HARRY HOWARD is a Melbourne-based musician and songwriter whose public career began when he guested on bass with The Birthday Party in 1982. He went on to play alongside his older brother Rowland S. Howard in Crime & The City Solution, These Immortal Souls, and the Shotgun Wedding touring band. Returning to Australia, he switched to guitar with CHABM and Pink Stainless Tail. He currently sings in the self-titled Harry Howard & The NDE (Near Death Experience), Duet, and the electro-punk three-piece ATOM.

MARC HURTADO is a musician, performer, poet, painter, producer, soundtrack composer, and filmmaker who co-founded the French duo Etant Donnes with his brother Eric in 1977. He has made more than thirty albums and twenty-six films (including three feature films), and has performed hundreds of concerts worldwide. His films have been screened across the world, and, beyond his solo and duo work, he has collaborated with many cult figures from music and cinema including Alan Vega, Martin Rev, Genesis Breyer P-Orridge, Michael Gira, and Z'ev, among others. He has exhibited paintings and video installations in major galleries across the globe.

PAT IRWIN was a founding member of 8 Eyed Spy and The Raybeats, later joining and touring with The B-52's (1989–2007). He also composes music for film and television and has contributed the scores for *Nurse Jackie*, *Bored To Death*, *Feed The Beast*, and *The Good Cop*. He has composed the music for hundreds of cartoons, including *Rocko's Modern Life*, *SpongeBob SquarePants*, *Pepper Ann*, and *Class Of 3000*. Most recently, he's recorded with SUSS and has released two records on Northern Spy—*Ghost Box (Expanded)* and *High Line*—as well as a duo with J. Walter Hawkes, *Wide Open Sky*.

JARBOE's prolific creativity has seen her release over thirty albums in addition to her work with Swans and numerous collaborative projects across a lifetime in music. As a multidisciplinary artist, Jarboe's oeuvre encompasses performance art, visual art, an award-winning video game soundtrack for The Path, theatre, and television voice work, as well as contributing audio elements to a range of art projects, her own and others. Jarboe's expansiveness has been inspired by experiences including her childhood in the Mississippi delta and New Orleans, her university studies in literature and theatre, and the life she has led since discovering the East Village scene.

JAMES JOHNSTON is a London-based musician and an acclaimed painter, a founding member of Gallon Drunk, and a former member of Nick Cave & The Bad Seeds. He has recorded and toured with a wide variety of musicians, including Lydia Lunch, Barry Adamson, Faust, and PJ Harvey. His solo album, *The Starless Room*, was released in 2016. Johnston has contributed scores to numerous film and television projects, most recently the *All About Eve* stage play, as well as collaborating with Ken Russell and acting for Olivier Assayas in his award-winning film *Clean*.

ROB KENNEDY could rest on his laurels for Da Chumps, the band that in 1976 introduced the world to Bad Brains and Half Japanese and Washington DC to no wave. He could rest on his laurels for Workdogs, the band that taught the Trash Blues to New York City in the 90s. But he would prefer you to check out his groundbreaking new duo, Jam Messengers; or the political arm of his music, The Robert Kennedy Assassination.

RICHARD KERN, photographer and filmmaker, remains first and foremost a portraitist. For more than two decades, Kern has worked with a shifting band of accomplices—including Lydia Lunch, David Wojnarowicz, Rita Ackermann, Lucy McKenzie, Marilyn Manson, Indochine, and Kanye West—to seek out, unravel, and illuminate the complex and often darker sides of human nature. Kern makes the psychological space between the sitter, photographer, and viewer his subject. With his dry, matter-of-fact approach, he underlines the absurdity of 'truth' and 'objectivity' in photography while playing with our reliance upon taxonomies surrounding sexual representation. (Written by Matthew Higgs.)

DAVID KNIGHT is a London-based musician born and raised in the World's End, Chelsea. After recording his first single in Delia Derbyshire's studio, he continued his fascination with all things electric and eclectic, working with Five

Or Six, Danielle Dax, Shock Headed Peters, Lydia Lunch, and current project UnicaZürn, among others.

MATT KORVETTE is a vocalist, performer, writer, and artist residing in Philadelphia, Pennsylvania. He is best known for his work with the group Pissed Jeans.

KAMIL KRUTA (aka Koonda Holaa) is a California Mojave Desert rat who fattens up his diet of sun half of the year in Toulouse, France. His current sound has been branded 'mystic-noir Americana' or psychedelic country & western … but it may well be world music beamed in from a world that does not yet exist. The Koonda Holaa sound is a dark, heavy flow at the end of the month, orchestrated with a looper and crowned with lyrics whose comedy redeems the darkness of its own messenger.

CHRISTOF KURZMANN is a Vienna-based musician existing in the spaces between electro-pop, improvisation, and 'new music'. A sometime soloist, he prefers to be part of a collective or a working group and has played concerts in all continents except Australia. Christof has worked with several great musicians such as Robert Wyatt, but unfortunately never with Ornette Coleman or Annette Peacock, while leading several groups including Orchester 33 1/3, The Magic ID, Schnee, and Disquiet. He is a member of Made To Break. A conscientious objector of military/civil service, Christof is politically active.

DAVID LACKNER was born in 1985 in New Jersey and is a composer and multi-instrumentalist (saxophone, piano, flute, EWI, synthesizers) specializing in jazz, minimalism, and pop music. In 2008, David founded Galtta as a vehicle for producing, film scoring, and releasing music by various like-minded artists. Informed by jazz and his study of North Indian vocal music with La Monte Young and Marian

Zazeela, David's music often explores just intonation and long durations.

MIRIAM LINNA has run the independent record label Norton Records since 1986. She was a founding member of The Cramps, then went on to join Nervus Rex, perform with The Zantees, launch The A-Bones, and guest on numerous releases. She co-edited the book *Sin-A-Rama: Sleaze Sex Paperbacks Of The 60s* and started a paperback book company, Kicks Books. Linna owns one of the world's largest collections of vintage paperbacks and featured many of the covers in her book *Bad Seed: A Postcard Book*.

LYDIA LUNCH is passionate, confrontational, and bold. Whether attacking the patriarchy and their pornographic war-mongering, turning the sexual into the political, or whispering a love song to the broken hearted, her fierce energy and rapid-fire delivery lend testament to her warrior nature. Queen of No Wave, muse of the Cinema Of Transgression, writer, musician, poet, spoken-word artist, and photographer, she has been on tour for decades, has written hundreds of songs, released dozens of albums, published numerous articles, half a dozen books, appeared in twenty films, conducted workshops, taught at universities, and refuses to just shut up.

SADIE MAE is a dyslexic artistic octopus. A synesthetic heart filled with countless inclinations. A floating mind magnetized by visual and musical emotions. Her wicked sense of humour is now taking her on the road of Mexico.

MIRCO MAGNANI is an Italian Berlin-based music composer and video artist, co-founder of Minox since 1984, then Technophonic Chamber Orchestra and 4Dkiller, besides his solo project TCO. In 1996, he co-founded the independent label Suite Inc., and he has performed onstage with Steven Brown, Blaine L. Reininger, Lydia Lunch, Mad Professor, and others. In 2009,

he moved to Berlin with the painter Valentina Bardazzi, launching the new label Undogmatisch in 2012 and producing releases in collaboration with Ernesto Tomasini and Lukas Trzcinski, and as Carlo Domenico Valyum.

ZAHRA MANI is a multi-instrumentalist who creates pulsing, shifting, psycho-ambient soundscapes out of found and recorded sound. She collaborated with Lydia Lunch and Mia Zabelka in the trio Medusa's Bed. They released an eponymous CD on Monotype, created a radio art piece in Vienna, and performed inter-medial sets across Europe with visuals by Elise Passavant. Zahra also played a one-off trio with Lydia and Weasel Walter in Trieste, and there may be more to come. In the six years the Medusas were recording and touring, Zahra and Lydia conducted a comprehensive survey of airport prawn sandwiches in numerous European cities.

CLIFF MARTINEZ moved to California in 1976, landing in the middle of the punk movement, and went on to stints as drummer for The Weirdos, Lydia Lunch, Jim Thirlwell, Captain Beefheart & The Magic Band, Red Hot Chili Peppers, and The Dickies. He has gone on to be a Grammy Award–winning creator of soundtracks for TV and film; he won a Best Soundtrack Award at the 2016 Cannes Film Festival and a Cesar Award for Xavier Giannoli's *A L'origine*, and was inducted into the Rock And Roll Hall Of Fame in April 2012 with Red Hot Chili Peppers.

CARLO MCCORMICK is a critic and curator based in New York City.

RICHARD METZGER is the editor and co-publisher of the long-running outsider arts blog DangerousMinds.net.

MURRAY MITCHELL met Lydia while touring with Siouxsie & The Banshees, went on to tour with

The Gun Club, and played guitar for Jeffrey Lee Pierce and Kid Congo, respectively. He has subsequently concentrated on offering technical and logistical assistance to Public Image Ltd, The Orb, Primal Scream, The Pogues, The Kills Archive, Super Furry Animals, Butcher Babies, and Catfish & The Bottlemen, to name a few. He returned to Lydia in 1990, as tour manager of the Harry Crews tour, and continues touring to this day, with 'quality' artists only.

THURSTON MOORE has existed in a state of continuous creative tumult since first plugging into the wild charge of mid-70s New York City. Best known for his work in Sonic Youth, his musical endeavours have spanned several hundred releases, with scant regard for the artificial divide of genre and a constant appetite for innovation. In 2019, he released *Spirit Counsel* to significant acclaim and continued extensive touring with The Thurston Moore Group. Moore continues to work extensively as a poet and spoken-word performer, as well as running the publisher and label Ecstatic Peace Library.

JAMES NARES has investigated, challenged, and expanded the boundaries of his multimedia practice that encompasses film, music, painting, photography, and performance over the course of a five-decade career. He continues to employ various media to explore physicality, motion, and the unfolding of time. Nares has been the subject of numerous solo exhibitions, including at the Metropolitan Museum of Art, New York, and a career-spanning retrospective at the Milwaukee Art Museum.

JOHNNY NATION toured with Lydia Lunch then joined the legendary, and very influential, LA trash rock band The Joneses. Leaving his punk past behind, he currently writes, records, and performs with his wife, Jewels, as The Nations, playing blues-based Americana.

ELISE PASSAVANT is a wandering visuals collector in perpetual quest for inspiration. As a photographer, VJ, and video manipulator, she has straddled the underground music and alternative art scenes, as well as mainstream media, for more than twenty years, in locations across Europe, Japan, and the USA. By employing a variety of film and still cameras, occasionally pirating images, and using her own textural post-production techniques, Elise creates a sensual visual poetry uniquely her own. This French nomad is taking the road south and will be opening a multimedia production studio in the Yucatan. Hedonism and transformation are the keys.

PHILIPPE PETIT likes to introduce himself as a 'musical travel agent', and, since the early 2000s, has performed throughout the world playing modular synthesiser, plastic sound-objects, the electric psalterion, hackbrett cimbalom, and Caterpillar drum guitars, as well as more conventional instruments such as the piano, turntables, and the Theremin. He has recorded with a dream team of collaborators and musicians while running the labels Pandemonium Rdz. and BiP_HOp. In 2019, he celebrated thirty-five years of musical activism and sharing his passions with the world.

KEMBRA PFAHLER is an American filmmaker and artist best known as lead singer of The Voluptuous Horror Of Karen Black. After appearing as a child actress in TV commercials for Kodak, she moved to the East Coast, became associated with the Cinema Of Transgression movement, and appeared in numerous films. She has since founded the art movements 'availabilism' and 'antinaturalism', with her work being shown at major institutions worldwide.

KID CONGO POWERS's open-tuned guitar is one of the more readily identifiable sounds in the history of underground rock. Best known for The Gun

Club, The Cramps, and Nick Cave & The Bad Seeds, Kid has spent fifteen years as a sideman to various artists; as a partner in Congo Norvell and Kid And Khan; a member of garage-rock supergroup Knoxville Girls; and as the leader of Kid Congo Powers & The Pink Money Birds. Kid has always had a knack for not only playing with some of the best bands but doing so during their finest hours.

RUDI PROTRUDI helped resurrect the feral abandon and savagery of primitive garage-rockers such as The Fendermen and The Kingsmen, when he founded The Fuzztones. His dedication to sexual outrageousness and the ethics and aesthetics of garage rock remains to this day.

LEE RANALDO's four decades as an artist encompass numerous musical recordings and performances, various poetry books and journals, visual art, music production, and composition. Active in the New York music scene from 1979, and a co-founder of Sonic Youth, recent highlights of Lee's work were the 'contre-jour' sound/light in-the-round performances with his partner, Leah Singer; and his 'Hurricane Transcriptions', based on wind recordings made during Hurricane Sandy in 2012, written for the Berlin Kaleidoscope orchestra and recently performed by Brooklyn's Dither Electric Guitar Quartet. His *Lost Highway* drawings and *Black Noise* prints have been widely exhibited worldwide.

BERNIE ROMANOWSKI is the guitar player for the American band Cable. They have toiled away in obscurity for over twenty-five years and plan to do so for another twenty-five years. Bernie lives in Manchester-by-the-Sea, Massachusetts, and greatly enjoys the company of his family and friends.

MATT SCHULTZ is an artist working across numerous mediums, including sculpture, music, design, and film. At the core of all his works is a desire to address the function of belief systems—to

ask where faith becomes industry, mantra turns into repetition, sculpture becomes manufacture, and the point where entertainment is transmuted into truth.

JIM SCLAVUNOS is a multi-instrumentalist, producer, and songwriter. Grammy-nominated, he has been a member of Nick Cave & The Bad Seeds since 1994. Alongside Lydia Lunch, he was an integral part of the no-wave scene in the bands Teenage Jesus & The Jerks, Beirut Slump, and 8 Eyed Spy, before joining Sonic Youth. Since then, Sclavunos has recorded with a diverse host of artists, including Grinderman, The Cramps, Marianne Faithfull, and Iggy Pop, along with his solo albums as The Vanity Set and his upcoming duet album with Nicole Atkins.

ROBERT SINGERMAN is known for developing iconic international talent, music export offices, trade missions, conferences, and new music business technologies. His main mission, however, is giving music subtitles, so music becomes truly global, through universal translation and understanding of lyrics as SVP, International Publishing at LyricFind. He travels and speaks globally, and in 2020 is helping launch as partner the new top-level domain: .music, (e.g., LydiaLunch.music.) IP-protected, no cyber-squatting, take down, stay down, .music will be 'Fair Trade music on the web' and stands to benefit all music creators and the entire music community.

VANESSA SKANTZE followed a serpentine path through spoken word and performance art to arrive at Butō dance. A seasoned improviser, she collaborates frequently with astonishing sound artists. She is a co-founder of Teatro De La Psychomachia, a performance space in Seattle that hosts many local, national, and international sound and movement artists. In recent years, her work teaching yoga and movement in prison has shaped her psyche deeply.

WIKTOR SKOK lives in Łódź and is a graduate of the Media & Audiovisual Culture Institute of Łódź University and the Institute Of Art History at Jagiellonian University, Kraków. He is an author, curator, and promoter, and has created music and exhibitions while also writing his own zines (*Zygoma*, 1988–1992; *Plus Ultra*, 1999–present). He is the founder of the group Jude and an active underground DJ devoted to all forms of extreme mechanical music. Since 1989, he has been promoting the concert series Wunder Wave, as well as combining a range of visual art productions with his love of music/noise.

DONITA SPARKS is an American vocalist, guitarist, songwriter, and creative director best known as co-founder of the band L7. She continues to perform with her band Donita Sparks & The Stellar Moments. In 2019, L7 released *Scatter The Rats*, their first album in almost twenty years, following the band's 2014 reunion.

GLYN STYLER is a completely disillusioned recluse who has no need for an audience.

BOBBY SWOPE (aka Bobby Berkowitz) was singer and lyricist of Lydia Lunch's short-lived but influential second band Beirut Slump. Post-Slump life has included co-founding the twentieth-century design gallery Full House in the 1980s in New York City, and, in 2005, co-editing the now iconic photography book on transvestites of the 1960s called *Casa Susanna*. He currently lives in Mexico City with long-time partner, now husband, Michel Hurst, and in 2019 they will publish the first book of their photographic collaboration in Mexico called *Pictures For Muriel*.

LIZ SWOPE is currently a lavender farmer living off the grid in Taos, New Mexico.

J.G. THIRLWELL is a composer, producer, and performer based in Brooklyn. He has released over thirty albums under his own name, as well as pseudonyms including Manorexia, Foetus, Xordox, Clint Ruin, and Wiseblood. Thirlwell has featured in various capacities for artists including Karen O, Zola Jesus, Tony Oursler, Melvins, Swans, Coil, and many more. He has also completed commissions for Kronos Quartet, Bang On A Can, String Orchestra Of Brooklyn, and others, and is a member of the Freq_Out sound-art collective. J.G. also creates the scores for the TV shows *The Venture Bros* and *Archer*, and has composed several film scores.

CATHI UNSWORTH is the author of six pop-cultural noir novels largely based on strange, occult, and unsolved murders, and the co-author of *Defying Gravity*, the life and times of punk icon Jordan. She lives and works in London.

WEASEL WALTER was born in 1972 and has done a lot of stuff. He leads a band called The Flying Luttenbachers and has played with Lydia Lunch Retrovirus, Cellular Chaos, Behold The Arctopus, Burmese, XBXRX, Hatewave, Lake Of Dracula, and many other groups and projects. As a proponent of improvised music, he has collaborated internationally with hundreds of improvising musicians, including Evan Parker, Roscoe Mitchell, Marshall Allen, Henry Kaiser, Elliott Sharp, Mary Halvorson, and Tyshawn Sorey. He appears on almost 200 commercial releases and has performed almost 2,500 concerts since 1990. There's more, but that's probably a good start.

IAN WHITE made the big move from Newcastle to London, determined to play the drums at any cost. He is still playing … and still paying the price. He remains forever exciting and always seeking more, much more.

LINK WRECKAGE Shapeshifter, unrepentant underground radical multi-instrumental(ish), enabler of miscreants, malcontents, and the maladjusted. One time cohort to D.K. Sale, D.J. Macdonald, Lydia Lunch, RSH, Sub Zero, Iron Curtain, The Spitters, Shotgun Wedding, Unto Ashes, and author of the prose poem 'The Omniscient Sea'. Partners in current endeavours with Ahna Anomali, including LA Vs LW. Shaker of trees, Blesser of bees.

WAJID YASEEN is a Manchester-born, London-based artist whose work draws on an interdisciplinary approach to develop sound-based works encompassing installations, live performances, acousmatic music, graphic scores, and sound sculptures. His work as a music producer (2nd Gen, Uniform) saw him release albums working with Lydia Lunch, Alan Vega, Franko B, Meira Asher, and Dälek. He is director of the sound-art research cooperative Modus Arts, the co-founder of the destructivist Scrapclub project, and director of the Ear Cinema project. His work has been exhibited and performed at the ICA Gallery, Arnolfini, Queen Elizabeth Hall, and the Freud Museum, among others.

MIA ZABELKA is a violinist and vocalist from Austria known for her experimental style. Educated in classical music from an early age, she has explored the limits of sound to build a language all her own based on the de- and re-construction of the violin's sonic possibilities. Expanding the range of the instrument using electronic devices, objects on/between strings, and innovative performance techniques. She is a three-time

winner of the Prix Ars Electronica, was recently awarded the Akademia Music award, and is artistic director of the Phonofemme festival and of Klanghaus Untergreith.

NICK ZEDD spearheaded the Cinema Of Transgression film movement and has directed forty-four movies since 1979, including *Police State, War Is Menstrual Envy, Ecstasy In Entropy*, and *Lord Of The Cock Rings*. He produced and directed *The Adventures Of Electra Elf* from 2004 to 2008. Mr. Zedd currently resides in Mexico City, where he paints, writes, and shoots videos. In 2013, he was presented with the Acker Award For Lifetime Achievement, a tribute given to members of the avant-garde arts community who have made outstanding contributions in defiance of convention or else served their fellow writers and artists in outstanding ways.

PAUL ZONE turned thirteen in 1970 and was already attending concerts with his brothers. He photographed shows by all the key players and countless icons of the NYC glam-rock era. Alongside his brothers, Paul formed The Fast, an influential headlining group that released five classic singles and two LPs, and he was a resident DJ at Max's Kansas City. In the 80s, he was part of the duo Man 2 Man, scoring numerous worldwide chart singles. His book *Playground: Growing Up In The New York Underground* is a pictorial and biographical memoir of his life across those wild years.

SELECTED WORKS

The following is a listing of key works in the varied and extensive career of Lydia Lunch.

FILMOGRAPHY

Guerillere Talks—a film by Vivienne Dick (1978)

Rome '78—a film by James Nares (1978)

She Had Her Gun All Ready—a film by Vivienne Dick (1978)

Black Box—a film by Beth B and Scott B (1978)

Beauty Becomes The Beast—a film by Vivienne Dick (1979)

Alien Portrait—a film by Michael McClard (1979)

The Offenders—a film by Beth B and Scott B (1980)

Vortex—a film by Beth B and Scott B (1982)

Like Dawn To Dust—a film by Vivienne Dick (1983)

The Wild World Of Lydia Lunch—a film by Nick Zedd (1983)

The Right Side Of My Brain—a film by Richard Kern (1985)

Submit To Me—a film by Richard Kern (1985)

Fingered—a film by Richard Kern (1986)

The Invisible Thread—a film by Penn & Teller (1986)

Submit To Me Now—a film by Richard Kern (1987)

Mondo New York—a film by Harvey Keith (1987)

The Gun Is Loaded—a film by Merill Aldighieri (1988)

Kiss Napoleon Goodbye—a film by Babeth Van Loo (1990)

Thanatopsis—a film by Beth B (1991)

The Thunder, The Perfect Mind—a film by Tom Richards Murphy/Marta Ze (1992)

Visiting Desire— a film by Beth B (1996)

Lydia Lunch: The War Is Never Over—a film by Beth B (2019)

THEATRICAL WORKS

South Of Your Border—written and performed with Emilio Cubeiro (1988)

Smell Of Guilt—written and performed with Emilio Cubeiro (1990)

BIBLIOGRAPHY

Adulterers Anonymous—written with Exene Cervenka (1982)

The Right Side Of My Brain—illustrated by Knut Odde Sørensen (1987)

Blood Sucker—illustrated by Bob Fingerman (1992)

Incriminating Evidence—illustrated by Kristian Hoffman (1992)

As.fix.e8—written with Nick Cave and illustrated by Mike Matthews (1993)

Paradoxia: A Predator's Diary (1997)

Toxic Gumbo—illustrated by Ted McKeever (1998)

Amnesia (2009)

Will Work For Drugs (2009)

The Gun Is Loaded (2008)

The Need To Feed: A Hedonist's Guide (2012)

So Real It Hurts (2019)

SELECTED DISCOGRAPHY

'Orphans'/'Less Of Me'—Teenage Jesus & The Jerks single (Migraine, 1978)

No New York—compilation featuring Teenage Jesus & The Jerks (Antilles, 1978)

'Baby Doll'/'Freud In Flop'/'Race Mixing'—Teenage Jesus & The Jerks EP (Migraine, 1979)

'Try Me'/'Staircase'—Beirut Slump single (Migraine, 1979)

Teenage Jesus & The Jerks—Teenage Jesus & The Jerks EP (Migraine, 1979)

Pre-Teenage Jesus & The Jerks—Teenage Jesus & The Jerks EP (ZE Records, 1979)

Queen Of Siam—album (ZE Records, 1980)

Live—Eight Eyed Spy live album (ROIR, 1981)

Eight Eyed Spy—Eight Eyed Spy half live/half studio album (Fetish Records, 1981)

Drunk On The Pope's Blood / The Agony Is The Ecstasy—split EP with The Agony Is The Ecstasy and The Birthday Party (4AD, 1982)

'Some Velvet Morning'/'I Fell In Love With A Ghost'—single with Rowland S. Howard (4AD, 1982)

'Thirsty Animal'—guest appearance with Einstürzende Neubauten (no label, 1982)

13.13—self-titled album (Ruby Records, 1982)

'Der Karibische Western'—guest appearance with Die Haut (Zensor Records, 1982)

In Limbo—album (Doublevision, 1984)

'Death Valley '69'—guest appearance with Sonic Youth (two versions of the song: Iridescence Records, 1984 and Homestead Records, 1985)

Hard Rock—split spoken-word cassette with Michael Gira (Ecstatic Peace, 1984)

Heart Of Darkness—guest appearance with No Trend (Widowspeak/No Trend, 1985)

A Dozen Red Roses—guest appearance with No Trend (Widowspeak/No Trend, 1985)

The Drowning Of Lucy Hamilton—album (Widowspeak, 1985)

The Uncensored Lydia Lunch—spoken-word album (Rough Trade, 1985)

Hysterie—compilation (Widowspeak, 1986)

Honeymoon In Red—album (Widowspeak, 1987)

Oral Fixation—spoken-word album (Widowspeak, 1988)

Stinkfist—EP with Clint Ruin (Widowspeak, 1988)

The Crumb—EP with Clint Ruin, Thurston Moore and songs from Honeymoon In Red (Widowspeak, 1988)

The Death Of An Asshole—guest appearance with Emilio Cubeiro (Widowspeak, 1989)

Our Fathers Who Aren't In Heaven—spoken-word album with Henry Rollins, Hubert Selby Jr., and Don Bajema (Widowspeak, 1990)

A Girl Doesn't Get Killed By A Make-Believe Lover ... 'Cuz It's Hot—guest appearance with My Life With The Thrill Kill Kult (Wax Trax! Records, 1990)

Extended Versions—guest appearance with Extended Versions (Nur Sch. Rec!, 1990)

Naked In Garden Hills—live album (Widowspeak, 1990)

'Twisted'/'Past Glas'—single with Z'Ev and Clint Ruin (Inspipid Vinyl, 1991)

Don't Fear The Reaper—EP with Clint Ruin (Big Cat, 1991)

Shotgun Wedding—album with Rowland S. Howard (Triple X Records, 1991)

P.O.W.—spoken-word album (Sovo Records, 1992)

Workdogs In Hell—guest appearance with The Workdogs (no label, 1992)

'Unearthly Delights'—single (Clawfist, 1993)

Sweat—guest appearance with Die Haut (What's So Funny About, 1993)

Unhealthy—guest appearance with Lab Report (Invisible, 1993)

Fear Engine II—guest appearance with Shock Headed Peters (Cyclops Prod, 1993)

Crimes Against Nature—spoken word album (Triple X Records, 1994)

Rude Hieroglyphics—spoken-word album with Exene Cervenka (Rykodisc, 1995)

Everything—compilation of Teenage Jesus & The Jerks (Atavistic, 1995)

Arkkon—guest appearance with Arkkon (Tonus Kozmetica, 1995)

Universal Infiltrators—spoken-word album (Atavistic, 1996)

York (First Exit To Brooklyn)—guest appearance with The Foetus Symphony Orchestra (Thirsty Ear, 1997)

The Desperate Ones—EP with Glyn Styler (Atavistic, 1997)

Pariah—album by Vanessa Skantze produced by Lydia (Hija Del Fuego, 1997)

Matrikamantra—album (Crippled Dick Hot Wax, 1998)

U-Turn—guest appearance with Minox (Suite Inc., 1998)

Re-Up—guest appearance with Etant Donnes (Les Disques Du Soleil, 1999)

Gutter Queen—guest appearance with Cable (Hydra Head Records, 1999)

Rotunda—guest appearance with Arkkon (Soleilmoon Recordings, 2000)

The Devil's Racetrack—spoken-word album (Almafame, 2000)

Hangover Hotel—album (no label, 2001)

Downwords—guest appearance with Minox (Suite Inc., 2001)

Champagne, Cocaine, And Nicotine Stains—EP with The Anubian Lights (Crippled Dick Hot Wax, 2002)

Memory And Madness—album with Terry Edwards (Sartorial Records, 2003)

In Our Time Of Dying—spoken-word album (Widowspeak, 2003)

Smoke In The Shadows—album (Atavistic, 2004)

OperettAmorale—guest appearance with Black Sun Productions (Divine Frequency, 2005)

Willing Victim—DVD live album (Atavistic, 2005)

Solo Cholo—guest appearance with Kid Congo Powers (Trans Solar, 2006)

Protocol—guest appearance with Uniform (Planet Mu, 2006)

Live At Max's Kansas City 1977—Teenage Jesus & The Jerks live album (Widowspeak, 2006)

Touch My Evil—album with The Anubian Lights (Widowspeak, 2006)

Deviations On A Theme—compilation (Provocateur Media, 2006)

Omar Rodriguez Lopez & Lydia Lunch—album with Omar Rodriguez Lopez (Willie Anderson Recordings, 2007)

Ghosts Of Spain—album (Widowspeak, 2007)

'Frankie Teardrop'—split single with Suicide (Blast First Petite, 2008)

The Milky Smell Of Phantom Sperm—guest appearance with Black Sun Productions (Old Europa Café, 2008)

Dead Man—split EP with Les Aus and the Weasel Walter Duo (Gaffer Records, 2008)

Shut Up And Bleed—compilation of Teenage Jesus & The Jerks/Beirut Slump (Cherry Red Records, 2008)

Big Sexy Noise—self-titled album (Sartorial Records, 2009)

Forgive Us Our Trespasses—guest appearance with A Storm Of Light (Neurot Recordings, 2009)

We Are Only Riders—guest appearance on The Jeffrey Lee Pierce Sessions Project (Glitterhouse Records, 2009)

Twist Of Fate—album with Philippe Petit (Monotype Records, 2010)

Sniper—guest appearance with Marc Hurtado and Alan Vega (Le Son Du Maquis, 2010)

'Still Searching'—guest appearance with Les Aus (OMS-B, 2010)

In Comfort—album with Philippe Petit (ComfortZone, 2011)

Trust The Witch—Big Sexy Noise album (Le Son Du Maquis, 2011)

Phantasmata Domestica—Black Sun Productions (Old Europe Café, 2012)

The Journey Is Long—guest appearance on The Jeffrey Lee Pierce Sessions Project (Glitterhouse Records, 2012)

Retrovirus—self-titled album (ugEXPLODE, 2013)

Taste Our Voodoo—album with Philippe Petit (RustBlade, 2013)

Don't Pressure The Man With The Knife—album with Lydia Lunch's Putan Club (UnJourPeut-Etre, 2013)

Collision Course/Trust The Witch—Big Sexy Noise album and live album (Cherry Red Records, 2013)

Medusa's Bed—self-titled album (Monotype Records, 2013)

A Fistful Of Desert Blues—album with Cypress Grove (RustBlade, 2014)

Twin Horses—split album with Cypress Grove; Spiritual Front on the other side (RustBlade, 2014)

Axels And Sockets—guest appearance on The Jeffrey Lee Pierce Sessions Project (Glitterhouse Records, 2014)

Synthetic Love Dream—guest appearance with David Lackner (GALTTA Media, 2014)

3X3 EP—Lydia Lunch Retrovirus EP (no label, 2015)

Urge To Kill—Lydia Lunch Retrovirus album (Widowspeak, 2015)

Live 1977–1979—Teenage Jesus & The Jerks live compilation (Other People, 2015)

Live In Zurich—Lydia Lunch Retrovirus live album (no label, 2016)

Ultimate Obedience—guest appearance with Jude (Requiem Records, 2016)

Brutal Measures—EP with Weasel Walter (Widowspeak, 2016)

Under The Covers—Cypress Grove (RustBlade, 2017)

The Avant-Age Garde I Ams Of The Gal Luxury—guest appearance with Heroes Are Gang Leaders (Fast Speaking Music, 2017)

Why Love Now—Pissed Jeans album produced by Lydia (Sub Pop, 2017)

Eulogy—album with Family In Mourning (GALTTA Media, 2017)

Cellular Resonance—album by Mia Zabelka with Lydia composing and producing (Little Crackd Rabbit, 2017)

Marchesa—album (RustBlade, 2018)

The Strange World Of Suzie Pellet—guest appearance with Transmaniacon (New Heavy Sounds, 2018)

Lost In Blue—guest appearance with Anni Hogan (Cold Spring, 2019)

CHRONOLOGY

The following summary of the career of Lydia Lunch is based on the extensive work conducted by Hans, curator of and powerhouse behind the FromTheArchives.org website. The author would like to offer his thanks to Hans for his help, support, and astounding endeavour.

JUNE 2, 1959 Lydia Anne Koch is born in Rochester, New York.

1976 Lydia moves to New York City and lives with James Chance for a year at addresses on East Second Street and Twelfth Street.

JANUARY 1977–JULY 1979 Lydia attempts to form

The Scabs with James Chance, Reck, and Jody Harris; the band then mutates into Teenage Jesus & The Jerks. The line-up would change several times, with Chance leaving in September 1977, and Reck leaving in November; Gordon Stevenson joins that same month, in time for shows in the UK in December; then Jim Sclavunos replaces Stevenson in June 1978. The band play their first show on June 27, 1977, at CBGB's; they disband in July 1979 after a European tour.

SPRING 1977 Lydia, Miriam Linna, and Bradly Field live together at Twelfth Street and First Avenue, then move to Warren Street.

1978 Lydia, Sumner Crane, and Bradly Field move into an apartment on Delancey Street.

JUNE 1978–JUNE 1979 Beirut Slump form, then play a first show under the name Belfast Ghetto in July. They perform four concerts in total, disbanding before Lydia departs on the final Teenage Jesus & The Jerks tour.

AUTUMN *Queen Of Siam* is recorded.

SEPTEMBER 1979–AUGUST 1980 Eight Eyed Spy form and play around sixty shows across the USA and Canada, as well as three shows in Italy.

NOVEMBER 17, 1979 Lydia presents a lecture on 'music theory' in Buffalo, New York City—her first spoken word performance.

AUGUST 5, 1980 George Scott III dies from an accidental drug overdose at age twenty-seven.

AUGUST 1980–FEBRUARY 1982 Lydia lives in Topanga Canyon from August to September, then moves to Venice, California.

OCTOBER 1980 8 Eyed Spy temporarily reconvene to record various songs in studio.

NOVEMBER 1980–FEBRUARY 1981 Devil Dogs perform fewer than twenty shows. Michael Paumgarden, San Adler, and Jim Sclavunos play in the first line-up in November, then Robert Maché, Rudi Protrudi, and Kristian Hoffman play a further handful of shows.

JUNE–NOVEMBER 1981 The first line-up of 13.13 (Johnny Nation, Greg Williams, Alex MacNicol) play ten shows together; Dix Denney and Cliff Martinez replace Nation and MacNicol in July.

NOVEMBER–DECEMBER 1981 Lydia arrives in London (living initially on Westbourne Grove, then at an address in West Kensington) and forms

The Agony Is The Ecstasy with Steve Severin, Murray Mitchell, and Kristian Hoffman. After seven shows, Severin leaves; the rest of the band perform ten shows in Europe in December, finishing on Christmas Day in Antwerp.

JUNE–JULY 1982 Lydia accompanies The Birthday Party to Berlin and takes part in their *This Is The Last Day Of the Rest Of Your Life* and the *Oops! I've Got Blood On The End Of My Boot* tours.

OCTOBER 1982–MAY 1983 Lydia lives in New York City, then returns to Baron's Court Road, London.

OCTOBER 1982–JANUARY 1983 Lydia forms and records with In Limbo: Pat Place on guitar, Thurston Moore on bass, Jim Sclavunos on sax, and Richard Edson on drums. The project ends after roughly ten shows.

NOVEMBER 4, 1982 Lydia performs her spoken-word piece 'Daddy Dearest' alongside a further work with Thurston Moore. Further spoken performances will take place nearly every month from this point on.

MARCH–APRIL 1983 US reading tour.

MAY 5, 1983 Lydia performs in a one-off band with Jim Thirwell, Norman Westberg, Michael Gira, and Roli Mosimann at the Speed Trials Festival at the White Columns Gallery in New York City.

MAY 19, 1983 Lydia performs with Jim Thirlwell and Jessamy Calkin at a festival in Vienna, then lays down the first version of *Stinkfist* with Thirwell at a studio in London.

OCTOBER 1983 The Immaculate Consumptive (Lydia with Marc Almond, Jim Thirlwell, and Nick Cave) perform a show in Washington DC, then two shows at Danceteria, New York.

NOVEMBER–DECEMBER 1983 Lydia Lunch, Jim Thirlwell, and Cliff Martinez tour *Swelter*, a piece they initially worked on with Norman Westberg.

JANUARY 1984 Lydia and Henry Rollins stage *Why You Murder Me*.

APRIL AND DECEMBER 1984 Lydia, Jim Thirlwell, Jessamy Calkin, and John 'Tex' Tottenham perform three dates in Europe, followed by a December date in Italy, then two US shows.

MAY 1984 Lydia moves to Spanish Harlem, New York City.

MAY 1984 Lydia records with the band No Trend; live dates follow in March 1985.

JUNE–DECEMBER 1984 Lydia joins Sonic Youth to perform 'Death Valley '69'. She joins them again for the recording of an accompanying video in March/April 1986 in Topanga Canyon, and guests at a small number of Sonic Youth shows during 1984–86.

AUGUST 1984 *The Intimate Diaries Of The Sexually Insane* spoken-word tour. Further dates take place under that name in 1985.

OCTOBER–NOVEMBER 1984 Lydia supports Marc Almond & The Willing Sinners on their *Vermine In Ermine* UK tour.

MARCH 1985 First screening of *The Right Side Of My Brain* at the Kitchen, New York City.

JULY–NOVEMBER 1985 Lydia supports Scraping Foetus Off The Wheel (Jim Thirlwell) at various live dates across Europe, the USA, and Japan. She continues to tour with Foetus into 1986.

MARCH 1986 First screening of Richard Kern's *Submit To Me*.

APRIL–JUNE 1986 Lydia works on *Stinkfist* in California and New York.

JULY 6, 1986 *Fingered* premiers at the Cat Club, New York City.

AUGUST–SEPTEMBER 1986 *Yank 'Em, Crank 'Em, Don't Stick Around To Thank 'Em* tour.

MAY 1987 Lydia works on *The Crumb* with Thurston Moore and Jim Thirlwell, while preparing *Honeymoon In Red* for release.

JUNE 1987 Lydia performs *The Gun Is Loaded* at the Performing Garage, SoHo, with Merrill Aldighieri filming one date.

DECEMBER 1987 Lydia is in the studio with Jim Thirlwell, working on a further piece for the *Stinkfist* EP.

JANUARY 1988 *South Of Your Border* runs for ten performances at the New Theater, New York.

JUNE–SEPTEMBER 1988 The Harry Crews band start rehearsing in New York City with Pat Place on second guitar (alongside Lydia), Kim Gordon on bass, and Sadie Mae on drums. After Place departs, the three-piece tours Europe for thirteen live dates in September 1988.

FEBRUARY–APRIL 1990 The *Conspiracy Of Women* tour of the USA and Europe. Additional dates follow later in the year.

OCTOBER 1990–MARCH 1991 Various recording dates with Jim Thirlwell.

DECEMBER 1990 Lydia leaves New York City and moves to New Orleans.

MARCH 1991 Lydia and Rowland S. Howard start a band called Gashouse, soon renamed Shotgun Wedding. An album is recorded in May; a tour follows in November–December. A different line-up tours Australia in September 1994, and a farewell show takes place in Melbourne in July 1998, at the last ever These Immortal Souls concert.

OCTOBER 1991 Lydia joins Die Haut for a one-off date following her guest appearance on the *Head On* album. She then tours with them in August and October 1992.

MARCH–APRIL 1992 Spoken-word tour of the South.

MAY 1992 *Smell Of Guilt*, Lydia's second theatrical production in collaboration with Emilio Cubeiro, has an extensive run in San Francisco, having premiered as a one-off performance in New York City in June 1990. The play has a further run in August–September 1993.

JUNE 1993 Lydia leaves New Orleans and subsequently settles in San Francisco.

JULY 1993 Lydia takes part in *The International Theater Of Poetry And Pain* with Emilio Cubeiro and others at Knitting Factory, New York.

JUNE 1994 *Universal Infiltrators* UK tour.

FEBRUARY 1995–MAY 1996 A yearlong (off and on) tour with Exene Cervenka. The March dates are labelled the *Terror Twins* tour.

APRIL 1995 Lydia moves to Pittsburgh.

JANUARY 1997 Lydia produces Vanessa Skantze's *Pariah* album, then begins work on *Matrikamantra* with Joe Budenholzer and members of Backworld. Certain songs were premiered live in 1996, but the formal debut takes place in March 1997, with extensive touring in May–June 1998 (Europe) and November 1998 (USA, then France). An April–May 1999 tour follows, with Ian White and Terry Edwards.

OCTOBER 1997 *Paradoxia* is published in the UK, with a reading tour of Europe following in November. A subsequent US reading tour takes place in September 1998, with a further European tour in October, and various other dates scattered in between.

JUNE–DECEMBER 1998 Lydia takes part in two sessions with the duo Minox in Italy, then performs three dates with them in December.

JANUARY 2000 Lydia leaves Pittsburgh and moves to Los Angeles.

FEBRUARY 2000 The *Dirty Little Secrets* tour, on which Lydia reads from *Paradoxia* and from her internet sex advice column 'Tough Love'.

APRIL–JUNE 2000 *Tough Love* spoken-word tour.

NOVEMBER 2000 European spoken-word tour with Gene Gregorits.

MAY 2001 Recording work commences in California with The Anubian Lights. A tour with the band follows, with various dates worldwide during May–November 2002. A small number of US dates are played in 2003. In 2004, Lydia performs the music of The Anubian Lights with Ian White, Terry Edwards, and James Johnston.

SEPTEMBER–OCTOBER 2001 *Smoke In The Shadows* performances with Terry Edwards.

JUNE–JULY 2003 *Willing Victim* tour.

FEBRUARY–APRIL 2004 *Memory And Madness* tour.

APRIL 2004 *Smoke In The Shadows* tour with Terry Edwards.

APRIL 2004 Lydia moves to Barcelona.

OCTOBER–DECEMBER 2004 European tour with Ian White, Mark Horse, Ntshukumo Bonga.

MARCH–DECEMBER 2005 European tour with Ian White, Terry Edwards, and Marc Viaplana. The last performance of the *Smoke In the Shadows* material takes place in December 2005 in the UK.

MARCH–NOVEMBER 2006 *The Real Pornography* multimedia performance tours Europe (David Knight and Ian White perform, video by Marc Viaplana). A reduced line-up of Lydia and Marc performs 4 further dates in 2007.

SUMMER 2007 Lydia records three songs with Les Aus. She will perform with them once in 2007, once in 2008, and once in 2009.

JUNE–DECEMBER 2007 Lydia tours the *Hangover Hotel* project in Europe and the USA.

NOVEMBER 2007 *Paradoxia* is published in the USA, ten years after its UK publication. Lydia performs a reading tour in November.

2008 TO 2015 Around a dozen Teenage Jesus & The Jerks shows take place involving performers including Jim Sclavunos, Thurston Moore, Al Kizys, James Johnston, Ian White, Terry Edwards, Weasel Walter, and Tim Dahl.

FEBRUARY 2008 Lydia performs five dates under the title *Blood Is Just Memory Without Language: Songs Of Sex, Sorrow, And Rage.*

JUNE 2008 Ian White suggests the idea of Big Sexy Noise; recordings begin in late 2008.

MAY–DECEMBER 2008 Various performances under the *Ghosts Of Spain* title. The same title is resurrected for performances in 2009 and January 2010.

2009–11 In 2009, Lydia records extensively with Philippe Petit then subsequently tours with him for various dates April 2009 to May 2011.

MAY–AUGUST 2009 Lydia records in London for the Jeffrey Lee Pierce Session album *We Are Only Riders*. She subsequently makes further recordings with Cypress Grove July–August 2009. She records for a further Jeffrey Lee Pierce Session compilation in 2010–11, and tours with Cypress Grove for various periods between August 2012 and November 2017. Their collaboration is ongoing.

APRIL 2009–APRIL 2013 Lydia collaborates with Mia Zabelka periodically across this period.

SPRING 2010–DECEMBER 2012 Lydia performs various dates and line-ups under the title *Sick With Desire*. Other performances happen under names such as *Toxic Lust* and *Battle Scars*.

MAY 5, 2011 A single performance of *Queen Of Siam* takes place at Austria's Donaufestival.

JUNE 2011–JUNE 2012 Sister Assassin, with Jessie Evans and Beatrice Antolini, play five dates in 2011, then a final show in Lisbon in June 2012.

MARCH 2012–APRIL 2013 Putan Club's first performance in Toulouse (March 2012) is followed by a tour of France in November 2012, then a wider European tour January–April 2013.

MAY 2012 The first *Post Catastrophe Women's Workshop* takes place in Rennes, France. Further iterations follow across 2013–14 in the USA.

SUMMER 2012 Recording of the *My Lover The Killer* album.

NOVEMBER 2012–PRESENT Retrovirus play their first show in California, featuring Al Kizys, Bob Bert, and Weasel Walter. In November 2013, Tim Dahl replaces Kizys.

NOVEMBER 2, 2012 Johnny O' Kane kills Michelle Stamper and commits suicide.

JANUARY 2013 The debut performance of *My Lover The Killer* in Limoges, France, with Lydia and Marc Hurtado supported by François R. Cambuzat and visuals created by Elise Passavant.

JUNE 2013 Readings to support *The Heroin Chronicles* compendium edited by Jerry Stahl.

JULY 2013–PRESENT Lydia tours *Dust And Shadows* with Elise Passavant's video art.

AUGUST 2013 The gloriously titled *Horribly True Confessions* debuts in Europe with subsequent dates in 2014 and 2015.

NOVEMBER 2013 Lydia forms Medusa's Bed with Mia Zabelka and Zahra Mani following the recording of an album earlier in 2013.

JUNE–JULY 2015 Lydia Lunch is a guest at the Jack Kerouac School Of Disembodied Poetics at Naropa University in Boulder, Colorado.

NOVEMBER 2016–OCTOBER 2018 Lydia performs four *No Wave Out* shows with Omar Hassan,

Weasel Walter, Tim Dahl, Don Babatunde, and Shaun Kelly.

AUGUST 2015–PRESENT Lydia's duo with Weasel Walter, under the name Drums-Voice-Brutality, mutates into Brutal Measures, an ongoing project.

JUNE 2017 The Coven convenes at Soho House, Brooklyn, for a first performance, with further shows in 2017–18.

SEPTEMBER 2017 Lydia leads *From The Page To The Stage* spoken-word workshops in Sweden. The series is expanded and repeated in 2019.

FEBRUARY 2018 The second performance of *My Lover The Killer* takes place at the Deutsche Oper, Berlin.

FEBRUARY 2019–PRESENT Lydia and Marc Hurtado's *Play Alan Vega And Suicide Songs* tours extensively. The project debuted in April 2014.

JUNE 23, 2019 Big Sexy Noise play their final show in Larvik, Norway.

BETH B FILMOGRAPHY

The following is a listing of key works in the five-decade career of Beth B.

G-Man—co-directed with Scott B (1978)
Black Box—co-directed with Scott B (1978)
Letters To Dad—co-directed with Scott B (1979)
The Offenders—co-directed with Scott B (1980)
The Trap Door—co-directed with Scott B (1981)
Vortex—co-directed with Scott B (1981)
'The Dominatrix Sleeps Tonight'—music video for Dominatrix (1983)
'I Need Someone'—music video for Joan Jett (1984)
'In The Middle Of The Night'—music video for Taka Boom (1984)
Salvation! Have You Said Your Prayers Today? (1987)
Belladonna—co-directed with Ida Applebroog (1989)
American Nightmare (1991)
Stigmata (1991)
Thanatopsis (1991)
Shut Up And Suffer (1991)
Amnesia (1991)
Two Small Bodies (1993)
Under Lock And Key (1993)
High Heel Nights (1994)
Out Of Sight/Out Of Mind (1995)
Visiting Desire (1996)
Voices Unheard (1997)
Breathe In, Breathe Out (2001)
Hysteria (2001)
Nerve.com: Downloading Sex—TV documentary film (2002)
The Investigators—TV documentary series (2002–07)
Crime Scenes Uncovered—TV documentary film (2003)
Exposed (2013)
Call Her Applebroog (2016)
Lydia Lunch: The War Is Never Over (2019)

ALSO AVAILABLE FROM JAWBONE